# CROSSOVER

## A LOOK INSIDE A MANIC MIND

# BRETT STEVENS

PAGE PUBLISHING, INC.
New York, NY

First originally published by Page Publishing, Inc. 2019

Some of the names and identifying details have been changed to protect the privacy of individuals.

ISBN 978-1-64544-049-9 (Paperback)
ISBN 978-1-64544-050-5 (Digital)

Printed in the United States of America

Crossover: a basketball maneuver in which a player who is dribbling the ball switches the ball rapidly from one hand to the other, to make a change in direction.

Bipolar Disorder: a mental illness marked by alternating moods characterized by periods of mania and depression.

*How I remember it…*

## The Release

"Everybody, shut the fuck up! I've had enough of you all talking behind my back!" I screamed, looking out at a public crowd having lunch that day at a packed pizza shop in Texas. "Shut the fuck up!" I yelled even louder, as loud as I could. The place went silent, except for Twenty One Pilots' "Heathens" playing on the pop station in the background.

*♪Please don't make any sudden moves,*
*You don't know the half of the abused♪*

I had the crowd's attention: five foot eight, white skin, black hair, strong build, light beard. I was wearing gym shorts, Nike shoes, and a soft T-shirt that was a gift from my mom this time last year. I looked around and saw nervous college students, fathers ready to protect their wives and young children, and restaurant staff looking for the closest phone to call 911. I took a deep breath, enjoying the peace and quiet that hadn't existed in my world for the last week. A beam of sunshine shed through the window, landing directly into my eyes. *I've served you well, haven't I, God?*

Then a brave man, about my height, chubby, and friendly, joined me in the spotlight. "Hey, man, you all right? Let's take a walk outside." He represented everything I was going to change about the world, this fat, fake world. Then his face transformed, teeth growing into fangs, eyes widening, voice deepening. All the spectators disappeared. He put his hand on my shoulder and, in a deep voice, belted out, "Come on, man. There are kids here."

I felt his internal poison being transferred to my shoulder and saw his words floating in front of me. *Come on, **man**, there are kids here.* I pulled the letters that I needed to unscramble, and the words *hear me* lit up in the sky.

*This is your world, Brett. You are my son. Now, go take it.*

Then I was back in the pizza place, with the crowd of insignificant mortals. I looked at the man's hand on my shoulder and thrust my arms forward, with perfectly utilized force, knocking him back over the table behind him. A chair shifted, and silverware dinged on the floor. A woman shrieked. Kids cried. Now, about thirty men stood up, ready to physically remove me from the premises, fifteen of them standing in front of the exit. God showed me an image of myself as a high school basketball player running sprint after sprint to motivate me to escape. I got low and charged forward toward the door, like the crowd wasn't even there. I was met by punches, name-calling, "Kick his ass!" and the loud rip of my shirt. We were all looking for the same result, getting me out of the restaurant. Eventually, our combined force knocked me out of the front door and onto the street. I stood up like nothing had happened and went about my day with a ripped shirt, enjoying the sunlight, available to answer work e-mails if needed, excited for a blind date that I had planned that evening, and most of all, ready to accept the next challenge that God had in store for me.

## *Little League*

It was a sunny spring day as I drove to my first Little League game. I was excited, wearing cleats, white pants, black uniform, and a black ball cap. My life was great. I was the middle child between two awesome brothers. My parents were happy, and we all had more than we needed. I ran out of the car and was greeted by my friends, who were also excited about our game. My world was perfect and small as we laughed and got ready to play.

"We're going to try you out at catcher, Brett," said my friend's dad, who was the head coach of our team.

"Sounds good to me!" I replied.

Catcher, pitcher, outfield, bench—it didn't matter to me. I hadn't experienced much hardship, and I felt as though all of us were on a mini vacation called life.

I put on the catcher's chest pad, as well as the face guard, pounded my glove, and ran to my place behind the batter on the opposing team. I took a deep breath in and enjoyed the feeling of air brushing the inside of my nostrils. I glanced up at the clear blue sky and saw a cloud slowly moving in.

*Whoa, am I too close to the batter? He might smack me in the head with his bat.*

I slid back a few steps to make sure I was safe. I put my glove up, ready for the first pitch. Before the ball came, the batter dug his foot into the dust and kicked it up into my face without realizing it. I coughed a bit and closed my eyes. I felt a pop in my glove, and the ball was secured.

"Strike 1!" yelled the umpire.

"Good job, Brett!" shouted my parents from the stands.

*Well, that was lucky, but I'll take it!*

Pitch number 2 came a bit harder and caused another explosion of dust to come through my mask. "Strike 2!" repeated the ump. Loud cheers came from the stands. This time, the dust felt like it was clogging my throat. My pads and face mask were very secure and another pitch was on the way, so I hung in there, breathing heavily. The batter slid both of his feet on the third pitch, creating yet another cloud of dust. It felt like I was swallowing sand as I took a deep inhale. Then I started to panic.

The ball came fast, and the batter connected, sprinting toward first base. If he hadn't connected, it might have hit me in the head. The game was no longer a concern of mine—surviving was. I tried to get my pads off, but the panic was hindering my ability to help myself. The world was looking fuzzy as I lay on my back, not able to breathe, looking into the umpire's eyes.

"Can somebody help?" yelled the ump.

My dad sprinted from the stands and leaned over me, telling me to breathe slowly. My mom assisted by bringing cold orange juice for me to sip. I was lifted into the car and shipped to the emergency room.

After some yelling, medical equipment beeping, and the warmth of my mom's hand, I was calm, stable, and in the hospital. "This isn't a very big deal, and it happens to a lot of people," my dad said. "You'll be all right." I nodded and learned the underlying lesson that if you survive something hard, you move on without questioning how hard it was.

After the asthma attack, I was prescribed an inhaler.

"A lot of people have these," my mom said.

I accepted the truth that I had asthma, and it was not certain if I would grow out of it. I was down about it, although it didn't show. This experience drove home the point that my life was not perfect. I was thinking about myself an awful lot and paying no mind to the fact that my family had the means to put me in the league in the first place. Not to mention a car to drive to the emergency room, a father who was a doctor, and the means to get everything I needed to treat asthma.

*Why me?* Every time I asked this question, I wasn't comparing myself to all others, only to my brothers. They were the only two on the planet who had been brought up how I was, with all other things being equal. *Why me and not them?* This was what I was really asking.

## Inner Anger

I was in fourth grade, watching my little brother, Russell, play basketball at the North Gym of our suburban high school along with my parents. Russell was in third grade and the best one on the court. He could dribble with both hands, had serious quickness for his age, and was a great shooter with perfect form.

I had only played soccer and baseball up to this point but figured I could play basketball if Russell could. I guess I didn't realize until now that Russell was the reason that I started. I'm not sure my interest was even in the game itself. Seeing my little brother get attention from my parents, the coaches, his peers, and other spectators was the driving force. It was not until later that I would discover other passions within the game.

I was not very good when I started. First, I was typically the shortest one on the court. Second, it took me some time to fully grasp the rules. I remember a teammate passed the ball to me at half-court, and I thought I wasn't allowed to move. I must have mixed up the order of when I was allowed to dribble versus not. Everyone, including my dad, in the gym was screaming at me, "Go!" and I just kept my feet planted, because that was what I thought was right, and I was too nervous to go away from that. The other team crowded around ripping the ball from my hands, and I fell to the ground. I did not feel sad or confused in this moment, but I recall having an overwhelming sense of anger and a serious adrenaline rush to do something about it. I hopped up, and before I could take action, the buzzer sounded and the game was over.

"Good game," my mom said to me as I walked off the court. I said nothing and took slow breaths as this unfamiliar feeling slowly faded away.

I stuck in there with the rest of the fourth-grade season and settled in a bit. Although my jump shot and ballhandling were not on the same level as Russell's, I was able to channel my in-game anger to defense. I liked playing defense, because I had nothing to lose. If I went for a steal and missed, I could always sprint back and get ahead of my man. If I took the ball from my man, then the crowd went wild. Scoring was never my strong suit. I remember the scariest thing in a game was when I would steal the ball at half-court and have a wide-open layup on the other end. This was undoubtedly the easiest way to score in the game, which was precisely why it made me the most nervous. I recall preferring to have two opposing players defending my layup instead of having a wide-open court, because of the fear of missing and being embarrassed. Everyone can understand a miss with defense, but missing a wide-open layup is laughable.

My older brother, Jerry, was bigger and stronger than both Russell and me. I am about two years older than Russell, and Jerry is about two years older than me. Jerry was both physically and mentally tough on us. We'd play a game called 33, which is essentially a game of one-on-one-on-one. Most of the hobbies, activities, and general interests I had were because one of my brothers had them first. With Jerry, I piggybacked onto everything he did. When Jerry bought the new 311 CD, 311 became my favorite band. When Jerry got a good grade on a test, I knew I had to. When Jerry called a foul on me in our game of 33, he got the ball back and we played on. But when I called a foul on him in our game of 33, he called me a pussy. It was this hypocrisy that brought out my inner anger in a new form, mentally. I could not fathom how something could be so unfair yet also accepted. I could not bear to remain quiet in these times of injustice, even in fourth grade, while Russell was able to. I felt like I was speaking out for both of us. My challenging of Jerry's calls only made the situation worse, and sometimes our games led to physical fights. Boys will be boys. But when the game was over and we had resolved our issue, I became obsessive, giving myself a mental beating about why it all happened. I'd replay what happened and cry to my mom about how unfair it was. She had all the answers and was able to settle me down. While the uncontrollable ping-pong match in my head about how to handle these situations was nowhere near resolved, these experiences proved useful in life down the line.

## Deep Thoughts

Outside the asthma scare, life was calm and predictable for most of my childhood. All three of us did well in school, and for a few summers, we went to a private summer sports camp in New York. Camp gave us the opportunity to get outside the bubble we lived in and mingle with peers from all over the world. Once again, I took for granted how privileged I was to be able to attend the camp in the first place.

Maybe having fully engaged parents with a mixture of tough love and support from my brothers was the reason that I had a boatload of confidence those summers at sports camp. I couldn't wait to e and show off my stuff. For example, when the quiet kid was orner, reading by himself, I'd be proud to walk up to him and make a friend. Then I'd bring him into the group and ensure that others knew he was one of us. On the basketball court, I couldn't wait to get out there and compete with campers way older than me. Also, I thoroughly enjoyed getting to know my much older counselors and learning from them. I followed every rule and didn't have a complaint in the world.

At night, I'd create mind games, enjoying the process of connecting far-off dots. *If I'm eleven years old right now, then Russell is nine and Jerry is thirteen. My counselors are seventeen, which means they are eight years older than Russell, six years older than me, and four years older than Jerry. Take me out of the picture and Russell is four years younger than Jerry, who is four years younger than my counselors. When Russell is my counselor's age, I'll be nineteen and Jerry will be twenty-one. My counselors will be twenty-five. At that time, there will be another group of campers and counselors that are nine, eleven, thirteen, and seventeen. I wonder if in the history of this camp there have been three boys that have the same age differences as Russell, Jerry, and I. I wonder if it will ever happen after us. Of all the camps in the world, I wonder if three boys with our ages are attending right now. I'm certain no one else in the world has asked this question.* I'd snap out of this train of thought with some anxiety and take some deep, slow breaths. Then I'd fall asleep.

At the end of each summer, there was an award ceremony. Camper of the Year was a big deal. The winner would have his or her name engraved on a trophy that would stay with the camp forever. Camper of the Year also got free snacks and drinks for the entire next summer.

"What an amazing summer!" said the owner of the camp at the podium on the final day. "We've created bonds that will last a lifetime. This final award will last a lifetime as well. Camper of the Year goes to the camper who has truly embodied the values of our sports camp. This camper has been respectful, honest, engaged, friendly, and a delight to be around. Camper of the Year goes to...Brett Stevens!" I stood up and smiled. *Really? All I did was follow the rules and I win Camper of the Year?* I walked to the podium and accepted the trophy. The hundreds of campers and staff were looking at me, but I did not feel anxious, more confused. *You're telling me that I outniced all these other people? I told the truth and did what I was told more than all these other people? That was easy.*

That summer at sports camp added to the confidence that I already had. I realized that I was wired to be well-liked by many. I hadn't yet made it to middle school, but I was not afraid. There were still so many unknowns, like, why did my mind wander so far at night? I was okay not having the answers at this point and enjoying the pleasant feelings, but it was certainly something that was mysterious to me. I received praise from my friends and family after winning the award, but something seemed off. *I get the Camper of the Year award for acting normal all summer? Literally anyone could have won this. All people can win this award. There is nothing unique or special about me.* My mind churned the whole car ride home.

## Inner Rage

The three of us had hours of 33 in the driveway and at least one season of formal basketball under our belts, as our parents drove us to our first summer at basketball camp. There were hundreds of players ranging in age from fifth grade all the way to high school as we pulled up. DMX's "Ruff Ryders' Anthem" played loudly from our car.

> ♪*All I know is pain, all I feel is rain. How can I maintain? With that shit on my brain*♪

My parents let us listen to whatever we wanted. We turned off the car and walked in to register.

I was really anxious because I had never done anything like this before. I knew I'd be all right when I was actually on the court, playing. I'd learned from my fifth-grade travel basketball experience that I'd usually be the shortest one on the court, but also unafraid of the other team, who were predictable as guards and clumsy as big men at this level. What had me anxious was all the nonsense surrounding the game itself. For example, when they passed out large T-shirts that were way too big for me, would they tell me I had to wear it? Another uncontrollable concern was whether my alarm would sound at the correct time, or would it fail me, forcing me to run in late for morning stretches? When I finally got settled in, I realized that I could easily tuck my shirt in and my alarm clock was reliable.

The camp was about a week long, and I was able to adjust quickly. I found that there were others like Russell, Jerry, and me, but some of the kids weren't really sure if they wanted to be there and seemed mentally weak.

The structure of the game was basic. Coaches were asked to put their best players in for the second and fourth quarters of the game and keep their weaker players on the first and third quarter lineup. As I stood at five foot two and the ball was bigger than most of my upper body, my coach put me on the first and third squad. He was about six foot two and wore a cowboy hat. I could understand why he would take one look at a five foot two skinny white kid and put him on the first and third squad, but what really pissed me off was that he thought I was dumb. He thought I didn't understand that I was on the shitty team. He thought I was happy to be there and my rich parents made me attend the camp. I had a flashback to Jerry fouling the shit out of me in our games of 33. No matter how many times I had tried to score or get in close, he would relentlessly smother me or block my shot. I thought about Russell draining threes in my face if I gave him an inch of space.

"Good luck out there and have fun!" yelled my coach as the first quarter was about to begin. I gave him a smile. *I'll show you, motherfucker.* I had heard the language from DMX and liked how it felt to think it. We matched up with the other first and third team.

I felt bad for the point guard on the other team. He was even shorter than I was and chubby. As he walked onto the court, his left shoelace was untied, so he had to pull up his Rex Specs to his forehead to bend down and tie it. He wore black shoes, high socks, and a yellow shirt with the sleeves cut off, where his pale, flabby arms were on display. My minirage for being judged and put on the first and third team only got worse when I saw whom I'd be matching up with. I saw blood.

The ref shouted, "Have fun, guys!" and the jump ball was in the air. The clumsy, big man on the other team tapped the ball back to

Rex Specs. I sprinted up to him and ripped the ball out of his hands with ease. I took it the other way and scored; I'd been working on my wide-open, full-court layups all summer and felt more comfortable this year. I slowly started walking back on defense, fully knowing that the opposing team would make a lazy inbounds pass and not expect me to be waiting. As expected, I was able to jump in front of a telegraphed pass for the steal and scored again. They finally got the ball in on the next attempt, and I took the ball from Rex Specs again for another layup. The second and fourth players on my team were going nuts from the bench. I was in a state of mind where I could do this all day. I wasn't getting tired, I had rage inside my blood, and my target was weak and underprepared. Finally, the opposing coach called a time-out, and I jogged back to the bench, where I was greeted with high fives. The rage began to go away, and I felt bad for Rex Specs. For the rest of the game, I paced myself and didn't go for the kill. I had an understanding that there would be a time and place to unleash this rage inside me, but not against a defenseless opponent. We won the game, and my coached moved me to the second and fourth team moving forward.

## *Taking a Step Back*

Unlike the first and third team, where I could take advantage by overpowering, the game on the second and fourth team required some figuring out. On my first attempt to steal the ball like I had previously, my man blew by me and scored. I felt helpless and lost a bit of confidence. As I brought the ball up the court on the very next play, the same player on the opposing team ripped the ball from me and scored. *Do I belong here? Am I the Rex Specs of the second and fourth world?* My coach called a time-out, bent down on one knee, and got in my face. I could smell his nasty breath as he said, "Pass the ball! If you turn the ball over one more time, then you're back on the first and third team!"

I was ready to give up. I walked back slowly onto the court with my head down, and the much taller, stronger, and more athletic fifth grader put his shoulder into me, knocking me down. No one really saw, but it sparked another helping of rage. *Does this asshole really think he's better than me?* As we set up to break the press, one of my teammates pointed up the court as a signal that he was going deep. I received the ball on the inbounds pass and began to dribble like I would on any other play. I even put my head down a bit to sell the idea that I was going to try to beat my man up the court. As soon as I moved forward, my teammate sprinted toward the hoop. I looked up and fired a full-court pass that was caught and scored by him. *Boom!* This was a great feeling and opened up a world of opportunities. It became clear that I could still be on the second and fourth team without needing to be as big and strong as the others. I could use clear communication and timing to score.

I don't remember if we won or lost the game, but I was feeling good. I attended all the activities throughout the week and was dedicated to improving my game.

On the last night of camp, before tomorrow's final award ceremony, Russell and I heard a knock on our door in the dorms. "Come with me," our neighbor and friend said. He walked us a few rooms over to the sight of old pizza slices lying on the floor, bed, and dresser accompanied by about six other campers crowded on the bed. "If I Ruled the World" by Nas was playing, and clothes were everywhere.

*♪Life. I wonder. Will it take me under? I don't know♪*

Everyone was a bit giggly and glancing over at the minifridge against the wall. Our friend Eric was usually the butt of our jokes, but we liked him. Our neighbor said, "We froze Eric's boxers!" and the crowd erupted with laughter. "We stole a pair from his room, drenched it with cold water, and have kept it in the freezer for three days!" The crowd went wild, again. Russell and I awkwardly smiled, knowing that it was funny but could get us in trouble. There was no way we were missing the big moment, however.

"Quiet!" yelled the captain of the goon squad as he crept up to the fridge. As he pulled the handle and opened the freezer, a triangular red-and-white slice of ice pizza struck the floor. This forced one of the sixth graders on the bed to hop up, grab the slice, and throw it in the microwave. "Ewwwwww!" the crowd roared.

"What? I'm hungry."

"Back to the matter at hand," said the leader. He went deeper into the freezer and carefully removed a pair of frozen-solid boxers like a surgeon taking a vital organ from a body. It was so cold he couldn't hold it and dropped them on the floor, shattering the ice and leaving the boxers to thaw. The immature group continued to laugh until Eric popped his head in from all the noise.

"There they are," he announced before grabbing them and taking them back to his room. We all had another laugh before dispersing back to our rooms to get some rest before the award ceremony.

Sunlight was shining through the glass walls on hundreds of young basketball players sitting on the court, with their parents spectating from the running track above. Coach, the owner of the camp, was standing next to the awards for the top ten players at the camp from different age groups. I was anxious because I knew there was a chance I could win. I contemplated if the stress of walking up in front of hundreds of people was worth winning the award itself. *If I do win, then I have to walk up and be embarrassed. If I don't win, then I suck.* Little did I know that this internal conflict would follow me around for many years to come.

"And the Shooter of the Week award goes to…Russell Stevens!"

The crowd cheered loudly as Russell ran up to accept his award, high-fiving peers as he went back to sit down. *He made that look so easy.*

Other awards were presented. Then finally, Coach said, "And the Playmaker of the Week award goes to…" It felt like I had just been punched in the gut and all my air was taken away. "The Playmaker of the Week award goes to…Brett Stevens! These bros can play!" I felt numb, but somehow I managed to walk up, take the award, and sit back down. I'm sure that I blanked out in that moment.

The stress of winning the award had vanished as Russell, Jerry, and I met our parents in the lobby. "Amazing job," said both of my parents. "Good shit, guys. You can thank me now for getting rough in our games of 33," Jerry said with a loving smirk. I remember not wanting that moment to end. We were all together, happy and making our way home as a team. I felt secure knowing that no matter what challenges were ahead in basketball or any other area of my life, I'd always have these people supporting me. As we approached our five-seater Jeep Cherokee, Jerry yelled, "Shotgun! Mom, you're sitting in the back-middle because you didn't win an award."

We all laughed, including my dad.

## Puberty

I walked into middle school on the first day of eighth grade and was surprised. *When did everyone get so tall? And why does it smell like my dad's dirty laundry in here? Doesn't anyone use deodorant?* I strolled through the halls and knew everyone. "Stevens, how was your summer?" "Brett, you playing basketball this year?" "Where are you going to sit at lunch?" I loved the attention—it was earned. When some of my friends were bullies, I was inclusive. When someone was having a bad day, I was there. I felt the need to make sure everyone liked me. In my simple world, this was majorly successful. I'd find out later that it would hinder me.

Not only had I won Camper of the Year at private sports camp, but I had also won Student of the Week a few times last year. I had a great combination of smarts and work ethic. "Your only job is to do well in school," my dad would remind me often throughout the school year. Not that there was any issue if I did poorly on an exam, but the overall grade needed to be competitive. In regards to school, Jerry was pure. I never saw him do a homework assignment or study for an exam, but he always had As. Russell was the polar opposite, always doing schoolwork, sometimes at the expense of his social life. Russell also had all As. I was somewhere in the middle, working as hard as I needed to get As, which was more than Jerry and less than Russell. The common theme was that we all did well in school, no matter how much effort was put in. This created an added layer of competition between the three of us: who was the smartest? The answer was unknown. But among our peers, we all stood out.

I walked to my first class, standing at five foot three. I paid closer attention to the girls this year. Many of them were much taller than I was, which was embarrassing. *Relax, that's one of those things that are completely out of your control.* I let this sink in as I stood up taller. I was tagged as "cute," which was a compliment in middle school, but I didn't like it. I felt that I was cute because I was short, while my friends where "hot" because they were taller and more mature. I tried to make my voice deeper when I spoke, but it was lame.

I developed a complex this year. *I don't give a fuck what anyone thinks about me.* It wasn't a pleasant, soft whisper in my ear. It was a loud roar that reminded me to control everything I could while also resisting and trying hard to control the things that I could not. As I strolled through the hallway, saying hello to most of my peers with a smile on my face, I was thinking, *I don't give a fuck how tall I am now or if I ever get taller. I don't give a fuck what you think about me or what you think about me.* I finally found my class and gave a warm smile to my history teacher. She was hot.

I glanced over to find my seat, and my two best friends, Jack and Roger, had that look on their faces. *We've died and gone to heaven getting this teacher.* They couldn't sit still. As I walked past them to find my desk in the back of the class, they were giggling. "We hit the jackpot, Stevens!" said Roger.

"I'm Ms. G, and I'll be your history teacher this year. I'm really looking forward to getting to know all of you, and I think it will be a great..."

The sound of a whoopee cushion went off from under Roger's desk.

"Year," she finished. "All right, who has the whoopee cushion?"

Roger and Jack could not hold back their laughter, but it got pinned on Roger.

"Roger, stand up."

Roger stood up and saluted Ms. G. "Yes, ma'am!"

"Where's the whoopee cushion, Roger?" she said.

He walked to the front of the class and put both hands on the chalkboard. "I guess you'll have to search me to find it."

I was in tears of laughter. I enjoyed lying low and not being the center of attention when it came to breaking the rules, but I definitely participated in the fun that came with someone else breaking a rule. Roger got suspended for a few days, and the whole incident blew over.

Like all my peers, I was learning more and more about my emotions in middle school. I never got into fights or felt the need to have to defend myself. I had basketball as a place to put most of my anger and rage. The rest was harmless. I told myself that I didn't give a fuck about what anyone thought about me, but that was far from the truth.

## Failure

Russell and I had heard stories about how Jerry led his team to the medal rounds of the Maccabi Games, and I couldn't wait to watch the tape when he got home from Florida. On the tape we saw Jerry make a perfect pass to a wide-open teammate under the hoop with two seconds left. Unfortunately, he blew the layup and they lost. I remember paying close attention to Jerry's reaction after the miss. I observed anger and rage, which made me grin. *That's my brother.* I was excited to have my shot on this stage soon.

The Maccabi Games are a yearly event similar to the Olympics, but only Jewish youth qualify to play. There are multiple venues across the USA that host the games every summer and also bigger events held in Israel every few years. Maccabi was awesome because it gave us an opportunity to shine even brighter. If you're familiar with the physicality and athleticism it takes to be great at basketball, you can see how playing with a smaller segment of the population, only Jewish youth, would be easier. Not to say that the game was easy, but when you narrow the playing field, five foot three is not as short as it used to be.

I walked into my first practice very confident about my skill and strength. After all, I'd already been one of the better players on my youth teams and won an award at basketball camp. I laced up my Iversons and looked around the gym, noticing that I wasn't the shortest one on the court anymore. I felt really good about that. I saw a lefty stroking three-pointers with little effort and swooshing every one. I started shooting close in and rebounding for him. He did the same for me, and we formed an instant bond. Before we got to talking, a five foot seven man with glasses strutted his way into the gym and blew his whistle. "Get on the line!" My new friend smiled and comfortably trotted to the baseline, while I felt a strong pang of anxiety.

"I don't care if you can shoot. I don't care if you can pass. I don't care if you can dribble. But you *will* not get tired. Take them through some stretches, Danny." My friend warmed us all up, and we were back on the baseline. "Al, explain to the team what a *suicide* is."

Al was about six foot two, and he looked like a giant among the rest of us. "A *suicide* is when we sprint to the foul line and back, then half-court and back, then to the opposite foul line and back, then to the opposite baseline and back." I had done one of these before and was determined to win the race. The other 70 percent of the team sighed heavily.

I won the first suicide. "Go again," said our coach. I won the second suicide. "Again." I won the third suicide. "Last one, go!" I looked to my left and right and saw most of the team essentially walking at this point. Dan and Al were still pushing. I heard a faint voice telling me that I had to win. I pushed so hard that I won by far, but I couldn't breathe. I rested my hands on my knees and tried to regain my breath. I looked up and no one else even appeared to be tired. Dan jogged over and asked if I was okay, and I pretended to be.

"Good," he said. "Practice is about to start now."

Over the next two weeks I learned how to pace myself, but the voice telling me to win never faded. At this point in my life, I saw having something to prove as being a purely good quality.

When we arrived at the host city for the games, the other teams were much bigger and stronger than we were. I'm not sure that we won a game. I recall being down by twenty points and still hav- mind-set that I wanted to steal the ball from my man even we had no chance of winning. He had been dominating me entire game, so I pressed all the way up on him against my coach's orders. He made one move left, then back right, elbowing me directly in the nose. I got a hand on the ball and he took it right back as I fell to the floor. Pathetic. We had worked so hard and put ourselves through so much pain only to be embarrassed in a far-off land. "Chill out," Dan said, although equally as upset at our showing. He always had a way of remaining calm while still competing at a high level. And here I was, all in or nothing, all the time. I felt numb to emotion as I sat on the bench and the clock went to zero. Confused, I wondered, *How could I put all this energy and effort into something and come out embarrassed? This is bullshit!*

My first experience at the Maccabi Games was eye-opening. I had worked so hard and came up so empty. I felt worthless and that I would never be able to get the things I wanted in life. What better proof was there than this? I finally made it home tired, bruised, and defeated. I hadn't had enough experience with losing to know how to deal with what I was feeling. So I did what any other sheltered adolescent would do, cried to my mama. As always, she reassured me and said, "Wait until next year!"

## *Weakness*

I pushed the ball directly down the middle of the court with one man to beat. With assassin-like precision, I moved the ball across my body, getting the final defender to shift left. Then I pulled the ball back with lightning speed to the right, causing the defender to slide back on his heels and topple over. I scored the layup and ran back on defense. "That's the Stevens!" my teammate said as we slapped hands on my way back. My friends had coined this in-and-out move as the Stevens because I used it so often with success.

I continued to develop physically in eighth grade, which led to a great season, followed by a better showing at the Maccabi Games the following summer. I was certain I wanted to try out for the high school team, which was only a few months away.

One day in the fall of my freshman year of high school, Jerry and I were shooting around in the backyard when we heard the loud thumping of 2Pac's "Hail Mary" coming from a vehicle parked in front.

♪*I ain't a killa' but don't push me, revenge is like
the sweetest joy next to gettin' pussy*♪

This song elevated my adrenaline, although I didn't really concern myself too much with the lyrics. Jerry threw the ball at my shoes and said, "Time for open gym."

I was shaking with anxiety in the back of the car like a freezing fan at a football game. Max was driving, and Jerry was in the front seat. "You brought your brother to an open gym?" questioned Max.

"Yeah," Jerry said. "He's a scrawny little bitch but can hang."

"Whatever you say," said Max as he turned the music up a bit louder and drove us to the high school.

The South Gym of the high school was vast and had bleachers on three of the four walls. You could smell the history. We were a bit late and changing our shoes while other players were already engaged in organized stretches. Standing at five foot four, I was the smallest one in the gym by far. Even the guards were five foot ten or taller. The three of us joined in, and right as we were about to warm up, a whistle blew.

At six foot four and an ex–college athlete, Coach D glided to the center of the court. He took one look around, and we made eye contact for a split second. "Ballhandling. Get 'em goin', Jerry." My brother was now a senior and had been to open gyms for the past few years. I sighed with relief that ballhandling was one skill that I felt strong in. I was breathing hard when Coach D walked by, and I dribbled off my foot. He threw the ball back to me and said, "It's okay," noticing how badly I wanted to impress him.

That was about all the attention I received from the head coach that day. I hung in there for a few more drills and wasn't able to work my way into the scrimmage. *What the fuck is wrong with me? Why am I so soft?* Jerry was playing well, and I felt good about that because he would be in a good mood on the way home and not add insult to injury about my weak showing.

The whistle blew, and everyone came together, clapping, until Coach D spoke. "How's everyone feeling? We're doing well, but we have a lot to work on if we're going to be the team that we can be this year. Max, do you agree?"

"Aye, aye, Captain," said Max to the roar of laughter from other confident, experienced seniors.

"All right!" Coach D said. "Before we go, let's try one more drill."

"Oh, boy!" shouted another player, already aware of the impending doom. Everyone had already run to their places before I had a clue of what was going on. I followed Jerry—thank God he was there.

In this drill, half of the players lined up under the hoop, and the other half lined up at the half-court line. *Fuck, we're taking charges.* This information sunk in my stomach like a bad burrito. I was in the back of the line, watching each player run out, get knocked over, and Coach D determined if it was a block or a charge. It was finally my turn, and I was matched up with a six foot six center. In this moment, I wasn't scared. It was an opportunity to show my toughness. *Bring it on, motherfucker.* The center couldn't hold his laughter as he trotted up, slowed down, and tried to push me over with his pinky finger. Everyone, including Coach D, laughed, except Jerry. I didn't want to be a baby about it, so I laughed as well. *You're all fucking idiots.*

The drill progressed, and somehow I was matched up to take a charge against Jerry. *This might be okay.* After all, Jerry had had my back more than once that day. "We'll end after the brothers' duel!" shouted Coach D, with an interested look on his face. Then the whistle blew.

Jerry was coming fast. Too fast. I expected him to put some decent velocity behind his charge, but this was too much. I was a helpless five foot four, 125-pound, scrawny freshman waiting to absorb a charge from my five foot eight, 170-pound brother coming full steam ahead. He lowered his head, turned his shoulder, and made contact. I flew backward a few feet and was knocked down. My perception went blank. The playfulness stopped, and the room went silent. After a few seconds on the ground, I hopped up and shook it off. My back was killing me, but I didn't let it show. After I was able to collect myself, we huddled up. "Good work today, team," Coach D said.

On the drive home, Jerry and Max were having a great time while I sat in the back, hiding the pain. *Why did he have to do that?* When we got home, my parents asked, "How was open gym?" I walked right by them and took a shower.

## Full Control

"Throw me the ball, Billy!" shouted the assistant coach of the high school freshman basketball team as he stood at one end of the court. Billy had a great arm, but poor judgment.

"Yes, sir," he replied as he cocked his arm back from the other end like a quarterback and shot the ball from his hand directly at the coach. The rest of the team watched as the ball went through Coach S's hands, landing directly in his crotch.

"A…a…ahem," gasped the hunched-over coach. "Nice velocity on that one, Billy. Ahem, nice job, everyone. I think we've had enough practice for one day."

The group of ninth graders on the sideline erupted with laughter and jogged into the locker room.

I wasn't tall, strong, or mature enough to play on the varsity or even junior varsity team my freshman year of high school. It didn't bother me to be on the freshman team, because I viewed high school basketball as a four-year journey. Friends that I had played with growing up were all on the team with me, and we had a blast. We finished the season with both a great record and lots of memories.

That summer, Russell and I decided that we wanted to improve our games. I was going to be a sophomore, and he would be entering his freshman year. If I ever wanted a shot at junior varsity, this would be the summer to prepare. We had heard about a one-day skills clinic and convinced our parents to sign us up.

"Just do the best that you can," said our dad as we pulled up and saw hundreds of mature-looking players walking toward the gym. After performing well in most situations like this, I wasn't very nervous. Russell looked the same. We laced up our shoes as the coach addressed the crowd.

"Players and parents, thank you all for coming. This clinic was my million-dollar idea. Oh, no, I'm not a millionaire, but in the thirty years that I've been teaching these dribbling techniques, I've earned about a million dollars!" The players were a little bit lost, but the parents chuckled. "Today you will be learning a proven system for becoming proficient in all areas of ballhandling. In all my years using these practices, I've found that THE PLAYERS WHO WORK THE HARDEST WILL GAIN THE MOST!" I sensed frustration in his voice that most of the players didn't work their hardest.

I was mesmerized. *The players who work the hardest will gain the most.* This line sank into the depths of my soul. Suddenly, I felt like I had control over my own destiny. *All I have to do is work harder, and I can win.* I was excited and couldn't break eye contact with the coach. The rest of the room went blurry, and all I could see were the actual words coming out of his mouth. What I heard next was, "Let's talk about a few housekeeping items," but what I saw was an old man's mouth moving and bold black words floating into the air: *The. Players. Who. Work. The. Hardest. Will. Gain. The. Most.* It was like watching a puppet moving its mouth while words drifted out.

I snapped out of my trance and looked over at Russell, who was also paying attention. What I saw next was mind-boggling. A majority of the other players weren't even listening! They were pinching one another, looking around, making noise, or just bored. *This man just gave us golden advice, and you missed it!* I then felt the urge to whisper to Russell, "Did you hear that?" His smile confirmed that he did without him even speaking. *At least Russell gets it.*

A whistle blew and the rest of the day was spent performing intricate ballhandling drills. If one didn't know any better, they'd think we were at the circus. "Why do we have to juggle? What's the point of dribbling with three balls? When do we get to start shooting?" The other players complained. Russell and I immediately saw the value in these exercises, and we tried our best to do what the coaches were asking. I made so many mistakes that day! The drills were new to me, and I found myself dribbling off my foot every time the coach walked by. Unlike my mistakes in front of other coaches, these mistakes didn't bother me at all. *The players who work the hardest will gain the most.*

When the day was over, my dad asked the coach how his kids performed. "Which is the one that's going to be a sophomore?" asked the coach.

"Over there." Dad pointed to me. I pretended that I wasn't listening.

"Oh, him?" Coach asked. "He'll never play varsity."

Surprisingly, I had no reaction to hearing his words. The coach had given me more than he knew that day.

On the way out, both Russell and I received a towel, water bottle, T-shirt, and what would become the most important item in our basketball careers, the drill book. I hopped in the front seat and yelled back to Russell.

"We're doing drills out of this book every day."

Before I could finish my sentence, he shouted, "Obviously!"

Then I mused out loud, "Apparently, I'll never make the varsity team. Should I get into rugby?"

The three of us laughed as we drove back to home base to get organized, as Wu-Tang's "Tears" played softly in the background.

♪*After…laughter…comes tears*♪

# Hard Work

A bead of sweat dripped from my forehead onto a worn-out drill book, smearing the pen marks in a box across CROSSOVERS: *3 × 50.* "How many reps of crossovers did you do again, Russ?"

"Fifty," he replied.

I wrote over the old pool of ink and ensured the number 50 was legible. I tossed the crinkly paper binder to the side and took my turn pounding the ball from one hand to the other, working aggressively on the most useful ballhandling move in the game of basketball: the crossover.

For the two months after the clinic experience, we did what we said we were going to do and significantly improved our games. Wake up. Eat. Shoot. Eat. Lift. Ballhandling. Eat. Go to the local courts at night and play pickup. Repeat. We'd swap out an occasional night at the courts to hang out with friends or adjust our routine on family vacation, but for the most part, this was our entire summer. Both of us could dribble two balls at the same time with our eyes closed, juggle three balls, fiercely bounce one ball through our legs and catch it behind our neck, and most importantly, we were lights-out shooting from behind the three-point line.

"Do well in school and you won't have to get a summer job," my dad would say. He was a successful dermatologist who was able to support our basketball endeavors. He even put a basketball court in our backyard. I'd invite my friends over to play and get sarcastic comments about being a rich Jew. This fueled my fire to work hard even more. *I'm a rich Jew, and that's the only reason I'm good at basketball? Do you have any fucking clue how hard we work out here?* I'd laugh it off externally and go back to playing while this inner rage would eat at me.

It was not all fun and games that summer. Russell and I had spent essentially every waking minute together pushing each other, dribbling in the rain, going for long runs after sundown, and also playing one-on-one. As July turned to August, we had both become stronger and more competitive. We had an understanding that the more we pushed each other, the more systematic we were with tracking our drills, and the more physical our sessions were, the better off we would both be.

It was extra humid after we finished shooting jump shots one morning, and I casually asked Russell, "Wanna play one-on-one?"

"Sure," he said.

I pulled my left leg back to my butt, released, pulled my right leg back the same way on the other side, then jogged over to the boom box and turned up "Da Mystery of Chessboxin'" by the Wu-Tang Clan, extra loud.

♪ *The game of chess is like a swordfight. You must think
first [sound of sword swinging] before you move*♪

"Ugh, not another Wu-Tang song," Russell whined.

"This game will be over quickly," I said, annoyed. "I'll shoot for ball." I fired a deep three-pointer to see who would get the ball first and bricked it.

"Your shot isn't even that good," Russell remarked. He moved to the top of the key and I got low on defense. "We're playing to five. I'm tired," he said.

"So soft, as usual. Fine," I answered.

♪ *Raw Imma give it to ya, with no trivia, we're
like cocaine straight from Bolivia*♪

He took his shirt off and showed off his newly gained, built upper body. I was wearing a yellow cutoff and Nike shorts. "Let me guess, you are wearing sunscreen because Dad scared you."

"Yeah, I'm not an idiot like you."

♪ *Well, I'm a sire, I set the microphone on fire,
rap styles bury, and carry like Mariah*♪

I could feel equal parts adrenaline and anger building up inside me. Russell threw the ball to me, and I threw it back a bit low and too hard on purpose. I pressed up on him unexpectedly, took the ball out of his hands, and went in for an easy layup. "1–0, make it take it." We checked the ball again, and I jabbed right at him, then pulling up for three. Swoosh. "3–0, really, Russ?" I got the ball back and was loving the music. I could feel no pain.

♪ *My peoples, are you with me? Where you at? In
the front in the back, killa' bees on attack*♪

I faked a jump shot, Russell bit, and I went in for another layup. "4–0." I looked Russell in the eye and felt slightly bad for how big of an asshole I was being. The second I let my guard down, he stole the ball from me and swooshed a three pointer. "4–2," he said with no emotion. Then we checked the ball. He shot again. Swoosh. "4–4." Just like that, we were tied and Russell had the ball. I felt anxious and not in control anymore. When Russell got the ball back, he fired up another three before I could even get a hand in his face. The ball was moving in slow motion and looked good. *Please don't go in.* Then it rimmed out. I was able to retrieve the rebound and take it back to the top of the key. Russell was now aggressively going for the steal and scratched my arm, opening up the skin. I felt no pain. The next random Wu-Tang song came on.

♪*Shaolin shadowboxing, and the Wu-Tang sword style.*
*If what you say is true, the Shaolin and the*
*Wu-Tang could be dangerous.*
*Do you think your Wu-Tang sword can defeat me?* ♪

I felt another burst of adrenaline as the song projected, "Bring da mothafucking ruckus," and repeated a few times.

♪*Bring da mothafucking ruckus. Bring the motha, bring*
*the motha, bring the mothafucking ruckus.*♪

With my bloody arm, I backed Russell down into the paint. He was taller, but I weighed more. I aggressively jumped into his body and grazed his face on the way up. I tossed the ball up toward the rim, and it went down. "Game!" I yelled in his face as I pushed him onto the grass with perfectly utilized force. I started walking slowly back into the house, leaving him there. Then everything went black.

A few seconds later, I gently opened my eyes and let some light in. I found myself confused on the ground, with a basketball next to me. I rolled over and saw Russell still on the court about thirty yards away.

♪*Bring da mothafucking ruckus.*♪

I put it all together and hopped up like a madman. Then I sprinted directly at Russell, where we brawled on the concrete for a few minutes.

Finally, we were both out of energy, lying on the concrete court. Me with a bloody arm and him with a rip in his shirt, both of us out of breath. On cue, we started laughing hysterically.

"How in God's name did you hit me directly in the back of the head from all the way back there, you asshole?"

"Got lucky," he said with a smile on this face. "I think that's enough for one day."

I picked up the drill book and headed inside. Russell turned off the music and shot a few more foul shots before following me in.

## Jeffrey

The summer was winding down, and the open-gym cycle would start over in a few weeks. Russell and I had managed to get ourselves ready for the upcoming season and even squeezed in another week of basketball camp. On the last day of camp, my dad said, "There's a more exclusive type of camp that I can get you registered for if you want, Brett. There's only one spot, so you'll have to wait for next year, Russ. It starts next week."

"Okay," I replied without having a clue what I was getting myself into.

I had one night of sleep at the house and was still a bit sore from last week's camp, but I was up and ready to go at seven o'clock the next morning. When we got to the college campus, where the camp was held, the rain came down on our front windshield violently. "I'll be back at the end of the week to get you. Have fun." I grabbed my bag from the trunk and sprinted to take cover as my dad drove off, leaving a wake behind him.

I managed to navigate the rain and find my dorm, which was about a half mile from where I was dropped off. I dragged my bag up to my floor and heard the new Beanie Sigel album playing from one of the rooms.

*♪ Still got love for you, though you left me in the cold, and face this world alone, and make it on my own. ♪*

I matched my registration papers with the number on the room and found a muscular black adolescent enjoying his music in our room. "Hey, man, I'm Brett. Nice to meet you."

He sat up and gave me a pound. "You too. I'm Jamal."

I threw my bag down and lay on my unmade bed with my shoes still on. "You ever been to this camp before?" I asked, trying to gather as much information as possible.

"Yes. Just be on time to everything and you'll be all right."

We then sat without speaking until the entire album played out.

*I'm drowning in a pool, fighting for my life with whistles blowing all around me. With every breath comes a mouthful of water. I'm slowly sinking down, down, down, until my eyes rip open.*

"Get your asses to the top of the hill!" screamed a coach as he exhaled into his whistle from outside my window. Jamal was nowhere to be found. I panicked and scrambled to find my outfit. I threw on a blue cutoff, white socks, Under Armour spandex, black Nike shorts, and my Iversons and hustled outside. There were a few other stragglers, but most of the camp had already made it to the top of the hill for morning stretches.

When I scaled the hill, I found hundreds of campers stretching in unison to the tune of what sounded like an army general counting, expecting a response from his troops. "One!" *Clap.* "Two!" *Clap clap.* "Three!" *Clap clap clap.* "Four!" *Clap clap clap clap.* "Five!" *Clap clap clap clap clap.* I had never seen anything like this before. I found my place in the back and ran through morning stretches, which were performed on concrete.

What made this camp so great was the quality of coaches, lecturers, and training that each camper received. There were rumors that Michael Jordan, Ron Artest, and Mike Krzyzewski would be on campus. They even had an open draft to select the teams. I recognized a theme that had become standard as I showed up to the draft selection games. *Big surprise, I'm still short.* I had trained very hard this summer with Russell and was unafraid. When I walked into the gym, I saw Jamal slam-dunk the ball on a far-off court that had already started playing. *Damn.*

I was put on a draft team to play an open game so coaches could evaluate and make their selections later that evening. On the first play, I went to get the ball as usual to bring up the court. The player on my team took one look at me and passed the ball to a different player to bring the ball up. *Dick.* I jogged up the side of the court to watch this player pull up from way behind the three-point line and completely miss. The other team got the rebound and quickly scored on the other end. This time, I ran up and said, "Give me the fucking ball!" This got my teammate's attention, and he passed me the ball. *Idiot.* I made eye contact with a six foot light-skinned teammate, and he responded by pointing his finger up toward the rim. I dribbled down the middle of the court and looked to my left, where I faked a pass to the player on my left. Out of the corner of my eye, I saw the same six foot light-skinned figure about to launch into the air. I continued to look to my left but threw the ball on the right side of the rim, where the astronaut was approaching and slammed it down. We pointed at each other as coaches were yelling, "Dunker, what's your name? Point guard, what's your name?"

"Jeffrey!" he shouted.

"Brett!" I yelled.

"Brad?"

"No, Brett."

"Brent?"

"Brett, B-R-E-T-T!"

"Got it!"

After the game, Jeffrey and I had a chat and became friends. "Most of these dudes suck," he said. Even though I was half as tall and half as strong as most, I was right there with him.

### Front and Center

There was still 2:17 on the clock at the end of the second quarter in the field house, but all players froze as NBA great, six foot seven Ron Artest towered into the gym. He was wearing windbreaker pants and a loose-fitting white T-shirt and found a spot in the bleachers, taking up three vertical rows. His arms were sprawled out, covering three more seats on each side. The man was taking up the surface area of about twenty seats. The players snapped out of their trance and played on.

I swear that when Ron Artest entered the gym that day, we made eye contact. It felt like he was branding my soul with his gaze, and an instant connection was formed. I was in the corner, and the defensive player guarding me got up in my face, spitting, "That's my cousin over there." *I'm being guarded by Ron Artest's cousin!* This excited me because I knew I was quicker than him. I sprinted toward the top of the key and got the ball. I jabbed at his right shoe, and he stumbled back a bit. Then he tried to recover, lunging at me, while my body lowered and arms went up for the shot fake. Before he landed, I took one hard dribble to the right. He barely found his footing but stepped over to try to get in front of me with all his momentum moving right. I crossed the ball aggressively back to my left hand, and he fell on the floor. The crowd went wild, and Ron sat up in his seat. Another defender charged at me, and I used the coined Stevens to make him miss. Then I took one more hard dribble and spun off the final defender for the layup. Everyone in the crowd, including Ron Artest, clapped. I ran back on defense with a tense look on my face, feeling awesome.

That night, Ron Artest was to give a presentation to the entire camp of 1,200 on what it takes to succeed. I was in line, waiting to walk up the bleachers for the presentation, when I saw Ron walking toward me. I got anxious. *What's this guy doing? Shouldn't he be front and center?* He then asked, "What's your name?"

"B-Brett," I choked out.

"Thanks," he said and walked away.

*Holy shit, why?* I brushed it off and found my seat.

"And now, for the main presenter of the evening, explaining to all of us what it means to be successful, Ron Artest!" The crowd cheered as Ron walked to the microphone.

"Before I get started," he said, "where's Brett?"

My heart sank to what felt like the bottom of the ocean.

"Brett, where are ya? Come on down here."

My legs and arms were shaking as I stood up.

"There he is! Get on down here!"

The crowd of 1,200 awkwardly clapped and judged me as I toppled over other campers to get to the aisle.

Ron put me through a workout in front of the entire camp. I still don't remember what I was doing out there, but it might have been a bunch of sit-ups and layup drills. When he was done with me, he announced to the camp, "Thanks, Brett!" Then he came in close and said, "Nice move today, dude." I ran back to my seat, feeling overwhelmed and relieved at the same time.

When the presentation was over, Jeffrey ran up to me and said, "Holy shit, dude, that was awesome!"

"Thanks," I replied. "I almost shit myself."

He laughed and followed. "Hey, listen, my dad is going to be on the outdoor courts tonight during pickup. Do you want to meet him?"

"Sure," I said.

Later that night, I was playing pickup, minding my own business, when I saw a mountain of a man wearing all white approaching. Campers and coaches were screaming and following like schoolchildren as this six foot six figure moved onto the court I was playing on. *Oh my god, that's Michael Jordan!* I couldn't move. I wanted to, but I couldn't. My feet were planted to the ground like a mailbox in front of a mansion. Jeffrey appeared behind him and grabbed his hand, pulling him toward me. "Brett, meet my dad, Michael Jordan." I couldn't talk. I wanted to but couldn't.

"Nice to meet you, Brett," he said, and he shook my clammy hand.

On the last day of camp, there was an award ceremony. My mom and Jerry showed up to the cafeteria, where 1,200 basketball players were looking at the front table. The noise quieted, and the head of the camp started with awards. "And the Playmaker of the Week award goes to Brett Stevens, a rising sophomore!" I felt somewhat comfortable walking up in front of the group to accept my award. Later, I would learn that Jerry's reaction was, "How?"

The exclusive camp experience built my confidence on the basketball court and off. I was prepared to try out for the varsity team, and life was good.

## Initial Buzz

I was well-liked in high school, a good student, and an excellent basketball player. Our family took a trip to the Jersey Shore the summer after my freshman year for vacation. My parents led the caravan for the six-hour drive, followed by Russell and me listening to Jadakiss in the Acura, and Jerry and his friend Colin were in the back. Jerry was able to purchase a flashy blue Subaru WRX after a summer of being the top seller at his summer job and was excited to get it on the open road. As we drove into the main stretch of the shore, we were surrounded by mini golf, ice cream, beach, and basketball courts. We settled into our extravagant rental house.

"Let's go get booze," Jerry said. My parents looked at each other and laughed, not terribly concerned. Jerry, Colin, Russell, and I piled into the WRX and headed to the liquor store. None of us were over twenty years old. On the drive over, Colin pulled out what looked like a magic wand. I had tried beer before and didn't like it. I knew what marijuana was but had never tried it. Before I could look out of the window, the wand was being passed to me in the back seat. Like everything else I did in front of Russell, I acted confidently. I took a huge hit and coughed uncontrollably. I passed it to Russell, who took a tiny puff and passed it back to the front. Then the music in the car started tickling my ears. I could feel my heart beating. The wind from the open window felt like a full-body massage. *This is awesome!* I looked over at Russell, and before I could fully turn my neck, we both started laughing uncontrollably.

"You guys are so gay!" Jerry giggled from the front seat. "Nolia Clap" by Juvenile was blasting from the car.

♪*Y'all hear that Nolia Clap? [Clap, clap, clap, clap]*♪

We all knew the words, even though we couldn't relate to them. We pulled up to a red light, and a car pulled up to our right, with an African American driver. Colin, a little stoned at this point, turned the music down and closed his window. "Chill, chill, chill," he said. Jerry looked at him like he was nuts and continued onto the liquor store. *Someone is going to catch us. Why did we do this? I can't feel my legs—how can I run?* My buzz was fading, and paranoia was setting in. Jerry used a fake ID to purchase a handle of vodka, and we made it back to the house.

I sneaked past my parents and locked myself in my room. I was so excited when the door locked, ensuring no one would see me like this. I went back to enjoying the rest of the buzz and took a nap.

I woke up to a loud knock on the door. "We're circling up and going out!" Jerry yelled. I walked to the outside deck and found the bottle of booze in the center of a round table, with four seats and one lonely shot glass. We sat down as Jerry explained the rules. "Circling up. You don't have to drink fast, but you do have to drink." He poured a shot for himself, downed it, and passed the shot glass to Colin, who did the same. The shot glass and bottle came to me. I mirrored what the others did, felt the poison go down my throat, and passed it on to Russell, who did the same. The level of booze in the bottle looked the same as it did before we all had our shots. Jerry took another and let the shot glass sit in front of Colin. Colin took his time on this one. He grabbed the speakers and put on a different Juvenile song. After that, we sat in a circle, laughing and getting drunk for the next hour or so.

Jerry and Colin went to the eighteen-plus club, and Russell and I went to the under-eighteen club. "Go stand over there," I told Russell, and he complied. Sure enough, two girls found him attractive and walked close to him. I came in and introduced us as brothers. This tactic would work out well for us on more than one occasion. Send Russell in as bait with his height and good looks, followed by me with my charming personality and wit. The rest of the night was a blur of dancing, laughing, making out, dizziness, and nausea. I woke up in my bed the next morning to another knock on the door. "Get your ass up, we're playing Monopoly." I felt terrible but found my way to the same table where we had just polished off a full bottle of vodka the previous night. Colin hit the music and we started the game, five dollars a head, winner take all. After less than an hour of play, I had won the game. It would go down as the fastest game of Monopoly in the Stevens family history.

After Monopoly, we moved on to No-Limit Texas Hold 'Em. I understood how to play poker, but this game was different. I learned about the blinds, flop, turn, and river. I used my Monopoly winnings to get into the poker game; I might have even spotted Russell as well. The game made sense to me right away. Over the course of the week, we found a few other things to bet on, mini golf, which I won, and two-on-two basketball.

"Ten dollars each for basketball, boys. You practice all the time, so it's fair," Jerry announced. Jerry and Colin were much stronger than us. Every time we'd get close to the hoop, they would foul us hard and start the play over again. I was getting more and more angry with every play. Finally, when the game ended and they won, I had a meltdown.

"I'm running home," I said.

"Get in the car," Jerry replied.

"Fuck you! Russell, are you coming with me?"

Russell looked at both of us and sided with me.

We started the five-mile run back to the house on the sidewalk. Thirty seconds later, Jerry pulled up to our left and yelled, "Get in the fucking car! Mom's going to kill me!"

"Don't even look at him," I said to Russell. We kept our heads straight until Jerry finally peeled off in frustration.

Having an older brother on this trip allowed me to experiment with liquor and marijuana before most of my friends had. I didn't crave the experience again, but I did learn that partying with drugs and alcohol was certainly more fun than partying without. I came back from this trip with an added social confidence. I overlooked the paranoia and anxiety that the weed had caused and summed it all up as good, clean fun.

## First Game

I came out swinging and showed strength, hustle, smarts, and mental toughness in the open gyms prior to my sophomore year, not allowing myself to get too caught up in the fun that I had at the Jersey Shore. The junior point guard in front of me had natural skill and was a standout his entire life, but he didn't take the time to work as hard as Russell and I did over the summer. I found it natural to run the offense even with him all over me on defense. I also had moments of taking the ball off him and scoring at the other end. Regardless, he was a great mentor and there were no hard feelings between us. I wasn't expecting Coach D to put me on the varsity team that season, but he did. I felt a sense of power in that moment. *The players who work the hardest will gain the most.* I took a second to thank my drill coach in my mind for the advice that he had given the group just months earlier, even though "He'll never play varsity" echoed in my mind. I took another second to let the rage inside me pass for him doubting me.

The whiteboard in the visitor's locker room at the predominantly black high school was clean except for a list of player initials with their height, position, and short description written in red marker. Our group of twelve crowded around the whiteboard like eager students, wearing shiny blue snap pants and white warm-ups with blue stripes across the chest and a gold streak down each side. "Zach, you'll be guarding DJ," said Coach D with confidence. Zach was six foot five, wide, and our biggest player. I glanced up at the board and saw *DJ, 6'9", center—won't shoot from the outside, powerful, box him out.* I saw one of our bench players smirk, which usually meant, "We're so fucked."

*Not so bad,* I thought.

"Chris, you'll be guarding RD." *RD, 6'7", power forward—may shoot, good skills, box him out.* Chris was six foot three.

*Oh, shit, that's not good.*

Two others on their team were matched up against two of our other physically inferior players before all eyes were on me. "Brett, you'll be matched up against DR, 6'3", point guard—can do it all.

DR turned out to be Darrelle Revis, a talented high school athlete then that turned out to be an NFL Pro Bowler.

*Fuck it,* I thought, shaking in my five foot five tailored warm-up gear.

"Let's go, Blue! Bring it in!" said Coach D. We crowded in, clapping, and then ran up to the court.

Not only had I made the varsity team, but I was also the starting point guard. We made our way to the corner of the court, and the coaches walked toward our bench. One of the seniors on our team brought us together and proudly voiced, "Fuck these n——!" The other eleven of us reacted with, "Whoa, whoa, whoa. Chill out." I took the ball and ran around the outside the court, with the varsity team running behind me in a single-file line.

"Get off the court, you weak crackers!" yelled a hometown fan.

"Is this really your team?" shouted another.

I led the team to the middle of the court and began the tip drill by charging to the basket and throwing the ball off the backboard while the teammate behind me jumped, caught it, and repeated the process until all twelve players had tipped the ball off the backboard. We then ran a few warm-up drills while an edited version of the familiar 2Pac song "Hail Mary" blasted in the background.

♪*I ain't a killa', but don't push me, revenge is like the sweetest joy next to gettin' [bleep]*♪

I was feeling pretty good, believe it or not. The ball felt the same as it always had, the hoops were the same height, and I knew that we'd be underestimated, which might give us an advantage. A buzzer sounded, and the music stopped. We all lined up for the national anthem. I found it interesting that all the derogatory name-calling halted during this moment. *Just because this song is playing, we all become civilized?* I also developed a weird habit of counting the fifty stars on the flag slowly during the national anthem, trying to hit the last one right as the song ended on the word *brave.* I never liked to wait for anything, and I had to keep my mind occupied for these few minutes.

The national anthem ended, and the other four starters and I sat in our chairs, waiting to be introduced. The other four starters got their names called one by one to the sound of loud "Boos," ran over to shake the opposing coach's hand, and then came back to our side. "And now, a five foot five sophomore point guard, Brett Stevens!" I had a brief flashback to having my name called at basketball camp for awards, but this was much different. I hopped up to the crowd booing and laughing at the same time. "Hit puberty!" yelled one fan. *Fuck all these people.* I trotted over, shook the coach's hand, and headed back toward my team, feeling excited. *I'm fucking starting varsity, holy shit!* The announcer called the other team out, and boy, were they fired up. The starting five for each team walked to center court for the tip-off.

I was walking straight ahead when I felt a shoulder hit directly into mine, knocking me off course. I looked up at a forty-five-degree angle and found DJ looking down at me, smiling. Then I felt a tap on my shoulder. "Are you the point guard?"

I laughed nervously. "Yeah."

It was Darrelle Revis. He smirked as well and got into position for the tip-off.

I must have been crazy, five foot five, 150 pounds, and standing confidently. *I don't give a fuck who you are. I'll fucking beat you!* My mind was in a very dark, aggressive place. We won the tip somehow, and the ball was in my hands. After having a ball in my hands all summer and most of my childhood, I realized it never felt like this. I was dribbling, approaching the most athletic person I'd ever seen in my life, and I couldn't feel my arms, legs, or the ball. I attempted a pass to the wing, and the ball went out of bounds, nowhere near any of my teammates. "Get your head in the game!" Coach D yelled at me. Darrelle got the ball on the inbounds and came directly at me. *Oh, shit.* Before I could even look up, he was already scoring a layup behind me. I ran up and got the ball back to run the offense again, feeling slightly more comfortable after the initial surge. Darrelle stole the ball from me at half-court. Previously, when this would hap-
n, I'd be able to sprint and stop the layup on the other end. With
·relle Revis, he was already at the hoop before I turned around.

Coach D called a time-out, and I was on the bench. We went on to lose the game.

"Don't sweat it," Russell said later that night. "That dude is going to be pro in something."

"Yeah, I just thought I was ready."

"You still are. Just keep showing up."

We spent that evening in our comfortable home, watching reruns of *Family Guy*, letting the difficult moment pass.

## Serious Injury

After the tough first game, I was able to gain my footing. It didn't hurt that I had one of the best players in the area as my shooting guard. We developed a good sense of where each other would be on the court, and I racked up assists by passing to him. Our success after the initial letdown was not surprising to me, because most things in my life had gone this way. I'd get anxious and underperform to start, then begin to understand and gain a feel for whatever the activity might be. Then I'd find a sweet spot and become the aggressor. Standing at only five foot five, I was able to put intense pressure on many older, stronger opponents and find the advantage at the varsity level.

Up to this point in my basketball career, I had been able to avoid serious injury. In fact, I'd become lazy with stretching because I didn't see the immediate rewards. We finished the season with a record good enough to make the playoffs, which was a big accomplishment. *Starting point guard for a playoff team. Not bad, not bad at all.* Before the playoff game, we had a scrimmage with a nearby school to get additional in-game experience. We were all feeling pretty good about ourselves and came to the scrimmage underprepared. We were joking, moving slow, and when the scrimmage began, we were on our heels.

"You think you're all hot shit?" yelled Coach D. "Run the damn offense!"

We snapped into action, and I called out "Motion!" from the top of the key. Then the wings simultaneously ran deep toward the baseline and set screens for the two others moving toward where the wings once were. I passed the ball to the right wing and set a screen for the left wing, knowing that I would be wide-open if I cut hard toward the hoop. I made the cut, and the right wing shot a bounce pass through the defense, directly to me for the layup. I landed on my man and stealthily hit my shoulder into his jaw so no one could see. He frowned and got the inbounds pass as we ran back on defense.

I harassed him, jabbing at the ball and smirking at him as he dribbled the ball past half-court. Everything moved in slow motion as he crossed the ball from his right to left hand, almost as if the ball were stuck to the floor and not coming back up. I swiped my hand in, took the ball from him, and headed the other way. I had a wide-open layup on the other end and soared through the air for the finger roll. I felt a smack on my arm and a push on my back as I came crashing toward the ground. It felt as if I was going to hit the hardwood headfirst, so I twisted my body and landed directly on my lower back. I heard a crunch but hopped up like nothing had happened.

"You all right?" shouted Coach D.

"Yes!" I clapped my hands and once again pressed up on the goon that had tried to injure me. I was feeling no pain and having a blast.

When I woke up the next morning for school, I experienced a shooting pain in my lower back. The adrenaline had worn off. I hobbled out of bed and told my parents that I could barely move. My dad was concerned but went to work while my mom took me to the doctor. "You could make this worse by playing more basketball this season," said the doctor with a concerned look on his face. I was crushed, just like my L4 spinal segment.

I called my dad and told him the news. "Let's go see Dr. A." Dr. A was a close family friend and orthopedic surgeon.

"I'm going to give you Viox to ease the pain. It should get you through the next game, and then you can go back to the other doctor," said Dr. A.

"Okay," I said without questioning a word.

I took the pill before the game, and it didn't seem to help. On every possession, I was grimacing and trying to hide it. We ended up winning, though.

The pain got worse for round 2 of the playoffs, and we ended up losing. All in all, it was a terrific season for me. I had shown that I could play at the varsity level. We went back to the original doctor that week.

"You played, didn't you?"

"Yes," I said with my head down.

"Well, I'm reviewing your x-ray, and we'll have to put you in a back brace for three to six months. Come back in a week and we'll mold it."

*Fuckin' A! Well, at least the season is over. I'll wear this belt for a few months and I'll be fine.*

"Okay," I said.

We came back and sat in the room, waiting for the plastic mold. As my mom and I waited, we reminisced on what a great season it had been. My mom distracted me by playing tic-tac-toe on a piece of scratch paper. We were both anxious to get this thing over with. We heard a knock on the door and the doctor's voice. "Tammy, will you help me with this?" My heart sank, and I looked over at my mom, who was concerned.

The nurse pushed open the door as the doctor lugged in a two-foot-long, one-foot-wide body cast. It was practically impossible to carry with his chart in one hand. He unloaded it on the chair in the corner of the room and showed me how to strap on the three belts that wrapped around the front. "Wear this all day, every day, except when you shower and sleep. You can wear it when you sleep if you want to." *If I want to?* "I'll see you in three months." I glanced at the table with our tic-tac-toe game and wished I could go back to that moment, before getting the news that I would become Iron Man for six months.

"Well, I guess I'll need to start stretching," I said with a smile on my face and my new armor wedged under my armpit.

## *Blow to the Head*

The brace was bulky and made it nearly impossible to bend over without looking like a hunchback. I wore sweatpants and a hoodie for three months straight because my jeans didn't fit. In school, my friends would come up behind me and tell knock-knock jokes using the mold as a prop. It was all in good fun, but worst of all, the back brace made it much harder to do our drill routine the following summer, which led me to having an average junior season. When my senior year came, however, I was elected team captain. I was fully developed at five foot eight, 170 pounds, and broke the school assist record. We had a great season and made it to the championship at a downtown university.

I had some bad sushi the night before the big game. I was throwing up in the shower and didn't sleep very well. *Uh-oh, this could be bad.* I had baggy eyes and a tired look on my face as I stepped onto the bus that would take us downtown. I blasted "Go DJ" by Lil Wayne on my headphones to bring up my mood, which worked.

> ♪*Now you know I play it like a pro in the game,*
> *na better yet a veteran a hall of fame.*♪

We pulled up to the college arena, walked through the back entrance, and found a seat in the bleachers, wearing our warm-up gear. There was another championship game being played before ours. It was very close, heading into the fourth quarter, as we left to get ready in our locker room. I was still in good spirits and excited. As the clock was approaching zero, a player made the tying three-pointer, sending the game to overtime. From the locker room I heard a buzzer and fans cheering. The loud noise was irritating. "Let's go!" shouted one of our backup players in my ear. I looked at him in disgust and said, "Don't do that again." My head was spinning, and I was trying to keep it together.

*Bzzzzzzz!* the buzzer sounded again. *Okay, our turn.*

"Double overtime!" shouted an assistant coach of ours.

*Ugh, I'm going to pass out.* It felt like we were waiting in the locker room for hours. I found and chugged an energy drink to stay up.

*Bzzzzzzz!* "Triple overtime!"

*Wow, will I be able to play?*

Finally, the game ended in dramatic fashion with a half court buzzer-beater. I had no interest in who won or lost the game, only that it was our turn now. I took a deep breath and strutted out for the biggest game my career.

Everyone that I had ever known was in the stands. Teachers, students, friends, and even family had flown in from New York. The game would be televised. Our high school had not won a championship since the sixties. We happened to be playing against our hometown rival, USC. I pulled myself together for pregame warm-ups, "The Star-Spangled Banner," and introductions. My hands were in pain as I gave the other starters low fives before the tip. *Well, let's see what happens here.* The ball was tipped, and I felt a surge of energy. The game felt twice as fast as before. I was unsure if it was my lack of sleep, the sushi nausea, or the fact that this was the biggest game I had ever played.

Our rivals, USC, came out swinging and took the early lead. "K-I-L-L, USC. You can't spell *sucks* without USC!" chanted our fans.

"We can't hear you!" *Clap clap clap clap clap.* "We can't hear you!" *Clap clap clap clap clap.* The wave of USC students roared back.

After a few ups and downs, I felt woozy. Coach D called a time-out, and we huddled up. I saw a garbage can out of the corner of my eye and pretended to listen to Coach D's orders. "One second," I said. I ran to the first row of the bleachers and vomited into the garbage. *There's that tuna roll.* I looked up and found four kids watching me. "Stevens is puking!" I used my jersey to wipe my mouth and ran back to the huddle.

"You all right?" asked Coach D.

"Yep," I replied.

"Good, let's go!"

We broke the huddle and headed back onto the court.

I felt slightly better after throwing up, and we brought the game to a tie toward the end of the first quarter. I made a smooth pass to our best player, who scored. *Man, that feels good.* I got low in a defensive stance and was putting pressure on my man on the wing, without the ball. My man walked toward the baseline and made a sharp cut to the corner of the foul line. I followed him without looking up until I felt a crushing blow to the head. Everything went dark.

I felt my back on the hardwood, but my mind was somewhere else. *Why do the morning whistles have to be so loud? We get the point. I'll be sure to be on time for morning stretches at the top of the hill. Russell, how the hell did you hit me in the back of the head from that far away? Jerry, my back is killing me, and I have a headache now. Did you have to run me over like that?* I saw a white circle surrounded by darkness and felt at peace. Then the circle became larger, and bright light was blinding me.

"I'm so sorry, dude. I didn't mean to shoulder you like that," said the six foot three, 220-pound USC forward, who had knocked me out. Coach D's face was the only thing I saw until I sat up. Fans from both sides clapped as I was escorted to the bench.

We lost the game by a basket and stood in a line as we received second-place trophies. After the postgame, I met with my parents and headed to the hospital. While lying in the hospital bed, I pondered how I had dreamed about making it to this game my entire life and ended up in the hospital with food poisoning, no sleep, and a concussion. I connected this event with the struggle to wear a back brace a few years earlier. This was another moment where my perception of life had changed, just like in Little League after the asthma attack. *The players who work the hardest will gain the most?*

## *Releasing Anger*

It was nice to receive so many good wishes after getting a concussion in the championship game. I felt like my basketball career had meant something. We made the state playoffs but lost in the first round. I had a decision to make. *Go have a normal college experience or play division 3 basketball close to home?* It was an easy decision for me because I was barely five foot eight, feeling a little burnt-out, and I wanted to enjoy the college experience.

Before all that was figured out, I had an opportunity to try out for the national eighteen-and-under Maccabi team. The tryout would be held at Princeton University, and it was open to all Jewish players under eighteen in the USA. The event itself was a Jewish Olympics, if you will, with sporting events of all kinds held in Israel and medals going to the winners. I called my old friend Dan, and we both wanted to try out, so our dads drove us to Princeton.

When we arrived for the tryout, there were some really athletic, tall, and skilled players warming up. Dan had had an impressive career at his high school, and I felt good about mine. We laced up and joined the tryout, ready to compete. I learned quickly that almost all these players, including Dan, were planning on playing college basketball next year. Once again, I felt like the underdog.

The tryout lasted for a couple of hours, and then we headed back home, both uncertain as to whether we made the team or not. A few weeks later, I received a call from the man who would be the head coach of our team. "Is this Brett Stevens?"

"Yes," I replied.

"You've made the team! We'll have two weeks of practice before heading to Israel in August." He hung up, and I told my parents.

Dan called me shortly after. "I'm in!"

We showed up at Princeton at the same court we tried out on and met the rest of the team. Everyone was very friendly as we tried on all our gear. Each player got two pairs of shoes, two USA jerseys, two practice jerseys with shorts, socks, four shirts, and a bunch of other goodies that were customized for the event. This was pretty cool. I really had nothing bad to say about any of these guys. We worked hard in practice and played cards at night. After one and a half weeks of practice, I was still on the second team. I was calm about this and didn't really care, or so I thought.

We were lacing up our sneakers and stretching for one of the final practices before heading to Israel. We jogged around, did a couple of drills, and practiced the offense. Coach blew his whistle and shouted, "Okay! Team 1 versus Team 2, let's scrimmage. Run the offense." I was still calm as the ball was in play. Team 1 scored, then I got the ball and called out a play. I passed to the wing and ran to the opposite side to set a screen. Before I could look back, Team 1 had already stolen the ball and dunked on the other end. *Wow, you suck.* I sprinted back to get the ball again, still breathing smoothly. I called out another play, "Motion," and passed the ball to the left wing, then cut down the middle. Again, I looked up and saw a lazy pass that was stolen and going the other way for the score. *What the fuck?* I was already on the other end, so the ball was inbounded to my teammate, who dribbled off his foot and watched the ball roll out of bounds. *Oh my God.* Team 1 inbounded the ball on the wing, to a wide-open player, who made a three-pointer.

My blood was boiling. I had gone from calm and cool to raging, angry, and frustrated in a matter of minutes. I got the ball and called out another play. This time, I didn't run the offense; I drove down the center of the lane and twirled in for the layup. In the background I heard, "Run the offense!" Team 1 inbounded the ball. I harassed the point guard, suffocating him and taking the ball away. I scored again.

Team 1 brought the ball down and, again, went right past our defender for the layup. I was still raging. I didn't get the ball this time; I sprinted over to one of my favorite players on the team that just got burned and shouted in his face, "Play some fucking defense!" Then I got the ball and didn't even call out a play. I just dribbled down and shot a three from the top of the key. *Swoosh.* "This isn't the fucking Brett Stevens show!" said Coach. "Run the offense!" *Fuck you.* My other friend on Team 1 brought the ball up the court. I slapped him on the arm and pushed him over, taking the ball from him. Coach blew the whistle and called a foul. I looked down at my friend, and he looked scared. I was nearly crying at this point and breathing heavily. The rest of my teammates looked at me with confusion. "Let's take a break," said Coach.

I calmed myself, and Dan put his arm around me. "Stevens being Stevens," he said.

I fake-laughed and walked it off. The truth is that I had never felt like this before. I was amazed that I could lose my cool like that.

No one else said a word to me about my meltdown that night. It was like it never happened. I was right there with everyone as we played cards and joked. *Am I a psycho, or did I get respect?* The feeling I had passed, and on the final day of practice, I was moved to Team 1. I would be the starting point guard for the eighteen-and-under national Maccabi team. Even after all of the hard work, we had a subpar showing in Israel and my basketball career was officially over.

## Independence

I stood up and put knuckle to table in my kitchen, capturing the attention of my eight friends who were sipping on Natural Light in a circle around the table. "Turn that Akon song down." The floor was mine—it was my house, after all. I cleared my throat and pointed to the bottle of Vladimir Vodka standing alone next to one shot glass in the middle of the table. "Circling up. You don't have to drink fast, but you do have to drink," I projected loudly to my friends, word for word, like Jerry a few years ago at the Jersey Shore. I filled up the shot glass, took down the poison, and passed it to my left. "Turn it back up!" Akon's "9mm" came back strong.

♪*I got a 9 millimeter, ready to go off any minute so you feel it. Because of the law I had to conceal it, but if you fuck around, you gon' make me reveal it*♪

Laughing, storytelling, and more shots followed.

When we were good and drunk, someone drove us to a nearby house party filled with half of our high school, it seemed. I didn't have to try too hard to get my female peers' attention. I was the starting point guard and captain of the basketball team, did well in school, and was going to college next year. I was pulled into a circle of friends passing a bowl around, and I decided to partake. I had experimented with marijuana and alcohol for most of high school. Alcohol was amazing. It helped me dance and not feel accountable for anything I did or said. I would often wake up after a night of partying with dozens of text messages going out to whoever was in my contacts that I didn't remember sending.

Marijuana was a much different beast. I found myself thinking that I was hearing other people's thoughts. I was paranoid, believing that everyone knew I was high. When I was alone, I loved feeling high. It let my mind do whatever it wanted to with no restrictions, and I was intrigued by the creative places that it would go. I recall staring into the streetlights on the drive home from a party and pretending red meant "go" and green meant "stop." I'd listen to music and picture the entire band in the room with me; it felt real. What I liked most about marijuana were the munchies. I loved to eat to begin with, and when I was high, everything was intensified. We'd usually stay until the end of the party, looking for a hookup, or we'd head to the Wendy's drive-through, looking for a spicy chicken sandwich; both were equally satisfying.

After most parties, I'd have a slight headache the following Saturday morning and head over to a friend's house to play poker all day. Nothing cured a hangover better than friends, pizza, and poker. Sometimes we'd play for twelve hours straight. I developed a liking for poker and felt an intense yet balanced rush when I would win or lose. I was learning more and more about the game each time I played. Poker was a great source of entertainment in those years.

Overall, high school was a great time in my life. I was able to be successful with complete tunnel vision, keeping my eyes forward with blinders on both sides. I had few distractions and was surrounded with love from family and friends. I achieved a sense of balance, winning the respect of my friends through basketball and the respect of my parents through school. When I was asked where I wanted to go to college, my answer was, "Somewhere warm." It was that simple for me. Somewhere South seemed like a good option. My grades were solid, and I did well enough on the SAT to get a one-third tuition scholarship to college. I was very excited and was the only one from my graduating class heading to that part of the country.

When I arrived with my parents to school, it was 102 degrees. We got the registration squared away, walked by the state-of-the-art outdoor pool, and found my room. When I opened the door, my new roommate, Carter, was sitting in his chair, making music on his laptop. He was tall, light-skinned, with a lean, athletic build. We hit it off right away. I gave my parents a hug, and they left. Within thirty seconds of the door closing, Carter opened the door of his minifridge, which was filled with beer. "Want one?" A bond was formed as I took the bottle from his hand into mine. "Cheers!" *So this is why they say that college is the best years of your life.*

## Best Years of Your Life

College was amazing. I was accepted socially and had class four days a week for a few hours. One Sunday morning, after a night of drinking until 6:00 a.m., I was watching a marathon of *Scrubs* in bed when I heard a knock on the door. I crept out of bed and opened the door, finding a floormate wearing jeans shorts and a stripped collared shirt. "Yo, dood, the whole floor is going to a pahty tonight. Do you and Cahter wanna come?" I looked back at Carter, who was also curing his hangover with *Scrubs*, and he gave the thumbs-up from his bed without looking back.

"We're in. I'm Brett, by the way." I put my hand out.

"Bobby," he said as he shook my hand. He scurried off to the next room, and I closed the door.

I could hear through the wall, "Yo, Nate! There's a pahty tonight. Do you and Brad wanna come?"

I smiled and got back into bed.

Later that afternoon, I finally made it out of bed, threw some gym clothes on, and strutted to the community bathroom to brush my teeth. On my way, I noticed a light marijuana smell. I looked to my left and noticed a bit of smoke coming out of one of the rooms. I thought nothing of it and continued to the bathroom to get ready for the gym. On my way back, the smoky door opened like the tunnel before a WWE wrestling match, with three smiling students walking out. Then, a glazed-eyed floormate wearing a backward Yankee hat, shorts, and a white tank top stuck his head out. "Yo, dude, wanna play Mario Party?"

"I'm down," I replied.

I put my things back in my room and headed into the cloud. There were three more students sitting on beds with controllers in their hands. I didn't realize one room could hold so many potheads. "Close the door, turn the fan on, and plug the door with that towel. I'm John, by the way."

"Brett," I said.

I did as John instructed and took a seat on the bed. Next, I observed grown men talk into the Nintendo microphone, throw controllers at one another, and of course, pass around joint after joint. There was always a new one being rolled right as the last one was finished.

I focused intensely on the game and didn't talk much. It felt like I was inside the TV screen, with Mario on my left and Luigi on my right. My senses told me that if I stood up from the bed, I would fall one thousand feet into darkness. The sound of picking up a coin in the game felt like gold rushing through my body. This intense experience was interrupted by a knock on the door. My heart stopped, and I felt a punch of anxiety to my gut.

*Oh, shit, everyone knows I'm high. What if that's one of my professors? What if it's the girl I liked at the party last night? What if it's my parents?*

As the leader of this group, John confidently stood up, eyes red as ever, ready to handle the situation. He unplugged the towel, left the fan on, and cracked the door. He found a floormate wearing jeans shorts and a stripped collared shirt. "Yo, you dudes wanna come to the pahty tonight?" John laughed and pulled Bobby in between his forearm and bicep. "Let me get some of that!" Bobby called out.

The next thing we all knew, it was time to get ready for the party.

"Let's just leave without him!" shouted an irritated floormate. "He'll figure it out."

The group of ten freshmen began the walk to their first college frat party. I stayed behind. Bobby was the one who told me about the party, and I wasn't about to ditch him. "Thanks, B," he said after realizing I had waited for him. "Let's take a detour." Bobby pulled out a brown cylinder-shaped object that was hard to see.

"Cigar?" I said.

"No, blunt," he replied.

Up to this point, I had been able to take small puffs and get plenty high. With just the two of us smoking the biggest blunt I had ever seen, it would be tricky to hide my newness with all this. Bobby smoked like a fish and pushed me to keep up. I did my best but finally urged him to get to the party, where all the women were.

We showed up to the sound of a loud reggaeton beat, with Daddy Yankee's voice rapping in Spanish over it. *Boom. Bu bu bu boom. Bu bu bu boom.* The music was tickling my soul, and I started bumping my head. Then I realized how high I was and started drinking to find the right buzz. I glanced over and observed Bobby eating an entire tray of Jell-O shots that were meant to service the whole party. "Holy fuck, dude! Chill!" He smiled at me and had five more. I scanned the crowd for a familiar face and then heard a crash against the wall. Bobby passed out in the middle of the party, his eyes closed. I ran over to him and got him awake. "Heyyyy, Beeeeee," he said with a grin on his face. I picked him up, and we started walking back toward the dorms.

On our way back, I saw flashes of fire and ice out of my left eye. A police officer was on his way, and Bobby yelled at the far away cop, "Pig!" and started running. I watched him go and stumbled back to the dorm safely, avoiding the police. I stared at myself in the mirror for ten minutes. *What the fuck is wrong with you? Why are you all alone, again?* The room started spinning, and I threw up on the counter. I sneaked out of the bathroom and found my pillow. Everything went black.

*Knock knock knock.* I rolled out of bed and opened the door. I found Bobby, with a black eye, wearing nothing but a hospital gown. I started laughing so hard I cried.

"Wanna get some food?" he asked like nothing happened.

"What happened to you?"

"They tried to keep me in the hospital, but I broke out. They can't hold me, B! You should know that by now!" He had a smirk on his face, and we both laughed hysterically.

"Go put some clothes on and we'll eat."

Bobby scurried down the hall in his hospital gown, ass showing. As he moved past the smoky room, John popped his head out, eyes glazed, and asked, "You wanna grab some food?"

I nodded and went back into my room. *I love these guys.*

## Dealing with Bad News

Freshman year was not all about partying. Like in high school, I was very responsible when it came to showing up to class, doing assignments, and studying for exams. College was different, however. In certain areas, like psychology, I was able to do the work and get good grades. It made sense to me. I'd even show up to my psychology professor's office hours and debate optimism bias, nature versus nurture, and personality types. I had a strong black-and-white view, while he taught me that there is usually a gray area.

Most of my classes were pre-med, like biology, organic chemistry, along with the labs that came with them. I had never shown a true interest in this area, but my dad was a doctor, and it seemed like a good career path. No matter how much I studied for these classes, I could never get higher than a B. It deflated my ego and put me in a minor depression that I wasn't good enough. But the depression was balanced with a strong dose of partying.

"How's life down there?" my old friend from high school said on the phone.

I was kicked back at my desk in my dorm room, wearing sandals, shorts, and a cutoff shirt, ready to head to the outdoor pool. It was November. "Life is great, man. My hardest decision each day is whether I should go to the beach or the pool."

"You're an asshole," he said, laughing. "Are you on this dumb thing called Facebook yet? Apparently, it's an easy way to meet college chicks."

"Yeah, some kids here were on it since summer. They were already friends with the people in their classes before meeting them. Awkward."

"Ha ha, I agree."

"Well, I'm glad to hear you're doing well. I'll talk to you later."

I sat up in my chair and grabbed the towel on my bed, ready to hit the pool.

Then my phone rang again, and it was Russell. "Wassup keeed?" I said with an intentional Spanish accent.

"Did you hear what happened?" he replied.

"No. What's up?"

"Dad left Mom."

"What?"

"Yeah, he just took the dog and walked out. He already has another house set up. He had an affair with a woman who worked with them in the office. Mom was friends with her."

*What the fuck is going on? Why don't I feel anything?*

"Uhh, well, are you all right?"

"Yeah, I'm fine. I'm gonna go for a run. Bye." He hung up.

I was left sitting at my desk, alone, and in shock. Five minutes ago, I was completely relaxed, talking to a friend. Now I didn't know what to do. I called Jerry, and he already knew.

"How could he do this to us?" he said.

"This is only going to make our bond stronger. We'll be all right," I replied.

When alone I felt like the weakest person on the planet, angry and anxious, with low confidence. For some reason, when talking to my brothers, I had to be strong, suppressing my real fear, pretending that I was in control. I called my mom, and she was in the same amount of shock that I was in. "Don't worry about me," she said. I had talked to the people that would be most hurt by this, was unable to get in touch with my dad, and sat alone in my dorm room.

Then I heard a knock on the door. "Yo, doood, wanna grab some food?" Seeing Bobby brought it out of me. He represented everything that was fun and perfect about my personal life, which was now breaking apart. I leaned against the door and cried. He walked me onto my bed and closed the door behind us so no one would see me like this. "Tell me all about it, man." He sat there and listened to me talk about how great my childhood was, how support-ive my dad had always been, and how much he loved my mother. He listened to me get angry. Why would he do this? What was wrong with him? He listened to my rationalizations.

"Well, I guess this happens to a lot of families."

Then he said, "Let's get fucked up. Wait here." He ran out and came back two minutes later with a full bottle of Southern Comfort. "Let's drink the whole bottle." We went back and forth, taking swigs for the next couple of hours. We took a walk to the lake when the sun went down and smoked another Bobby blunt. I made myself sick and puked everywhere until I finally fell asleep.

When I woke up the next morning, I felt a box around my head. Nothing in and nothing out. If I had a thought about my dad, I kept it in the four walls of my mind. If a family member called, asking how I was, I blocked them out and said I was fine. It was the closest my mind had been to the raging state during that final Maccabi practice a few months ago—only I had no way of releasing it in this environment. It all stayed inside.

Over the next few weeks leading up to winter break, I got comfortable with the notion that no one was holding me accountable anymore. Sure, I had partied without the consent of my dad in the past, but now who cared if he found out? I actually started to enjoy this independence and didn't think him leaving was so bad, having no idea of the long-term pain this experience would cause. I was looking forward to being with my mom and brothers and booked a flight home.

## Confrontation

The sky was gray as I descended into my hometown. My carry-on felt heavier as I dragged it through the airport to baggage claim. I noticed less joy in others and more stoic, hard faces at the carousel. My mom and Russell swung through the passenger pickup lane, and I hopped in the back seat.

"How's everyone doing?" I asked.

"We're fine," they both replied.

*Not a chance.*

When we arrived at the house, I noticed empty space on the wall where beautiful artwork once lived. "What happened to the painting?"

"Dad took it," Russell said.

Roxie, our cocker spaniel, who was famous for peeing on everyone who entered the house, trotted up slowly, peeing, of course. "Where's Kobe?" Kobe was our yellow Lab.

"Dad took him," Russell said.

*Is he serious?*

The mood was gloomy as we sat around the kitchen table and ate the brisket that my mom had prepared. Cooking always made her feel comfortable, no matter what.

Jerry showed up a few hours later, and the four of us sat in shock for a while. Finally, Jerry said, "Let's figure this out. I'm calling him." We put the phone on speaker and got an answer.

"Hello?" His voice sounded different. I remembered how he grew his beard out for the Israel trip, which was out of his character. This visual paired with his voice now made me feel like a stranger was on the phone.

Jerry continued, "We're all here. Are you going to see us?"

"Of course," he said. "Nothing will change. I'll always be there for you guys and your mother. Why don't you come over to my house?"

My mom sighed heavily. He gave us the address to his secret home, and we drove over.

Jerry drove, I was in the front seat, and Russell was in the back middle with his head forward so he could be in the discussion. *Why are we even doing this?*

"All right, we're going to explain to him how fucked up this is and maybe he'll come back," Jerry said. Russell's facial expression showed a glimmer of hope as he rationalized the thought of him coming home. *No fucking way that's going to happen.*

We pulled up to a modest house that was ten minutes from where we lived and knocked on the door. The three of us shared a collective, new anxiety as the door opened. An average-height blond woman opened the door, wearing an oversize T-shirt and sweatpants.

She had a big smile on her face. "Come on in, guys!" I felt nauseated. The living room had two recliners, a love seat, and was carpeted brown. It smelled like an old bar. I looked to my left and saw an ashtray with a cigarette butt dying. I had a flashback to all the jokes that were made about people who smoke cigarettes and how disgusting it was, always initiated by my dad. I scanned the room and noticed an abundance of Christmas lights, stockings, and a fully decorated tree. *Are you fucking kidding me?* I had another flashback to my dad tearing apart the holiday in general. "So you're telling me that this virgin woman had a baby? Really?" he would say around the holidays every year.

Caroline—*my new stepmom, my new friend?*—left the room, thank God, and we sat in silence. I looked over at this bearded, sad-looking man in astonishment. Russell sat quietly. After all, he had been here when it happened, had witnessed the painting and Kobe abduction, had seen my mom get abstractly abused in real time. I was focused, sitting up, ready to have this hard conversation and attempt to empathize.

Jerry started, "Sooooo what's going on?"

Our heads turned, and six eyeballs stared directly at the man who had been so perfect up to this point.

"Your mother and I are having some issues. Nothing will change."

"Well," said Jerry, "some things are going to change. You live here now."

"Everything will get better in time." my dad said.

I chimed in, "You realize that when we all get married and have kids, you and Mom won't be together? We'll have to explain to everyone what happened?"

"Yes," he replied.

Then the anger came out. Jerry said, "You're sitting in a house with a fucking Christmas tree! Cigarettes are everywhere!"

Caroline had been eavesdropping from the kitchen. She came out to defend him.

*This bitch has no clue what she's walking into.*

"Leave us alone, you whore!" Jerry said.

*I think it's time to go.*

Jerry stood up, and we both followed, leaving the front door open on our way out.

On the drive home, we all expected and secretly wanted him to call us and make sure we were okay. This did not happen.

The next morning, we were certain he would reach out and smooth things over. No, this didn't happen either. We didn't know it at that time, but the grieving process of losing our perfect family had begun. We were lucky to have one another, and it could have been worse, as they say. All bets were off, and the three of us brothers would need to lean on one another to survive.

"You were always the ideal family. What? He did what?" said Tony, my lifelong friend, when I confided in him the next day. "You guys are strong. You'll be okay."

I was numb after the previous night's experience and the whole event in general. My mind was in a robotic state, feeling no emotion. We survived the next few weeks, and when the time came to head back to school, I couldn't wait to get the heck out of town.

## On the Edge

I was looking down from the corner of the ceiling, observing a group of my floormates in a circle by the elevator, laughing. "Why would he say that?" "What's with his haircut?" "He's such a Jew." "I heard his dad left his mom." "Who?" "B?" "Brett?" "Brett!" They all at once looked up at me with evil grins, laughing louder and louder. I woke up in a sweat, breathing heavily. Carter was asleep, and the moon was shining through our window. A few drunk peers were laughing in the hall. The sound faded, and I fell back asleep.

I made it back to the Southern sunshine and had trouble sleeping for the first few weeks. Almost every night, I would have some sort of dream where I was paranoid about others talking behind my back. I thought nothing of it and continued to work hard in class, play pickup basketball, and enjoy the college experience. I noticed that I spent most of my time running around, trying to please everyone. If three of us wanted to go to the pool, I had to make sure that we asked others on the floor first. If my roommate needed our dorm room to make music, I'd get my stuff and go to the library. The semester went fast, which led to another summer at home, where all bets were off. No Dad. No rules.

Carter had planned to visit, and I agreed to have a house party in his honor. After one night out, I came home with a few friends to the sound of women giggling and the smell of marijuana. My mom was smoking pot with her woman friends.

"Hi, Mrs. Stevens!" my friends said.

"Hungry?" I chimed in to tease. We let them off the hook. "Is it cool if I have a few people over tomorrow night? I know you'll be out," I asked.

"I'm not going to stop you!" she said.

We told our immediate friends about the get-together at my house, and they told their friends, who told their friends. My mom left early, and we were all set. As the sun went down, my immediate friends, including Carter, circled up. Like clockwork, groups and groups of people, mostly strangers, started showing up. Before I knew it, the entire house was packed from wall to wall, including the backyard. I witnessed grapes being thrown in the kitchen and fights breaking out. It was getting out of hand. I told Carter that I needed help.

"I got you, B. Let me show you how we do it where I'm from." Carter ripped his shirt off, stood on the kitchen counter, turned off the music, and got the crowd's attention. "You don't have to go home, but you can't stay here!" The crowd went right back to partying like it never happened.

Carter wanted to be heard and have my back at the same time. He tried again—only this time he grabbed a kitchen knife and held it up. "Like I said, you don't have to go home, but you can't stay here." The girls in our sheltered town had never had a hint of violence in their lives and thought they were going to die that night. The tough meatheads felt the same. After the knife came out, the crowd dispersed. I didn't know whether to thank Carter or run away from him.

Time seemed to move faster as I went back for my sophomore year. I decided to room off campus with John and another friend of ours, Kirk. This had its pros and cons. We were able to do whatever we wanted without campus security showing up, but we were isolated from the rest of our class. Our neighbors were friendly, and we had a beautiful apartment. I was focused on Biology 2 and Organic Chemistry 2. I was anxious every time I had to do a three-hour lab. I had no clue what I was doing and always needed my lab partner to pick up the slack. I dreaded the weekly lab, almost enough to avoid it altogether and take the failing grade. After all, my dad was not in the picture, and I wasn't afraid of my mom when it came to performance in school.

I made it home for another winter break and became hot-headed, fast-talking, and strongly opinionated. I'd wake my mom up in the middle of the night to discuss the meaning of life. "I just want you to tell me everything you believe in," I'd say, thirsty for her perspective. I'd pace back and forth, spouting out what were, in my mind, clear thoughts. I felt like I could debate with anyone about any topic, whether I had read up on it or not. The whole world was labeled, simple, and organized. I'd lie in bed at night, and my mind would race. *There was a time when this house wasn't here. It was a patch of land. No roads, running water, or neighbors. Someone figured out how to build. I wonder how many people died building things. Can you imagine living your whole life only to die in a building accident? I wonder how many times this has happened in the course of history. Millions?* My breathing was fast, and I was as anxious as ever, but so proud of myself for exposing mysteries of the universe like this.

My sleep had not improved as I headed back to school for my second-semester sophomore year. I continued to party, harder than ever. My alarm rang a bit late one morning for an 8:00 a.m. chemistry lab. I woke up. *Seriously, fuck this.* The culmination of my dad losing all credibility and my thoughts telling me I had something special pushed me over the edge. I found a packed bong in our living room, took a big hit, and went back to sleep. This was when my world started to shift.

# Birds

I woke up alone in my apartment to the sound of birds chirping and the sun blazing. *I cannot wait to get this day started.* I noticed a white smear on my car through the window, followed the line up to the sky, and saw a bird. I laughed to myself. *That bird tagged me as a friend and wants to follow me around today.* I widened my view out of the window and noticed several birds flying and perched at all different altitudes. I followed a shiny golden line bouncing from one bird to the other like a shooting star. I stared at this beautiful work of art for about ten minutes, interrupted by a tear dripping down my cheek. *It's so beautiful.* I was still in my sleep clothes but decided to put my sunglasses on to block the light, which was now overwhelming. I walked into the kitchen, with shorts and sunglasses on, alone in my apartment, but didn't feel hungry. *Do birds need to eat three meals a day? I wish I were a bird.* I had been very prompt for most of my life, but today, I lost track of time. When I saw the time on my phone, I panicked. I had class in ten minutes, and I was fifteen minutes away. I grabbed a few random notebooks and threw them into my back-pack. I found sweatpants and a hoodie to wear and ran out to the car. As I walked outside, I couldn't help but notice how many birds were in the sky.

I got in my car and felt panic about being late for biology. I opened all the windows and smirked as I saw the bird shit on my windshield. *Those tricky little bastards. Why are they targeting me? I'll try to scare them away.* I turned up Tom Petty's "Don't Come Around Here No More," hoping it would make them disappear.

♪*Hey! Don't come around here no more*♪

The panic got worse, and my chest tightened up. I still had a chance to be on time if I could catch every green light. The first one was red, and I waited, tapping my foot in anticipation.

It turned green, and I stepped on it as I made a left turn. I heard a startling honk, not realizing I didn't have the right-of-way. I sped through a few green lights and was almost there. The final light turned red, but I looked both ways and decided it was all right to go through. I found a good parking spot and jogged to class.

"Yo, Stevens! Why the fuck are you wearing sweatpants and a hoodie? It's, like, one hundred degrees outside." It was John, high as ever, busting balls.

"Can't talk right now. See you later!" I scooted off. *I wonder if John is aware of how these birds operate.*

I made it to the auditorium right as class was about to begin, drenched in sweat. I had a bird's-eye view of the whole lecture hall and could hear what they were all talking about. "Why was he late?" "Why is he wearing that?" "He may be the greatest man of all time for figuring out the bird secrets." I was proud of myself for the work I had done that morning. *Maybe we are all just birds and we don't know it.* The lecturer quieted his students and began. I looked into my backpack and saw that I had my notebooks for English, Math, and Spanish. *English, Math, Spanish. En. Ma. Spa. En-Ma-Spa. Ha ha ha.* I laughed to myself about how quickly I could come up with such a creative rhyme. *Maybe I'll be the next Eminem.*

"Today we're going to talk about evolution," said my professor as he showed an image of all different animals on the screen, including an eagle. *Oh. My. God. There is no way that this could be a coincidence. I've been thinking about birds all morning, and here I am in class, looking at a bird!* My professor continued, "Charles Darwin, the creator of the theory of biological evolution, was a pioneer. He went where no others had gone before in developing this theory. He was way ahead of his time." My interpretation of this statement sounded like, "He was a pioneer. He went where no others had gone before." *Could the professor really be talking about me in front of this large audience? Am I him?* I noticed a student look back, checking the time. *I'll sign autographs later. Keep your eyes forward, buddy.*

The first three minutes of class felt like three hours. I decided I had more important things to do, like conducting more studies on birds. I hustled to the second floor of an outdoor balcony that overlooked the quad. I perched over the railing with my elbows touching and hands covering my mouth. *Be a bird, Brett. BBB.* I didn't move my body at all, but my eyes were scanning the scene. I looked down on hundreds of students rushing to and from class. Some lying out on the lawn, others skateboarding. *Look at all these fools. Wasting their time with no perspective on how things really are. I'm the only one who knows how things really are.* I made eye contact with a finch that was at my level in a nearby tree. *See, we both get it.* This dialogue went on and on for hours until the sun started to set. I decided that I'd done enough amazing work for one day and headed back to my apartment.

When I walked back in, I found my roommates playing PlayStation. "Wassup, dudes?" I said.

"Yo," they both replied.

"You wanna get some food?" John said.

"Na, I'm good. Just going to call it an early night."

As I walked to my room, I heard a yell. "You realize it's only six o'clock, right?"

"Yeah, I don't feel like eating, and I'm just gonna pass out."

"Whatever, man," he said.

I lay down for the next several hours, balancing panic, anxiety, and euphoria. I called my mom to tell her how great I was doing, and she was so happy.

## *Perspectives*

I woke up at three o'clock in the morning bursting with energy. *When is Russell supposed to visit? She'll know.* I reached over and fumbled for my phone until it fell on my lap. I called my mom back. She answered after the first ring, a bit groggy.

"Brett? Is everything okay?"

*Aw, she's asking me if everything is okay because she is not okay. Alone in that big house.*

I chuckled. "Of course. What are you up to?"

"Brett, it's three in the morning."

"I know. I figured you would answer no matter what. I had such an amazing day yesterday, and today will be awesome also. I'm going to go back to my biology teacher to do more studies on the birds that I told you about. Also, I have to sort out the bills with my roommates. I'm writing a check as we speak! And when is Russell coming to visit?"

She started to reply, and I cut her off.

"It's going to be great to see him. I'm sure he'll want to work out and play basketball and go to the pool and go out to eat a nice meal."

I let her get a word in. "Russell is coming in a few days."

"Oh, good! I have so much to do!"

"Brett, you're a good brother. Are you able to calm yourself down a bit and get back to sleep?"

*Aw, she must be having trouble sleeping.* "Mom, don't worry about me. Good night."

"Good night, Brett. Love you."

I put my workout clothes on, laced my shoes, and went for a run. My iPod roared KRS-One's "Step into a World."

♪*Step into a world where there's no one left.*
*But the very best, no MCs can test.*
*Step into a world where hip hop is me,*
*Where MCs and DJs build up their skills*
*As they play every day for the rapture.*♪

I looked around at the beautiful, blinking streetlights and thought to play Kanye West's "Street Lights."

♪*Seems like streetlights, glowing, happen to be*
*just like moments passing in front of me.*
*So I hopped in the cab and I paid my fare, see I*
*know my destination but I'm just not there.*♪

Every time my foot hit the ground, a light would change. Then I looked at the sky and saw a full moon and hundreds of stars. I kept my right eye on the natural sky and my left on the man-made lights. *The perfect balance of nature.* A tear rolled down my cheek. Then I felt terribly anxious as all the streetlights turned red in the same instant. The music felt louder and the moon was getting closer. I picked up the pace steadily, working up to an all-out sprint, in the middle of the night, alone. *I'll show you, motherfuckers.* I turned around and sprinted all the way home. I took a hot shower and slept until the sun woke me up through my window, finally getting some sleep.

"Did you take a shower in the middle of the night?" John asked.

"Yeah, and went for a run."

"Well, that makes no sense at all," he said sarcastically.

"Johnny, there are just certain things you'll never understand." I got dressed for class and drove to campus.

*English is so dumb. My grade depends on some other person's perspective on something that she didn't even write. Honestly, I might just teach the class today.* There was a straight walkway through the quad to get to English class. It was an especially nice day, and students were roaming like ants on a popsicle stick. I got out of my car, and a young woman was walking toward me. *I see her face and the backdrop behind her. She must see me and the backdrop behind me.* I closed my eyes and tried to envision what she was seeing. I created a snapshot in my mind of my own face looking out, with my car behind me. I smiled. *So that's exactly what she is seeing. I'm figuring something out here.* She walked past me indifferently. *She must know that I know what she's seeing.* I started my walk through the quad, and it was very loud. Everyone was looking at me and telling secrets. I could hear all of them. *Look what he's wearing. Look at his haircut. He's like a celebrity. He's shorter than I thought he would be. I don't like that he's aware of my secrets.* It was getting very loud as I walked through the quad like every other student that day. Then I noticed a horde of twelve or so students walking toward me. *This will be fun.* After learning how to form the young woman's perspective earlier, I figured I'd give it a shot for this group. I pictured myself walking straight forward with students, grass, the pathway, and my car behind me. *This is what they are all seeing.* Then three students broke off to the left and three to the right. I gathered what they were looking at, turning my head left and right. I held the first view and added the two new views, cutting my perception in three. *Holy fuck, this is cool! I'd be jealous, too, if someone else had this much power.* I expanded to twelve visual squares with twelve different perspectives, all changing at once. I felt a thump on my shoulder and fell over.

"Watch where you are going, dude," said a frat boy.

*Do you have any idea whom you just bumped into? I will fucking beat you. Walk away, you peasant.* I had a flashback to losing control of my anger in basketball. *Take a deep breath. This is some next-level stuff you are solving for the rest of the world.*

I made it to English that day and sat in the back of the class day-dreaming about what everyone else was seeing. I had thought about every person in the room, including the teacher, then every combination of every person in the room, including the teacher. I took a few notes on what I was going to call "Life Theory: The Secrets of the Unknown." Then I got restless, grabbed my bag, and headed out of the class, which I sat in for a grand total of five minutes. The voices were really loud as I made it back to my car. I kept the radio off for this reason and drove ten miles per hour below the speed limit. I safely parked my car and saw smoke coming out of the window of my apartment; there was no fire.

## Paranoia

"Let's go to Kathy for weather."

"Thanks, Tom. As you can see, there will be a severe downpour later this evening. Be careful if driving and stay dry."

"Looks like we're staying in tonight, gentlemen," John said to Kirk and me.

I noticed how Kathy made eye contact with her TV audience as she said, "As you can see..." *As you can see. Hmmm. As I can see? Severe downpour of what? Rain is too obvious. Birds? A severe downpour of new ideas?* I knew that I needed to be careful with this newfound power that was like a drug. *Ohhh, stay dry, stay clean, don't use it too much. Understood, Kathy. Thanks for the message.* She nodded on the screen. I stood up to use the bathroom and shut the door behind me. I heard the sound of the TV and John and Kirk's voices, muffled through the door.

"Kathy, do you think he was ready for that message? He's so young to have this much power and be given these types of secrets," said John.

"Yeah! I thought we were the only two who would be able to decipher what you said," Kirk chimed.

"I'm the one that knows what's best for him. After all, I'm speaking to him through the TV," said Kathy. They all agreed that Kathy knew best.

*Once again, I'm ahead of the game. I was able to hear their conversation from the bathroom and now know that this is all real.* I looked at myself in the mirror with pride. I used the bathroom and walked out, noticing the looks of trying to hide something on their faces. "Anything you two wanna tell me?" I asked. *Don't let them know that you know about Kathy by asking about her. Remember to pretend to be like them.*

"No, dude," said John. "What are you talking about?"

"You guys want food? I'll go pick it up before the storm hits," I said.

They gave me their orders, and I headed out on another adventure.

Two neighbors were covered by the overhang, smoking cigarettes across the outdoor hallway. When I looked up at them, they giggled and walked away. *Why is everyone always making fun of me?* I walked down to my car and noticed that the bird shit was still on my windshield. *Well, that's good. At least someone is watching out for me.* I got in my car, closed the door, and put on the radio.

"He's pulling out and heading to get sandwiches for the whole group. Do you think he'll make it, Ron?"

"I don't know. He's been a bit cocky with his power and didn't show good composure back there at the apartment. The kid certainly has guts, though, I'll give him that."

*People, radio, and TV. I must be really special. That means that the whole world knows who I am. Keep it together, Brett. They want to see you fail, but you can be legendary if you keep it together.* I hooked up my iPod and let that play. Eminem's "Role Model" came on.

♪*I'm cancerous. So when I dis you, you wouldn't want to answer this*♪

The sound felt amazing, so I turned it up, loud. *Could I possibly be curing cancer right now?* I drove out of the lot and turned it up louder, vibrating my windshield and rearview mirror. Then I put all the windows down in my car. *Everyone should hear this.*

♪ *You beef wit' me, Imma even the score equally,*
*Take you on Jerry Springer and beat your ass legally*♪

I made my way to Quiznos. *I'm going to order these sandwiches so fast, the fastest that it's ever been done.* I walked in and there was a line of three people. "Oh my god, he's here!" I heard them say. *That's right.* I skipped the line and walked directly to order.

"I'll have three Italian hoagies, on white, toasted, with all the ingredients."

"Sir, you have to wait in line."

*Oh, shit, that's right. I have to pretend to be like everyone else. Okay, I'll play your game.*

I apologized politely and waited my turn in the back of the line, smiling. As I waited, I noticed a TV with a basketball game on and subtitles. It read, "This kid is really something special. He's smart, quick, takes the shot when he needs to, and also plays great defense." Then the camera cut to the head coach clapping for me. *Exactly. I am special. I am smart, quick, know when to use my power [take a shot] and can play defense, like I'm doing right now, pretending. What a smart way for them to get through to me, using basketball as a medium.* I waited patiently, walked up and ordered our sandwiches perfectly, and paid the bill. Then the Mims song "This Is Why I'm Hot" started playing, and I smiled.

♪ *This is why I'm hot, I don't gotta rap, I can*
*make a mil sayin' nothing on the track.*♪

*Whoever you are, you saw that, didn't you? Thanks for the acknowledgment.* I got to my car, which defaulted to the radio. "What a performance! He may be one of the best golfers of all time." *Ah, they have to hide the message with golfer or player or anything when they are*

71

*really talking about me. I see that.* I listened to the radio praise me for the rest of the drive home. I made it back to the apartment and found my roommates watching *Saw.*

I got a hit of anxiety. "The choice is yours, live or die." *If I fail, then they are going to kill me. John and Kirk knew this. That's why they put the movie on. They are trying to help me get ahead of these messages.* "Got your subs right over here, gentlemen. Don't worry, it's on me. You two deserve it. Thanks for all of your help."

## Danger

"Call me when you land. I'll be at the gate the exact moment that you walk outside. Seriously, the exact moment."

"Ha ha, okay," Russell replied.

I was especially excited today. Russell was visiting. I had a few hours, so I decided to go to the gym to pass some time. I was getting a handle on hiding the grandiose thoughts and fitting in, not to say that they weren't ever-present and getting more intense. I threw on an old high school T-shirt with cutoff sleeves, a shiny pair of shorts, high socks, laced up my Nikes, and headed to the gym.

The gym at the student wellness center was always busy. Lines of cardio machines, free weights, and circuit equipment filled the ten-thousand-square-foot gym. The facility as a whole was about sixty thousand square feet, including indoor and outdoor basketball courts, racquetball, pool, sauna, hot tub—you name it. I walked into the gym, again, hearing everyone's conversations. *Damn, he looks pretty strong. He's not that tall. I bet he won't lift that much.* I made it to the free-weight area, which had vast mirrors on three walls. I first looked at myself, noticing my eyes were red and glazed over. Then I expanded my view to the entire gym behind me in reverse from the mirror's reflection. I had a vision of ants covering a piece of candy on the ground. Then the people started moving faster and faster, doing sets, moving from machine to machine, changing weights. I could see the whole scene from the ceiling, a bird's-eye view. Then I zoomed out much further at hyperspeed. The people turned to ants, and the gym was the candy.

"Are you using that bench?" asked a fellow weight lifter.

"Umm, yeah. Sorry."

I snapped back to reality. I usually did flat bench with seventy-pound dumbbells. Today I decided to try ninety. I needed to test this newfound superhuman strength. I picked up the nineties, noticed a few people looking on with concern, and did five reps—no problem. *That was easy.* I had one of the best workouts of my life, and then my phone rang.

"Brett, we just landed."

"Okay, I'm on my way."

I had promised Russell I would be there right as he walked out, and although unlikely, it was possible. I ran to my car and cranked up Wu-Tang's "Duel of the Iron Mic," which had a loud piano as the featured instrument.

*♪Picture bloodbaths and elevator shafts, like these murderous rhymes tight from genuine crafts.♪*

The music was loud and added to my postworkout adrenaline. I sped off in my blue Honda Civic toward the airport.

The sky was crystal blue, with fluffy white clouds supporting it. My speedometer read ninety as I sped to the airport. *Ninety miles per hour, ninety-pound dumbbells. Maybe I should add them up and go for one-eighty?* My foot got heavier on the gas, but I had some sense that I needed to stay in between the lines and not push the Civic to exhaustion. The exit was near, and my promptness looked good. I glanced at the sky and noticed the clouds shifting. I saw the face of a lion looking directly at me. *Hey there, buddy.* I blinked and it shifted to a bunny. *Aw, how cute!* I blinked and it changed into a king wearing a crown. *More reinforcement right there. I am a king.* Then I saw a frown face that turned into an evil grin, with fangs for teeth. My heart sank. I looked back at the road and noticed I had missed the exit. *No! No, no, no!* I felt a weird arousal in my body that told me to do something about it. This mishap would take me five minutes off course, and I'd be late. *I can't be late picking up Russ. That's unacceptable.* The airport was on my left and getting smaller as I drove away in the wrong direction. The arousal, fear, and anxiety grew. I noticed no cars coming on the highway in the other direction. *Do it. You're invincible.* I turned left into the divot separating the multilane superhighway. My Civic smacked the grass in the middle, and I made it to the other side, heading in the opposite direction. I couldn't see very well, but no cars came. *That was meant to be. People like me don't need luck.*

I pulled up to the pickup area and found Russell waiting. "Sorry for making you wait, Russ," I said with a smile.

"It was, like, a minute. No big deal," he replied. He tossed his bag in the trunk and hopped in the front seat.

"My roommates are so annoying, always getting in the way," I said.

He laughed nervously. "Really? You said you liked them."

"Yeah, you'll see why this weekend."

We drove back to the apartment, where Kirk and John were watching TV. *If you two try to hurt him, I swear I'll hurt you.* In my mind, the rest of the evening was spent protecting Russell.

## Insomnia

We got back from the bar around two thirty in the morning. I made a bed for Russell on our white leather couch. "Let me know if you need anything," I said. "I'll set an alarm for 9:00 a.m. so we don't miss the day." He nodded and rolled over, and I found my way to my bed. I could barely keep my eyes open. It had been a long day. I turned to my right and was intrigued by the stars shining brighter than ever. I reached over to my desk and found my sunglasses. *I wonder what the stars look like with these on.* I put them on and noted the change in the light. Then I rotated them counterclockwise so the lens was only covering my left eye, leaving the right one free. The contrast was even more interesting. *Get some sleep.* I took the shades off and returned them to my desk. My eyelids felt heavy, and I passed out.

My eyelids shot open. It was still dark outside, but that layout of the stars had changed. I grabbed my phone: 4:00 a.m. *Man, I feel great. Sleep is overrated.* I hopped out of bed and turned the shower on. I undressed and got in, leaning one arm against the wall, letting the lukewarm water hit my back. *Let's test my pain threshold.* I turned the knob and felt a pleasurable burn, let my body get used to it, then turned it more. *Ouch.* I turned the knob all the way in the other direction and was burned by the cold. *Ouch! Note that both hot and cold can still burn me.* I washed up for sixty seconds, dried off, brushed my teeth, and noticed the red glaze over my eyes in the mirror. *How do I get rid of that?* I sneaked to my room and got dressed for the day, wearing a T-shirt, khaki shorts, and flip-flops. I grabbed my sunglasses and quietly left the apartment, leaving Russell to sleep. It was pitch-black, and my sunglasses made it worse, but the stars were so damn interesting. I drove to the local grocery store and got English muffins, ham, eggs, and cheese. *He'll love this.* I was the only one in the store except for the checkout employee. "How's your day going?" I said. She looked at me like I was crazy without responding. "Thanks so much!" I grabbed the bag and headed back to the kitchen. The clock on my car read four thirty. *Damn, will this day get here already?*

The kitchen in my apartment opened up into the living room, where Russell was sleeping. I grabbed a frypan, sprayed it with butter, and began to cook breakfast. I had not cooked breakfast up to this point in the one and a half years that I had been in college. I toasted the English muffins and cooked the ham and eggs to perfection. I added the cheese as a finishing touch, which melted on the piping hot ham and eggs. *Thanks for giving me these skills as well. I can do anything.* The clock in the kitchen read 4:41. The backdrop was looking a bit brighter through the window of the living room, so I grabbed my sunglasses. *Let's see how this perspective looks as the sun rises.*

I brought Russell's breakfast over to him and slammed it on the counter, making a loud noise, hoping to wake him up. It did not. "Russ," I said. Still nothing. I grabbed his shoulders and repeated, "Russ!" He rolled over and woke up.

"Dude, it's four in the morning. What are you doing? Why are you wearing sunglasses?"

"I made you an egg sandwich, and it's hot. Do you want it? You have to see what I'm seeing in these glasses. It's like a rainbow, whether you're looking at the sun or the stars."

"Umm, I'm going to sleep a bit longer. I'll eat that in a few hours. Thanks."

I went back to my room and watched the early-morning news. "What a nice gesture by this man." I changed the channel to sports. "He took a great shot there." I changed the channel to the food network. "You'll want to make sure the bread is nice and crispy before serving it." I needed to outwit the messages coming at me from the TV. *Let's see how you handle this.* I changed the channel every second, over and over, seeing and hearing blips of each station that were adding up clearly. "Breh..." Channel change. "Tis'..." Channel change. "The..." Channel change. "Wa..." Channel change. "Nnn..." *It all makes sense. It's all connected. Breh-tis-the-wa-nnn. I am the one.* Over the next three hours, I took another two showers, watched myself more on TV, tried to read, and listened to more music about me. It was eight o'clock, and I couldn't wait any more. I went back to Russell, his cold egg sandwich still sitting there, and woke him up again.

"All right, all right, I'm up."

"Wanna play NBA?"

"Sure," he said, a bit irritated.

I turned on the PlayStation, and we picked out teams. For the next hour, we played, Russell picking it up quickly and me hearing the announcers in the game evaluate my behavior. "He didn't have to do that." *Yeah, I guess I didn't have to wake him up. Could have gone for a run.* Then my 9:00 a.m. alarm went off on my phone. *We have to stop now. Something isn't right.*

"Wanna go do something else? Try these glasses on. They're amazing," I said.

"Yeah, slow down a bit. I'm going to shower."

I let him go. Then I walked onto our balcony with my sunglasses on, happier than ever, ready to watch more of the sun.

## *Getting Help*

I said goodbye to Russell at the airport and was excited to get back to my college playground. That night, Bobby and a few others came over to watch a movie. As I was sitting on the couch, I felt my right leg twitch. *Uh-oh, this is new.* Every time Bobby blinked, I would feel some sort of twitch in my body. I kicked him on the leg. "Can you move over?" I said in an irritable tone. I decided that the physical manipulation of my body by another's blinking eyes was too much and too bizarre. As I stood up to be alone in my room, my cell phone buzzed in my pocket: Dad. *How convenient. Everything I'm about to say will be recorded and broadcast to the world.*

I picked up. "Hello?"

"Hey, buddy, what are you doing? You feeling all right?"

"Yep, just watching a movie with some friends. I feel fine. What's going on?"

"Well, uh, I was talking to Russell, and he said things aren't going so well down there. John and Kirk said the same."

*Those disloyal bastards, all of them. And Russell? Wow.*

"Well, that's great, but I'm doing fine."

"I'm going to come down there and take you home to see someone. Just hear him out, okay?"

"I mean, why? Why can't I just stay here?"

"It's just to make sure things are all right. I'll be there tomorrow morning. Now go finish your movie and try to relax. I love you." He hung up.

*Well, I guess my dad wants to take an impromptu vacation this year. He must need my help with something.* I walked out to the movie room, noticing John and Kirk making eye contact, like I had just been given news that I needed to hear. "I'm heading home for a few days, FYI. Leaving tomorrow." John and Kirk looked relieved.

I hadn't eaten all afternoon but was not hungry. I had already worked out but was not tired. I had already showered, shaved, and packed but felt unprepared for the trip. I lay in bed that night in the darkness, breathing heavily, unable to sleep. I found a face in the moon and stared at it for most of the night. Before I knew it, my dad was at my apartment door.

"Where's your bag? We gotta go." He barged in and hustled into my room. "Is this it?"

"Yeah," I said, confused on why we were rushing.

He grabbed my bag and walked me into the rental car. "And he's off!" the car radio said.

*Well, I guess we'll see what happens now.*

We made it to the airport and returned the rental car. "You doing okay?" my dad asked as we waited in line at security.

"Yes, I'm good."

He was practically sprinting with his roller bag through the terminal. I followed about ten feet back. "Brett, keep moving." *What is the big fucking rush?* I was embarrassed, as the entire airport saw me tagging behind my dad like a child. We made it to the gate and sat down. I noticed a man wearing jean shorts, a white T-shirt, a blue hat, and sunglasses. He looked right at me.

I heard, "You're going to crash on this plane. He's leading you to your death." He pointed directly at me with aggression.

"Dad, do you hear that man in the blue hat?" I asked.

"What man? There is no man with a blue hat."

I looked back, and no one was there. *Making the man disappear? Real nice, you're making me look crazy in front of my dad. Thanks.* We boarded the plane, and I found a window seat. I looked forward and noticed a finger pointing backward at me from the seat in front on the left armrest. *Oh, fuck, he's back.* I looked on the right side and found a hand gripping the armrest tightly. *Hold on tight and everything will be fine.* I gripped both of my armrests with full force and saw the pointed finger disappear.

"You all right?" my dad said.

"Yeah, I'm good now."

We made it back home, where my mom was waiting to take me to see a psychiatrist. *Awkward to see these two together.* We drove a few minutes from my house, and I found myself in the waiting room. *Is this where the testing begins? I'm sure they'll want to question and congratulate me on uncovering the greatest mysteries of mankind.* I walked into the office and found a calm, middle-aged man sitting with his legs crossed.

"Have a seat, Brett. So tell me a little bit about school." *He knows.* "Why did your parents bring you here today?"

*I can certainly trust this man.*

"I think they needed me to come back to help them. My dad and mom have split, and I'm the only one who can bring them back together."

"I see," he said. "What else is on your mind?"

"Well, I'm just really sick and tired of people not giving it their all. I mean, I know I'm special and have been given this great gift, but other people really need to step it up."

"Special? How so?"

"Well, I'm getting crystal clear messages from birds, TV, and even radio. Sometimes when others blink, I can feel it make me twitch."

"Okay, Brett. I'm going to grab your parents now. You can go back to the waiting room."

I went back to the waiting room, and they made their way in with the doctor. Classical music was playing as I waited. *Thank you for the calming music.*

"Brett, will you come in here for a moment?" I got up and sat down with both of my parents in the room. "Brett." He put his hands chest-high and shoulder width apart. "Most people that I deal with are in this range." He moved his hands toward each other and then back out. "You are over here." He took one hand and pointed far beyond the boundaries of his hands. "I'm going to have your parents take you somewhere that can help you very much."

*This doesn't sound all that bad. Number 1, I'm obviously very special—he pointed that out. Number 2, I'm going to work with the smartest people in the world because those are the people I fit in with.*

"All right, Mom and Dad, let's do this!"

They both gave me a concerned smile. We found our way to the car and headed to the psychiatric hospital. I was excited.

## New Roommate

We parked the car and headed toward the entrance. I noticed cameras on the corners of the ceilings and the video footage on screens behind the check-in counter. My parents took care of paperwork and escorted me to a sitting area with others who were chosen like me. *I wonder what their powers are.* They were silent as we waited. I became a bit confused and didn't understand why everyone was so upset. After about thirty minutes, the door opened. "Stevens." We stood up and headed to the elevator, my mom, my dad, an escort, and me. I heard a lot of beeping, and my mom grabbed my hand, hard. When the elevator door opened, a rush of light came pouring in. The beeps got louder, and two escorts took me by the arms and walked me over to a locked white door with big windows. I saw a few people pacing back and forth on the other side. My parents were very concerned and said goodbye. It was not until they started walking toward the elevator that I realized they were leaving and I was staying. My excitement turned to confusion, and I got anxious. *Wait, why am I going into this locked room?* I slowed my walk, and the escorts moved me along. I brushed their hands off me and tried to back up a bit. Their force got stronger, and I stopped resisting. They left me standing in the hallway of my new home and closed the door behind me. I turned around and looked out, making eye contact with my mom, who was waiting for the elevator to come.

*How could you leave me here like this?* I stood with a blank stare as they got on the elevator. *Fuck 'em! I can figure this out on my own.*

I looked to my right and saw a payphone. There was an older man wearing a hospital gown talking loud and fast into the phone. "He's here, he's really here! We've delivered the package. The eagle has landed!"

*Oh, they are expecting me.*

I nodded at the man, like we were speaking the same language. He nodded back. *Okay, confirmed.* Another man with thick glasses and gray crew cut approached me, wearing a name tag with a key card. "Hey, Brett, let me show you to your room."

*Noted, key card on upper left pocket.*

I was planning my escape. Then I heard a loud screeching sound to the tone of "Shoooooooot!" coming from the end of the hall. I followed the employee closely down the hall. "Shoooooooot!" I heard again. As we walked down the hall, I saw three others gathered around the TV. They were facing me, the TV facing them. I could not see what was on. A very skinny woman with glasses, two teeth, and sitting in a wheelchair yelled at the top of her lungs, "Shoooooot!" On her left was a bearded young white adult with a face as hard as stone, frowning. On her right was an overweight black woman, laughing at the top of her lungs at whatever was on the TV. No matter how loud the yelling or laughing, the man's posture and facial expressions did not change.

We finally made it down the long hallway, and the yells got louder. "Shoooooot!" Then I was able to make out some of the sounds coming from the TV. "Well, Ron, he's made it down the long hallway, and they'll show him to his room. How do you think he'll handle tonight?" *Same old shit. Phew. They are here with me.* "You know what, Tom? Time will tell. He's had a much easier life than this woman in the wheelchair. He was born healthy, and it would just be unfair to compare the two." *Don't mess with Michelle in the wheelchair. She's had a hard life.* The employee showed me my room, which was right outside the main area, where the NHL hockey game was on. "Shoooooot!" I walked in and found my older roommate sitting upright in his bed, wearing hospital pants and a green turtleneck. Our beds were about ten feet apart in the small room. I had the window; he had a blank wall. We had a community desk in the middle.

"This is your roommate, Brett. I'll go grab you some towels." He left.

"Hi, Brett!" said my roommate.

"Hi! So why are you here?"

He stood up and towered over me, standing six foot four. He pulled the collar on his turtleneck down, revealing a deep, dark bruise around the front of his neck. "I tried to hang myself."

I stared blankly at him. *What a loser, giving up like that. He should die.* I thought back to a time, joking in middle school, when I said, "If you try to kill yourself and fail, then you couldn't even succeed at that!" My friends all laughed as we went back to playing in our protected, privileged neighborhood.

He pulled his collar back up and lay on his bed, sobbing. I looked out of the window and noticed cars driving and lights flashing. *This will all be critical to my escape.* "Shoooooooot!" *God, that's fucking annoying.*

"Time for meds," an attendant said, coming around.

I lay in bed. *I don't need meds. I'm totally fine. I can see why all these other assholes do, though.* They brought the pills to me because I didn't know the routine yet, and I took them. I started feeling tired. Only a few days ago, I was on the brink of uncovering the mysteries of the universe at school. Now there is a conspiracy, and I am locked up, looking for an escape. I turned on my back, staring at the ceiling. As my eyes were about to close, I heard "Shoooooot!" coming through the wall.

## Stay on the Psych Ward

I woke up on my back, groggy and confused. I rolled to my right and looked out of the window, noticing that the sun was blocked by a building. *Get through the building and you'll be able to see the sun once again. Find a way to get the fuck out of here.* I rolled to my left and saw my roommate, who had tried to hang himself. *I'd take Carter and the knife over this guy any day.* I rose to a seated position and heard a deep voice through the wall. "But blessed are your eyes because they see, and your ears because they hear. For truly, I tell you, many prophets and righteous people longed to see what you see but did not see it, and to hear what you hear but did not hear it."

I gained my footing and stepped into the common area, seeing an older man reading aloud from the Bible. He had a warm smile and appeared to be at peace. The moment was interrupted when a girl, about my age, stomped down the hall, furiously yelling, "So you're telling me that I have to ask you to unlock this door every time I have to use the fucking bathroom? Every time I have to take a shit? Shower?"

"Now, now, keep your voice down and follow the rules, or else," replied the staff member on duty.

"Or else what, bitch?" she said.

"Keep your voice down!"

"You can't tell me what the fuck to do!" Then she kicked a chair over. Before I could blink, two security guards grabbed her as she kicked her legs and squirmed in their hands. Her voice got louder. "Get the fuck off me!" The stronger men pulled her down the hall and out of sight. I felt nothing.

*When's breakfast? I'm starving.*

We lined up for morning meds and breakfast. I was one of about fifteen others wearing the same hospital clothes. A few were standing comfortably like me, but most were swaying back and forth, talking to themselves, or making random noises. Michelle went first in her wheelchair. "Is this the Gatorade that's going to make me feel better?" she asked as she held a cup full of what looked like orange Metamucil.

"Yes, Michelle. Drink it right up."

This put a big smile on her face as she downed the "Gatorade." *She would have done well in all those circle-ups.*

I finally made it to the front and had my meds presented to me. There were a few pills of different colors in a white paper cup. *Whatever this is, I know God wants me to have it.* I took the pills and had a vision of Jerry, Russell, and me playing with a Slip 'N Slide in our backyard. *My throat is the slide. The pills are us.* I grabbed a tray of eggs, cereal, pancakes, waffles, sausage, bacon, orange juice, and milk and made my way to the dining room. There was a seat open next to the emotionless, stoic guy from last night, and I sat down. "I'm fucking starving! What's your name?" No reply. *Well, I guess we aren't talking today.* I ate everything on my tray with no awareness of why I was so hungry. I went back to get seconds, and the food cart was gone. "Ummm, is there more food?"

"You'll have to wait for lunch."

*Wow, fuck this. Get back to the exit plan.*

I took a solo tour of the floor, walking by rooms with no doors, filled with broken-looking people, some sleeping, some awake, some in between. I found a corner that had every board game imaginable—puzzles, chess, Uno, you name it. The games were worn-out, with pieces missing and a creepy stench. I found another large window that would be critical to my escape. I memorized the layout and noticed that I could see the sun from this angle. *That's a good sign.* I kept to myself and protected the corner. I finally felt comfortable enough to make my way to the TV area. *Seinfeld* was on.

"If you're stuck in this place, how will you save the world?" said Jerry.

George replied, "If you're meant to save the world, how can you be stuck in this place?"

Elaine chimed in, "You two couldn't understand."

Kramer blew the door open. "I'm going to save the world!"

The audience laughed.

*What is this, some kind of joke?*

Just as *Seinfeld* went to commercial, the black woman from last night, who was watching TV, started laughing again extremely hard. *Is she laughing at the show, the commercial, or me?* I gave her a look.

Then I saw a white figure walking toward me down the hallway. *Who is that?* As she got closer, I noticed it was the girl who had the tantrum earlier. She was walking slow, wearing a straitjacket and clearly medicated. "Ask for a key before using the bathroom. Ask for a key before using the bathroom. Ask for a key before using the bathroom," she repeated over and over in a low voice. *I don't know what they did to her, but I definitely don't want them to do that to me.*

That night, the gang all gathered around the TV to watch *Forrest Gump. Of course they'd pick Forrest Gump. I'm Forrest and slightly slow, and they are all making fun of me. You must finish the entire movie to win the game. The true meaning will be at the end, and it will help you escape.*

"Med time!" an employee announced. A few sprinted to the front of the line, excited to get their meds. Most of us trudged down the hall, waiting for our turn to be poisoned. I made it back to the TV for the beginning of *Forrest Gump. Focus.* There was nice-sounding music during the initial credits. *Got it. Okay, that's a good sign.* Then my eyelids felt like ten-pound bricks. I tried to fight them, but

I couldn't. I asked for a key to use the bathroom to get ready for bed, lay down, and fell asleep with no problem.

## Brain Testing

I woke up to the clicking of static electricity swarming around my brain. *What. The. Fuck.* I was scared. *Why are they doing this to me?* I envisioned a group of white-haired scientists in a lab upstairs viewing our floor on monitors like lab rats.

"Turn the static up one notch," one scientist said to the other.

As he turned the dial, the click sounds become louder, and the pain was worse. I turned to my roommate, who was passed out and snoring. "Did you feel that?" He snored again. *Useless.* I came out of my room and noticed stealthy round cameras planted at every angle of the floor. *So we're all just lab rats? So this hospital is a place where you stick a great mind like mine in between a bunch of suicidal, mentally deficient, mute, assholes and conduct studies?* I kept my head on a swivel after figuring out that my body was being used for electrostatic testing. I spent the next couple of seconds thinking about how I could win. *The players who work the hardest will gain the most. The players who work the hardest will gain the most. It's all connected.* I practically sprinted to the puzzle area and found markers and some blank paper. I wrote in big letters, "I know what you are up to," and left it open for the cameras to see. I took a second sheet of paper back to my room. I wrote, "I'm ready to escape," and left it facing out on my window so the world could see. I coughed. *Oh, no, they are pumping in bad air, also testing the strength of our lungs.* The window was old and had a tiny socket that let air in and out. I sprinted down the long hallway to the dining room and grabbed a small straw meant to stir coffee. I sprinted all the way back to my room, hearing, "Time for meds," as I ran by the meds counter. I shoved the tiny straw in the tiny hole and took a breath in. The air was crisp and clean. A tear came to my eye. *Thank you for that challenge, but I'm ready to leave now.* A traffic light turned from red to green. *I'll take that as a yes.*

A white-haired old man wearing a white coat and carrying a clipboard entered the unit. He had words with the person at the front counter, pointed down the hall, nodded, and started walking my way. "Brett, I'm Dr. B. Please follow me to your room." *This is the guy responsible for all my pain. Maybe if I plead, he'll let me out of here.* The room was empty. He sat on my bed, and I sat on the desk chair. I saw his evil face with the backdrop of sunlight shining through the window. *The perfect balance of good and evil. Man versus nature.* I pictured his perspective, looking at my face, with a blank wall and an empty bed behind me. *Heh heh, whose view is better?*

"How do you feel, Brett?"

I looked at the ground. "I'm fine. I'm just feeling some of the pain of being here."

"I know, I know you are feeling pain. I'm so sorry about that."

"Well, can I go?"

"No, you have to stay here for a little while. I'm sorry."

My heart sank, like when I missed the exit to pick up Russell at the airport a few weeks ago.

"Hang in there." He stood up and walked back to the main area. "Michelle? Good to see you. Let's have a talk in your room." All the other patients tried to get a word in with Dr. B before he made it to Michelle's room. He was, after all, the one responsible for determining who stayed and who went. *Don't buy into his bullshit, Michelle. He's the one doing this to us.*

Wake up. Breakfast. Meds. Morning group. Boredom. Lunch. Boredom. Afternoon group. Boredom. Dinner. Meds. Sleep. I followed my regiment for the next few days.

One morning, a hospital staff member rolled a wheelchair to my room. "Hey, Brett. I'm going to put you in this wheelchair now. We're gonna get some tests."

I got up and sat down in a wheelchair for the first time in my life. He wheeled me down the long hallway, unlocked the door with his key card, and pressed the elevator button. *Step 1, make it to the elevator.* The door opened, and we rolled in and headed down to a lower level. We got off in a huge public waiting room. *Step 2, waiting room.* My instinct was to stand up, but he kept his hand on my shoulder, implying that I had better stay seated, or else. The action in the room brought me back to the student wellness center. Fast-moving ants on a giant piece of candy. I fell into this delusional state while I waited, envisioning millions of ants crawling on a large lollipop, until I was rolled into a private room. I saw a long table with a large circular plastic device wrapping around it.

"All right, Brett, the technician will take it from here."

I changed into a hospital gown, lay back on the table, and was mechanically moved inside the device. *This is it. My brain is either going to explode from all the radiation or I'll be more powerful than ever.*

"Brett, close your eyes and think happy thoughts. Completely let go."

*I'm at basketball camp, freezing boxers and eating pizza. I play against Darrelle Revis in my first varsity basketball game. My name is called for Camper of the Year, then Playmaker of the Week. I'm running out in front of thousands of people for the championship game. I hear a beep and feel the pain of Russell hitting me in the back of the head with the ball. Then Jerry running me over at open gym. Then getting knocked out in the championship.*

Then I woke up.

"How are you, Brett?"

Something smelled horrible, and I think it was me. "I think I shit my pants, but I'm fine otherwise."

"Go get cleaned up."

It turned out that I did lose control of my bowels during that memory trip. The good news was, I survived and my brain was stronger than ever. They rolled me back to the floor and dumped me behind the locked doors like manure in a wheelbarrow.

## The Jacket

Wake up. Breakfast. Meds. Morning group. Boredom. Lunch. Boredom. Afternoon group. Boredom. Dinner. Meds. Sleep. As the days passed, the patients were shuffled around. Some discharged, others moving to more restricted floors with crazier tenants. With patients on my floor moving around, it opened up room for new patients to be housed. I was watching TV one morning when a tall, young, white adult wearing hospital pants and a dirty white T-shirt came strutting down the hall, confident as ever.

"I know the drill," he said to the attendant. "Ask you for towels, soap, and to use the bathroom." My roommate had been discharged that morning, so the bed in my room was open. I observed from the TV area as this stranger set up camp in my room. He set his belongings down and sat next to me. "What are you in here for?" he asked. The Bounty quilted quicker-picker-upper commercial was on and in the background. I heard, "It's better and stronger than the other leading brands." *This guy must be better and stronger than me. Or it's a test.*

"I'm not supposed to be here. A few weeks ago, I was partying at the beach. I was the all-time assist leader on my high school basketball team. I'm not supposed to be here."

He laughed. "Well, I chose to be here. Good food, comfortable beds, and plenty of stuff to do. This is my third time! Wanna play Uno?"

"Sure."

We played Uno until dinner, played a little more, then took our meds. My new friend mingled with everyone that night like he was at a work party, introducing himself, shaking hands, and happy as ever.

"Well, I'm heading to bed," I said.

"Already?"

I washed up, confirmed my escape plan with the outside lights, and nodded off, facing away from his bed.

I awakened to a knocking sound a few hours later and rolled over. It was him. "Just heading to bed. Go back to sleep." I rolled back over and fell asleep.

*I'm back at basketball camp, eating pizza and laughing with friends. There are three of us jumping up and down on an old bed, seeing who can touch the ceiling. The bed makes a squeaking noise on every bounce, over and over.*

My eyes opened, looking out onto the still-dark sky. The squeaking noise continued. I rolled over and found my roommate wideawake, staring directly at me, masturbating. "Oh my god! What the fuck!" I yelled at the top of my lungs. I ran out into the common area and started throwing books at the wall. "Get me the fuck out of here!" I grabbed the same Monopoly board that I played with my brothers on vacation, stood on a chair, and threw it down the hallway, the pieces flying everywhere. Then two security guards ran toward me, stepping on the pieces, crushing a hotel. At first glance, they saw a short white kid throwing books. They slowed down a bit and asked me to calm down. I grabbed another book and threw it like a Frisbee into one of their guts. The much larger, stronger guard bear-hugged me from behind.

"He was jerking off in my room!"

I resisted, planted my feet on the ground, and jumped as high as I could. This was unexpected, and I almost got loose. Realizing that I was going to be feisty, the other guard helped and continued the journey down the hallway. Another guard walked toward us with a straitjacket, opened and ready to be put on, like a Men's Wearhouse employee, only from the front. I had no control over my body anymore as they forced my arms in and strapped it from the back. I was fully restricted, except my legs. They moved me into a padded white room and came in with me.

"Brett, you're going to stay in here tonight. I'm giving you one chance to get out of that jacket right now, and if you behave, I'll leave it off so you can sleep."

"Okay, okay," I said, defeated.

He removed the jacket, and I sat in the corner, confused and violated. The door closed.

I didn't sleep one minute that night and began to accept that something was wrong with me. But was this place really helping? *I think I'm getting worse in here.* My anxiety reached an all-time high as I scanned the four padded walls of my jail cell. For the first time in months, I was out of ideas.

## Visit

After being let out of my cage, I was able to find my bed and get some sleep. My roommate was moved to another floor, and I would never see him again. I was fixated on the idea that I was getting worse and needed to get out. I took a couple hits out of the straw poking through the widow and looked out onto the street. An eighteen-wheeler with a red Coca-Cola advertisement on the side drove past. *They are using me for marketing. Whatever I see, eat, drink, or use will be broadcast to the world and sell off the shelves.* Then a Pepsi truck drove by. *There's some serious competition for my attention.* The Pepsi truck moved on, and a Blue Honda Civic was parked with its flashers on. *That's my ride home!* I watched as a man got out of the Civic, holding a brown package, walked it into the building, looked up at me, and winked. *Okay, there's going to be some kind of package that I need to look for with the next clue.* I walked out into the hallway and saw a staff member leaving with a blue zipped bag. *That's it. That must be the top secret paperwork that gets me out of here.*

While I awaited my escape from Alcatraz, I had to play the part that this place was making me worse. If I did that, then they would let me out and I could go back to school. I was sure to choose my food wisely; if I chose Coke, then I'd get an endorsement from them and everyone at Pepsi would hate me, and vice versa. I tried to stay neutral to keep my options open for my big signing bonus when I got out of the hospital.

*How do I show that I'm getting worse? What can I do?*

A new patient entered the lobby, tall and well put together.

*There's the agent who will evaluate my behavior and get me out of here. Show that I'm getting worse and I'm out.*

I found a one-hundred-piece puzzle and put it together. I looked up at the camera and took it apart one piece at a time. *Is this what you want?* I set up a game of checkers and put one puzzle piece on each checker, pretending to play against myself. *I'm mixing puzzles and checkers now. That can't be good, right?* Then I grabbed a water and let it drip on each checker, sticking the piece to it. A staff member came over.

"Now, Brett, we don't want to pour water on the puzzle pieces. We need others to be able to use them after you."

*Why don't you go fuck yourself?* "Okay, thanks for telling me. I had no idea that water would mess up the pieces," I said with an attitude.

We had the opportunity to go to the in-house gym that afternoon. Visiting hours would be later. The Olympic-crazy team lined up and followed our staff leader to the workout facility. There was a carpeted room with a basketball hoop, balls, and cameras up top. *How clever of you to put me in this box.* I grabbed the ball and shot from deep. *Swoosh.* I dribbled a bit and pulled up. *Swoosh.* I spun and went in for a layup and finished. The staff member was impressed. *Now, let me show you what this place is doing to me.* I took the ball and threw it as hard as I could off the backboard, like Maximus from *Gladiator* sending a spear at the king in his private viewing box. *Are you not entertained?*

"Brett, settle down," said the attendant. I smirked and threw it harder. "Brett, last chance." I dribbled over to the side of the backboard and started shooting, hitting the exact same spot and intentionally missing each time. I shot this way for the next ten minutes. *See what you are making me do?* I looked up at the cameras. "C'mon, Brett! Shoot it like you were before. Don't you love basketball?" *Why don't you go jump off a bridge?* I threw another dangerously hard shot at the backboard. "I think I'm done." I sat against the wall until playtime was over.

I took a shower and got dressed in my finest hospital attire for the visiting hours. Jerry, Russell, Mom, and Dad would all be there. They walked proudly down the hall with concern on their faces. "The people are nice here, Brett. It could definitely be worse," said my dad.

I had a quick flashback to my roommate's eyes, the straitjacket, and the padded walls. "You have no idea."

We played a bit of Uno, somewhat normally, as I scanned the room protecting my family from the crowd. Then we went into my room, which was empty, and I played Jerry in chess. He won and wrote, "Jerry–1, Brett–0," on a piece of paper and left it on the desk. I wasn't going to tell them not to come, but I really didn't want them there. Russell asked me to call him so we could fill out our March Madness brackets together, something we had done every year since middle school. *Do you have any idea what it takes for me to make a phone call?* They all gave me hugs and said to hang in there. I kept a close eye on them as they walked down the long hallway. They were able to exit, and I had to stay. I was the first one in line that night for my meds. The thought of going home made me happy.

## Own Bed

The doctor came around again about a week later, met with me, and said I'd be discharged soon. *Yes! I'm getting out of here tonight.* I packed my belongings, took the sheets off my bed, and approached the front desk. "I'm being released today. Where do I go?"

"Brett, we don't have you as being discharged today."

"Oh." I went back and unpacked everything, becoming more restless by the minute.

This cycle repeated itself for the next four days. By the fourth day, I was convinced that I was never leaving. Then my mom showed up. I was escorted off the unit, down the elevator, and outside. The air was crystal clear, and it was a beautiful spring day. "So when do I go back to school?"

"We'll figure all that out. For now, let's just go home. I made you brisket."

I was sitting in the passenger seat of the car as my mother drove away from the hospital. I noticed smoke coming out of a pothole and felt anxious. *That's a bad sign. This is all smoke and mirrors.* I was glad to have mobile escorts in front and behind us. My mom was carrying precious cargo. I waved to the black Escalade behind us. *Good work, sir.* Lights were bright, and signs were everywhere. There was an independent plumbing service vehicle on our left as we got closer to home, with an arrow pointing backward. *We are not going back to that hospital. Leave us alone.* The light turned green, and he drove off.

I was expecting a big "Welcome Home, Brett" sign on the main road when we approached my house. There was no sign, but everyone on the sidewalk was chatting and pointing at our car, blown away that I was so close to them. I put on the radio and heard more reinforcement that the entire world had seen my hospital experience and was proud of me for making it out.

We made it back to the house, and everything was perfect. Basketball court in the back, brisket on the stove, and my own bed waiting for me. My mom put her things down and gathered a few different pill bottles with meds in them. "Brett, I'm going to help you and make sure you get the hang of taking these. We also have a doctor's appointment in a few days. You'll see a psychiatrist and a therapist for a while. Your job is to show up. I'm coming with you for now."

"Yeah, whatever. Can we eat?"

She smiled. "Yes."

I headed up to my room and was alone for the first time in about three weeks. I opened my bag and found my LG flip phone along with my shoelaces and some other items that were not allowed at the hospital. *Wow, forgot about this stuff.* I plugged in my phone, turned it on, and let it load while I went to the bathroom, without a key. When I came back, I found eighty-nine missed messages, some texts, and some calls. The messages were on all ends of the spectrum. "Did you do the chemistry homework?" "Are you going out tonight?" "What's your address again?" "I heard you disappeared. Are you alive?" On and on. *What did happen to me?* The phone rang, and it was one of my friends. I got anxious.

"Hello?"

"Brett, what's going on, man? You all right?"

"Yeah, I'm fine."

"What happened to you?"

"I just had to come home for a little while."

"Oh, all right. We miss you."

I realized that I had been removed from my life at school. The phone rang a few more times, and I did not answer, feeling bad. Then my dad called.

"Hey, Brett, you all right?"

"Yeah, I'm fine."

"I wanted to let you know that a similar thing happened to me in high school. I know what you are going through." *Why didn't you tell me about it before it all happened?* "Just make sure you work out. Russell and I are going to fly down to college, get your stuff, then drive your car back."

"Uhh, okay. Thanks."

"Hang in there. It could be worse."

I lay on my bed for a few minutes and became restless. I shouted, "Mom!" She came running up. "What am I supposed to do now?"

"It will all work out."

Sleeping in my own bed was no different from sleeping at the hospital that night. I rolled on my side and observed the stars through my window. There was a tiny red flashing light on my TV that I stared at. *Am I being watched?* I stared at it harder and longer until the red light changed to a green light. *I'm controlling this thing with my mind. Still got it.* Then I was able to blink and change it from red to green and green to red on demand. I was proud of myself for this mind trick, but it didn't feel the same.

On the very first night home, the buzz of it all began to fade. Just like in the padded room, I didn't get one moment of sleep.

## No Hope

"You have what we are calling psychotic disorder, NOS," said Dr. C sitting across the table from me. "NOS stands for 'not otherwise specified.' Any questions?"

*So you really don't know what's wrong with me.*

"Umm, why did this happen?"

"Well, we aren't really sure, but generally speaking, it's caused by drugs and alcohol and/or stress. We have you on an antipsychotic medication, Risperdal. That should help stabilize your mood and get rid of your psychotic thoughts. How are you feeling?"

"Fine, I guess."

"Okay. Well, I'm going to see you every week to monitor your medication, and you'll see Sue for psychotherapy. Have a good day."

I walked out, still confused, but with a place to be next week.

The boredom and restlessness were unbearable. I was too anxious to do anything but too bored doing nothing. I started doing puzzle after puzzle, day after day. My appetite had not slowed down, but my workouts did. I put on an easy fifteen pounds and started to feel depressed about that, month after month. My life was over. I didn't feel comfortable around people anymore, and I was living at home with my mom. *How lame.* I'd often lie with my back on the floor, head facing up at the ceiling, feeling overly dramatic that I had no options. On Russell's summer break, he would playfully kick me on the ground. That actually made me feel good.

"Brett, we don't think it would be wise for you to go back South for school this fall," said my parents. I actually agreed with them. I was afraid to leave the house. "Maybe we can look into taking a few classes at the local university next fall. No pressure." But then the thought of transferring schools, making new friends, and living at home, where I had spent almost my entire life, made me more depressed. The more depressed I got, the more anxious I became. In my most anxious moments, I would fall back and hallucinate.

One day, I decided to pick up a basketball and shoot around outside. The sound of a bird chirping brought me back. *I can't believe I thought the birds were talking to me.* I heard and saw a loud helicopter in the sky. *Could that be a sign?* As I was slightly distracted, I noticed a huge low-flying airplane come out of the clouds, heading toward me, engine roaring. I jumped back, and the airplane flew on. I was aware that the plane wasn't flying at me, that the helicopter wasn't a sign, and that the birds weren't relevant, but the delusional thoughts were replaced with boatloads of gut-wrenching anxiety. This continued in all the areas where I was formerly hallucinating. While watching TV and listening to the radio, I was aware that they were not talking about me, but I felt harsh anxiety instead. I could avoid people and was too anxious to even try to socialize. Even a bright light or familiar sound could bring me back to a psychotic place. I was crippled, and nothing felt normal.

I was finally able to get on a light workout routine, continued to show up for the doctor and therapist, and had the courage to enroll in a few classes at the local university. It took a few weeks to get used to driving by myself to class because of the amount of stimulation. I kept the radio off and both hands on the wheel. I was shaking as I walked into a small classroom. I sat all the way in the back by myself, hoping to never get called on or talked to. There was still a small fire inside me that wanted to answer the questions, wanted to be the confident, levelheaded person that I had always been. I knew the glow was there somewhere, smothered under layers of depression and anxiety.

I had dodged my friends as long as possible, as they continued to party and live out their normal middle years of college. I sat alone many days and nights, unsure if they'd ever see me as the same. It was communicated to me that drugs and alcohol were off-limits as long as I was on medication. The key words were "as long as I was on medication." So I asked, "Will I ever be off medication?"

"The way you are responding, pushing through some of your fears, and working out, I believe you'll make a full recovery. This means that we'll taper you off the meds, depending on how you are doing."

*Yes!* I saw a glimmer of hope. I'd be able to get through this and have my old life back. *Keep being patient and it will all work out.*

## Poker Rush

Over the next eighteen months, I slowly came back to life. I made a trip with my mom to visit Jerry, where he was doing a summer internship. We walked into his small, messy apartment, and he was on his computer.

"What are you doing?" I asked.

"I'm creating a website to enter fitness information for people who work out. I've been working on it for seven days straight." He kept typing.

"Cool," I said.

Taking a trip outside my local comfort zone was big for my confidence. I felt accomplished after arriving home.

I was getting more comfortable in my classes, meeting up with friends, and most importantly, I was tapering off the meds. I'd even met a new group of friends that took me in as one of their own. I'd often look up at the window of the University Psychiatric Hospital from campus, recalling how I used to be the one looking down.

With the newfound independence and finally being off all meds, I got back into partying. My goal was to recreate the life that I had before the episode. I didn't feel like I needed marijuana, because clearly, my mind could get pretty high without it. I had turned twenty-one, which officially made it okay for me to go to bars and drink.

Every so often, I'd get a flashback to the psychotic episode or hospital experience, but for the most part, I was able to move on with my life. The healthier I got, the more my dad explained what had happened to him.

"I was a mess. Didn't want to go to school. Didn't want to get out of bed. Was seeing green army men in the trees. I've been there, Brett."

"Wow."

*Again, why didn't you tell me this before? If I ever have kids, I'm going to make sure that they are fully aware of the genetic "thing" that happens to some of us Stevenses.* I later learned that my aunt on my dad's side had bipolar disorder. *So everyone is aware except me, the one who needs to be most aware.*

I had some pretty wild thoughts about how I was going to help other people who had had similar experiences as me without the means that I had. *Wouldn't it be nice if I did that?* I never did. I remained focused on school and my social life. My dad asked, "So are you going back into premed now?"

"Umm, sure."

I hadn't really thought about what I wanted to do. I was premed in the South because my dad told me to be, and now I was premed at the local university because my dad told me to be. What I hated most about premed were those damn three-hour labs. *If there were only a way that I could be premed without these damn labs.* A friend of mine was pre-PT (physical therapist), which sounded way easier, so I hopped on the bandwagon. Telling my dad would have been very difficult before his marital affair, but after it was a breeze.

"Okay, Brett," he said.

I was set up with pre-PT classes my second semester of junior year, had a great social life, and was ready to make the leap to move out and live on campus the next term. One of Russell's friends from high school was looking for a place, so we signed a lease confirming our residence.

The summer before senior year was a blast. Russell and I were both living at home, there wasn't much supervision, and I could go to the bar whenever I wanted. I had a lot of downtime and messed around with some online poker. One day, Jerry, who also played online, called me.

"Brett, log into my poker account and check the balance!"

I pulled out my laptop and logged in under his credentials, seeing a five-figure number. "Holy fuck! How did you do that?"

"This kid that I knew from college helped me. He's a professional poker player. Makes six figures per year. He has a friend that does the same."

"Wow, that's awesome!" I couldn't sleep the next few nights, dreaming about making money playing poker.

I called Jerry the next day. "Is there any way I can learn from these guys? What do they do?"

"I don't really want to bother them, but generally speaking, they go all-in or fold with twenty big blinds, raise with any two cards over seven, any pocket pair, any ace, and suited connectors. They don't invest more than 5 percent of their bankroll into any one buy-in. Start there." I wrote these notes down like a hyper scientist discovering a cure for cancer. I begged my mom to put money onto the poker site using her credit card and started with a low buy-in. I felt an adrenaline rush, similar to running late at night at school in the South, but much more under control, without hallucinating. *Let's do this.*

## Building the Bankroll

"Brett, can you come down here and eat? Your food is getting cold."

"No, I can't. I'm playing poker."

"Brett, we are all going out to dinner in an hour. Get dressed."

"I can't make it. I'm playing poker."

My uncle taught me how to play poker at a very young age at his beach house in New York. The game stuck with me growing up, carried over to the Jersey Shore, and was a huge part of my weekends in high school. Even at school in the South, I'd play online.

When my brother won that huge sum of money, I became even more obsessed. I had hundreds of questions for Jerry's professional friends. *How do I do this? What's the point of that? I know you said I'm supposed to do that there, but why?*

Then one day, after playing in the same online tournament for eight hours, I won $2,000. Both skill and luck played a role in my win. "You better get that money off the site right away!" my mom said. I told her I would, but I kept it on to reinvest in bigger tournaments. A few weeks later, I started playing three or more tables at the same time on my small laptop monitor. This gave me experience and was a more efficient use of my time. Then one Sunday, it all came together for me and I won $7,000 on a $55 buy-in. It was more money than I had ever had in my life. I took some off the site but left the majority on. I was more loose with my spending and excited to play my next session. Most of the summer was spent playing poker, and by the time I moved down to the local university for my senior year, I had accumulated over $50,000 in profit. At this point, I was playing six tables on my small laptop monitor at once, constantly clicking.

"You going in to play?" my roommate would say, playing NHL for Xbox.

"Yessir." I put on a Drake playlist, where "Forever" played.

> ♪It may not mean nothing to y'all, but
> understand nothing was done for me.
> And I don't plan on stoppin' at all, I want
> this shit forever, man, ever, man.♪

Six tables would pop up on the screen as I bumped my head to the beat.

> ♪Last name ever, first name greatest, like a sprained
> ankle boy, I ain't nothing to play with.♪

I'd go into a zone where everything became clear. *Bet. Check. Continuation bet. Raise. Fold. Fold. Boom.* Eight hours later, I'd come out to my roommate still playing NHL and he'd ask, "Did you win?"

"Yep, four grand."

"Yep, six grand."

"Yep, ten grand."

After the big wins, we'd go to the bars and I'd buy shots for everyone.

I realized that this was what I wanted to do for the rest of my life. *I'm going to be the best poker player in the world.* I called my dad. "Dad, I'm changing my major from PT to psych, just letting you know." It was easier than PT, and I could be a therapist one day as a backup. He was fine with it. I'd been so consistent with my poker winnings that no one could take a strong stance against it or tell me what I should do with my career.

I started putting poker over school and missed a lot of classes. One particular psych class was from six to nine once a week. I showed up only for exams and barely passed. My GPA dropped from 3.8 to 3.0 in one semester. It didn't matter to me. I was feeling pretty good about myself and had a lot of money. No one understood how I was able to play a game and accumulate such wealth. *I'll show you what I'm doing anytime, just ask. All these college kids, broke as hell, and not one of them wants to learn how to make money playing poker. Sigh.* I had one final paper to write before graduation and couldn't get myself to do it. *What's the point? I'm never going to use this degree anyway.*

"Dad, I think I'm going to drop out of college."

"In your last semester? That's ridiculous! You have the rest of your life to play poker. Write the last paper and finish."

*I guess that makes sense.*

"Russell, what's up, man?"

Russell was premed at his school. He and his frat brothers would pull up my poker tournaments while pregaming and take a shot every time I won a pot. They took a lot of shots. "Bsteven$087 [my online alias] is the truuuuth!" he would say.

"Wanna make $200?"

"Fuck ya!" he said.

"All right, I need you to write this paper for me. You'll get a bonus if I get an A. You in?"

"Fuck ya! Send it over."

I got an A and finished college, making over $100,000 playing online poker. I did things the right way and paid taxes on my winnings. My accountant almost fell out of his seat when I told him how I accumulated the money. I had a great life of poker, money, and independence ahead of me. I decided to bring my skills to Las Vegas for the World Series of Poker.

## *Main Event*

"You put up half, I'll put up half." I had an agreement with my dad on the $10,000 buy-in to the main event at the 2010 World Series of Poker. "Russell, you tag along." We all laughed. Russell and I got on a flight to Vegas with dreams of me getting on ESPN and making money in the main event. We had been watching this televised poker tournament since the Jersey Shore in 2002. We made it to the Rio All Suite Hotel and Casino a day early and rested up before the big tourney the next day in the afternoon.

We worked out and had a healthy breakfast in the morning. "You ready?"

"Yep, it's the same as every other tournament. Just gotta run the system."

We checked out the poker room, hundreds of empty, branded tables, ESPN camera crew setting up, analysts settling into their respective areas. I took my $10,000 cash and waited in line for an hour behind other hopefuls looking to achieve poker immortality. When I got to the front of the line, I traded the stack of cash for a thin piece of paper with my table and seat number. As the event came closer, I observed people of all shapes and sizes, some eating cheeseburgers, some doing jumping jacks, others bobbing their head with headphones. It was the closest I'd gotten to a pregame warm-up since high school basketball. I found my seat in the back corner of the room, hidden from the cameras. *This is perfect, start as an unknown, make it big later.* I settled in and found the game to be no different from online. I pictured an online table layered on top of my live table to get my bearings. A player would raise, I'd look into the space in front of my view to see a transparent online poker table, create the image of the player raising from his seat, his stack and the pot sizes changing, then I'd hold that image until the next player made a move. *It's literally the exact same game. They are all robots. Whoa, chill out with the robots. This is Vegas, not the psych ward.*

I was very comfortable at my hidden table. I wore a low light-blue hat, khaki shorts, and a Systems Fit T-shirt. Jerry's fitness website, Systems Fit, had reached a point where he was looking to raise money. I sat on a conference call a few months earlier with a group of wealthy adults. "What's he doing on here?" my uncle asked. I stayed quiet and ended up making a five-figure investment for a small percentage of the company. The sole reason for my investment was that Jerry was in charge. I knew he wouldn't accept failure and would push himself beyond reasonable limits to make this company succeed. With the chance of getting on TV, I had to represent and wear the Systems Fit T-shirt.

I played on, comfortable and doing well. Then a tournament director came over and announced, "We're breaking your table. I'm going to pass plastic cards around with your new table and seat numbers. It's completely random." Breaking a table is when there are enough open seats on other tables to consolidate. All tournaments break tables until the final table, where a winner is crowned. He passed nine white plastic squares facedown to each player. "Okay, flip your cards over and find your new seats." I watched as all the other players flipped, showing their table numbers in bold print with the same white background. I flipped my card over, and it was red. "ESPN-Featured Table," it read. *Holy fuck.* Everyone else at the table congratulated me. One player even asked to trade.

I saw Russell in the distance and gave him a look. I carried my backpack onto the main stage and saw his eyes light up. It was bright. I didn't notice anyone at the table until I sat down, spilling the loose change in my backpack all over the floor after forgetting to zip it. I looked to my left and saw Eric Seidel, a poker legend, famous for his appearance in the movie *Rounders*. *It's all the same. Just keep playing.*

I played for a few more hours and then undramatically lost with a good hand to a better one. I was a bit relieved and ready to head back to my cave, where I could get deeply involved in many games at once, alone, cut off from the world. I found out after my exit that Russell had taken a few pictures of the experience. Very cool.

"That's the side of his head!" my mom cheered, watching the footage of my featured table experience. I was on air for a total of three seconds, but it was still something to be proud of. Later that summer, I had considered moving to Las Vegas to get into more live games, but I decided to live with some high school friends on the West Side of the city instead. The West Side had a string of bars where college kids from the surrounding area went to party. I lived right in the heart of it. I bought $1,000 speakers and a $2,500, twenty-seven-inch Mac desktop. This gave me the ability to play up to twelve tables at once. I packed up the Civic and set up shop in my new home with new roommates. Life was good.

## Underground Game

♪*Move if you wanna, if you wanna, if you wanna move,*
*Move if you wanna, if you wanna, if you wanna move,*
*Move if you wanna, if you wanna, if you wanna move.*♪

Mims's "Move (If You Wanna)" was blasting loud, making my speakers shake on the wooden floor under my desk. I was wearing a comfy hoodie and some sweatpants, leaning back in my chair, engrossed by a twenty-seven-inch Mac computer screen. On my left sat a half-eaten Italian hoagie, and on my right, I was calmly moving and clicking the mouse.

♪*I don't understand how I can have so many haters,*
*Knowing I'm their father like my name is Darth Vader*♪

On the large screen, there were twelve small poker tables in constant motion. Chips moving every direction, alerts telling me when it was my turn. *Scan the table, boom. Watch the bottom left, click. Raise on the middle table. Check in the upper right. Be sure to count the chips on the middle left.* It was so natural that it felt like I was just sitting, listening to music. It was two o'clock in the afternoon, and I had started work for the day.

Hours would go by and I'd have no clue until my roommate, Aaron, would come in around five o'clock. "I hate my life," he'd say before face-planting on the couch. "Fuck you!" he'd continue jokingly. "How much you win today, asshole?"

"Not sure yet. I won't know until later tonight."

"Cool, man!" he'd say sarcastically. "Well, I worked all day and made about as much as that hoagie, so that's something."

I laughed, and he'd leave me alone.

More hours would go by. "How we doing now?" Aaron would say.

"Three tables left, close in all of them. We'll see what the poker gods have in store for me tonight."

"All right. Well, I'm going to bed. I'll see you at 5:00 p.m. and 9:00 p.m. again tomorrow."

This was how most of our days would go. Aaron and my other roommate, Warren, were up early and at work Monday to Friday. I'd wake up around eleven, maybe work out, and start poker at two. They would come home around five and go to bed around nine. I'd play poker until eleven to twelve at night. Repeat. I was profiting about $10,000 per month on this schedule.

On Friday and Saturday nights, we would hit the town and have a blast. I was happy to buy drinks for anyone at any time. We'd spark up conversations with college girls.

"So what do you do again?"

"I'm a professional poker player."

I'd get a weird look. "My cousin used to do that. He's in jail now."

"Oh, I'm sorry to hear that. I actually win, though."

"Yeah, sure you do." And they'd walk away.

I was having a real issue explaining what I did to people. Everyone had an uncle that played poker, but none of them called it their job.

Eventually, I just started saying, "I made $100,000 last year." This got their interest but made me feel like the ultimate douche.

I hadn't used marijuana at all but was drinking pretty heavily. Every so often, I'd get anxiety from the idea of what had happened a couple of years earlier. *The doctors said I'm good, so I'm good.* I'd suppress the feelings and continue living this lifestyle.

The money was always good in poker, but after a while, the lifestyle became a bit boring. Sure, I could do whatever I wanted, whenever I wanted, but I was alone most of the time. I recall getting a steak lunch at a high-end restaurant and calling Russell. "What are you doing?"

"I'm studying. You?"

"I'm eating steak at Ruth's Chris."

"Ha ha! You're living like a retired old man. Must be nice."

It felt like I needed to up the ante. My friend had told me about an underground game that took place about twenty minutes from the West Side. He said it was a big buy-in and to bring at least $2,000 cash and mention his name when I got there. I had played once every few weeks at the casino and was able to build a stack of cash that I kept in my room. I grabbed the whole roll, about $3,000, shoved it in my pocket, and started the drive. I had trouble finding the place, but eventually I did. I walked up, and the front door was locked. I noticed a camera in the upper right corner with a red blinking light. *No one's recording you, relax.* Finally, the door opened and a dirty-looking, plump man opened the door.

"Who do you know?"

"Hey, uhhh, Zach?"

He opened the door and nodded me in. I walked into a big room with one table in the center. Most of the seats were full. They had food, massages, and dealers.

"Deal the fucking cards!" shouted one of the regulars, unhappy with the pace of the game. He looked up at me. "Who are you, and do you have money?"

"I'm Brett, uhhh, Zach's friend? Yes, I have money."

"Why didn't you say so?" He smiled. "Have a seat."

I pulled out my wad of $3,000 and went into poker mode.

"Remember all the small people like me when you make it big, Brett," he said in a friendly tone.

I built my stack from $3,000 to $10,000 in four hours. "Am I able to leave now? I understand if you want me to stay."

"Nah, get outa here. You're welcome back anytime."

The cashier handed me $10,000 cash. I didn't have enough pockets to hold it all, so they gave me a plastic bag. I zoomed home, blasting "Power" by Kanye West.

♪*I'm living in that twenty-first century, doing something mean to it,*
*Do it better than anybody you ever seen do it.*
*Screams from the haters, got a nice ring to it,*
*I guess every superhero needs his theme music.*♪

I walked up the stairs to my apartment and found Warren and Aaron sitting on the couch, watching TV after a long day of work. "Where were you?" Aaron said.

"Oh, just working," I replied with a smile on my face.

"What's in the bag?"

"You really wanna know?"

"Yeah."

I took the bag and ripped it open, letting the cash rain on all three of us. Just another day at the office.

## *Marijuana*

♪*My chick bad, my chick hood, my chick do*
*stuff that your chick wish she would.*♪

Ludacris's "My Chick Bad" featuring Nicki Minaj played loudly.

♪*My chick bad, tell me if ya seen her, she always*
*bring the racket like Venus and Serena.*♪

*Swoosh.* A ping-pong ball splashed into the red cup, overflowing some of the beer. "Drink up, Aaron!" I yelled.

"Hey, Brett, can you not be a dick for five minutes? Okay, thanks."

Our apartment was packed with old high school and college friends and music blasting. An old friend showed up with a black backpack. I went to greet him. "Yo, man, how are you? What's in the backpack?" He smiled and nodded toward my bedroom. He unzipped the backpack and pulled out a collage of pills, weed, cookies, brownies—you name it. I thought about how many days in a row I'd been sitting alone on my computer during the day. *This will make it more fun. It will probably make me think deeper about the game too.* My buzz from alcohol tonight was strong.

"So what do you want?" he asked.

"Well, how much is the weed?"

"How much do you want?" He laughed.

"I have no idea. Pretty sure I've never bought weed before. How much would I need to buy right now to not have to buy it for a very long time?"

"Oh, you need an ounce." He pulled out a mason jar packed to the brim with sparkly green nuggets.

Looked good to me. "How much?"

"That's $400."

I went to my closet, took one look at the $10,000 cash sitting there, scoffed, and gave him $500. "For your efforts, my friend." We smoked a good amount, but not enough to make the smallest dent in the ounce. I went back to the party, eyes glazed like John from college, feeling extra good. I missed my next beer pong shot by far.

Although the poker hours were tough, it was nice sleeping in and having the luxury of working out midmorning. The gym was a ten-minute walk up the street and looked much different in the morning than at night. Dirty sidewalks, the smell of beer, and an overall sense that something bad happened there the night before were common. On one of my walks, I was stopped by a short skinny black man with tattoos on his arms and neck. "Take my album, man, it's amazing." I usually walked past a situation like this, but for some reason, I took it in my hand.

"Cool. Thanks, man."

Then he said, "Okay, that's five dollars."

I laughed and gave him the five bucks. What did I care? I tossed the album in my bag and moved on.

I made it back to my apartment on this September Tuesday all alone. *What would I have been doing on a Tuesday at this time in high school? Weird how life changes.* I showered, got in my work attire, and sat in my office chair, ready to do business for the day. The light shining through the window created a reflection that allowed me to see my closet. *Oh, fuck yeah! I forgot about that.* I took out my forest of weed and used the bowl and lighter that my old friend had left to set myself up. I took a big inhale and set it next to the mouse on the right side of my desk. I set up the music.

♪*If you're going to San Francisco, be sure to
wear some flowers in your hair,
If you're going to San Francisco, you're gonna
meet some gentle people there.*♪

I turned up the Global Deejays song with the techno beat in the background. Tables started popping up left and right. I got situated and felt like I had never felt before playing poker. *This is fucking awesome.* I was on autopilot, playing better than ever. I leaned back and experienced the table coming out of my computer screen in three dimensions. I tried putting the mouse on the left side of the desk so I could work on my left hand, just like in basketball. *Click. Click. Beep. Ding. Click. Shuffle.* I was in an alternate universe all because of a little weed.

*Knock knock.* "What the fuck is that smell?" Aaron asked.

I turned to him, grinning. "Want some?"

"Idiot." He sighed. "Look at you wearing a hat all alone in this place. Look at you making more money than I'll make all in one day." He laughed. Aaron did his usual check-in before bed.

"I'm kicking ass tonight, dude."

I ended up winning $20,000 that night, high as ever. I decided to go to the bar by myself on a Tuesday to celebrate. I walked into a dive bar. The lights and sounds were very intense. I felt slight anxiety but had no awareness that similar symptoms triggered my last episode. I had this feeling that I'd meet my wife in the bar that night. Turns out I sat there alone, hoping someone would ask me what I do for a living or how much money I'd made that night. *If they only knew, they'd be impressed.* I made my way home and slept it off, feeling completely normal the next morning. *Cool, I can handle the weed.*

Wake up. Eat. Work out. Eat. Smoke. Poker. Wake up. Eat. Work out. Eat. Smoke. Poker. Wake up. Eat. Work out. Eat. Smoke. Poker. By the sixth or seventh day in this routine, I was the happiest I had been in a long time. I experimented with different ways of seeing the game, like turning the computer monitor on its side and playing with that view. I started picturing the one hundred opponents at their homes, looking at their monitors. I strongly considered getting another mouse and figuring out how to play with two hands at the same time. *I'm ambidextrous.* I'd even do full workouts while playing, the second workout of the day. *I'm an independent man and have it all figured out. Who wouldn't want this lifestyle?*

## *Overly Proud*

I drove through the city with Immortal Technique's "Positive Balance" blasting through the speakers of the Civic, with all four windows down.

> ♪ *You need positivity like you need respect in jail,*
> *Because without positive balance, you'll be*
> *making negative record sales.*♪

There happened to be a jail close by. *Heh, what coincidence. It can't be the worst thing in the world that people might hear this song. It has a very positive message. And people can actually hear it. It's loud, and I'm driving near people. I'm not delusional like before.* I turned it up louder

> ♪ *I love when people think I'm psychologically disturbed,*
> *Because it means I overloaded their neurological nerve.*♪

I made it across town to the casino and headed to the poker room, where I'd go to break up the monotony of playing online, alone in my room.

Ninety-eight percent of people who play poker are not profitable. I was ranked in the 99.9th percentile and up over $200,000 at age twenty-two and well aware of the bad players. I walked into the poker room confidently, which had about fifty nine-handed tables full. *50 × 9 = 450. 98% = 0.98. 0.98 × 450 = 441. 441 players don't win money, 9 do.* I was in the top 2 percent and had played at a featured table in Vegas and an underground game with hustlers; the casino was not intimidating.

I was seated at an outer shorthanded table with only four other players; this meant that the hands would come around fast. *I'm going to raise every single hand just to get a rise out of these fools.* The action was on me. I raised. On me again, raise. Again, raise. Over and over until finally an older gentleman said under his breath, "This young prick has no clue."

"What was that?" I replied too loudly.

"I said you're a young prick and have no clue what you are doing."

I scoffed as the cards were dealt on the next hand. "Raise." This time, Old Man River called my raise and played the hand against me. I won the hand and he stood up. "This young prick is so lucky. I'm not playing against him anymore."

My blood boiled.

"Lucky? You think I'm lucky? How much money have you won playing poker? Ever been to Vegas? How old are you?" I looked around, realizing that most of the adjacent tables' players were turned around, looking at me. He walked away. "That's what I thought!" I sat back down, and my heart was racing. *Holy shit, what was that all about?* I had a flashback to myself freaking out on the Maccabi basketball team in practice. I did some slow breathing and decided to be done for the day. I racked my chips and drove back to the apartment.

My dad invited me to go to dinner that evening. "Catch a cab over here and I'll drive you back to the West Side later." I called a cab and got into the back seat, realizing that I still had the $3,000 that I brought to the casino in my pocket.

"How are you today, sir?" he asked.

"I'm fine. How are you?"

"Well, to be honest, I'm a wreck."

I noticed his long dirty gray hair, worn-out T-shirt, and ripped jeans. The car had a smell to it. "Why are you a wreck?" I asked politely.

"The government, man. No matter how hard I work, I can't get ahead. As soon as I make any money, they take most of it away. Also my ex-wife. She took the kids, and now I'm all alone. I can barely afford to pay rent and have been eating PBJ sandwiches and Ramen noodles for weeks."

"I'm sorry to hear that." I put my hand in my pocket, feeling the wad of cash, and already knew I would make his day.

"So what do you do for work, boss?" he asked.

"Me? I'm a professional poker player."

"Yeah, I have a cousin who does that."

"No, I, like, actually win a lot of money doing it."

"Yes, sure you do."

*The world will never understand.*

We made small talk for the next few minutes, and he pulled up to my dad's apartment, where he had been living since he left our home. "That will be $14.87," he said.

I pulled out two $100 bills. "Keep the change. Get a good meal on me."

His reaction was not what I expected. "Sir, I can't accept this."

"Trust me, I can afford it."

"Seriously, sir, I wouldn't feel comfortable."

"Do whatever you want with it, then. Give it to someone else." I walked away, leaving him confused.

As soon as I saw my dad, I told him that I had given $200 to the cabdriver because he needed it more than I did. "You did what?" *He wouldn't understand.* I called my mom and she had the same reaction. *She wouldn't understand.* I called Russell, and he was nice about it but didn't understand. *I guess I'm all alone on this one.*

## *Best Man*

I became more irritable by the day and developed a sense that smoking was not a good thing for me. I still had 90 percent of the ounce of weed in my room and decided to just give it away. But the damage had already been done. My ten-minute walk to the gym felt a bit different during that time. Strangers looked more suspicious. The traffic lights were creating meaningful patterns. Faces were forming in the sky. And worst of all, I was unaware. *Isn't it weird that when I click the mouse on my computer, I think of a mouse in my head? Now that I'm thinking about a mouse, I think about Mickey Mouse, the Disney character. Walt Disney, Wilt Chamberlain. Can you imagine being tortured in a chamber? As the torturer opens the door and it goes* click click click *like this mouse in my hand?* I'd snap out of it, still clicking the mouse. Then the music would start to tell me what to do in my game; 50 Cent's "Laughing Straight to the Bank" came to mind.

♪*I'm laughing straight to the bank with this.*
*Ha ha ha ha, ha, ha ha ha ha ha.*
*I see nothin' but hundred-dollar bills in the bankroll.*
*I got the kind of money that the bank can't hold.*♪

This line was relevant to my current financial situation. Sometimes I'd hear a song line up with what was going on in my game. For example, I really needed a heart to come one day, and Kid Cudi's "Heart of a Lion" came on.

♪*At the end of the day, day I'm walking with the heart of a lion.*♪

A heart showed up on the board, and I connected it all. That string of events happened often, but I held it together around other people and didn't let my symptoms show. It was my special little secret.

In my mind I was chosen, but I was also chosen as the best man for Jerry's wedding. We held the bachelor party in Vegas, obviously. I had thought about the best man speech for months in advance and wrote something nice. For the wedding, I stayed in the same hotel as Russell in the city where Jerry was living. I performed well at the ceremony. The reception was fancy, full of laughing and drinking high-end cocktails. I chose not to drink until after the speech was over. My uncle was close to the bar, and it was loud.

"Hey, Brett, want a drink?"

"No, thanks."

"Do you want some milk instead, you baby?"

"What?"

"Do you want some milk instead, you baby?"

"Huh?"

"Do you want something else?"

"Oh, no. I'm going to wait until after the speech."

He walked in the other direction.

*That motherfucker. He thinks I'm not old enough to drink?*

The music was getting louder, and the lights brighter. I found Russell, who was buzzed and having a great time. "Dude, Uncle E just called me a baby."

"What? That makes no sense," he said as he walked off.

I found my mom. "Uncle E just called me a baby."

"I'm sure that's not what he meant."

I found my dad. "Uncle E just called me a baby."

"What? No way." He took me aside and asked if everything was okay. I reassured him that everything was fine.

It was time for speeches. I was a bit nervous, but also excited. *Everyone will be focused on me listening to what I have to say for a change.* I stood up and talked about how Jerry did everything first before Russell and I tried it. The story about us running away from him and Colin at the Jersey Shore. I closed with a sentimental line and told them both I loved them. I did a good job and was relieved when it was over. I had a few drinks and headed out to the dance floor, where Lady Gaga's "Poker Face" was playing.

♪*I wanna hold 'em like they do in Texas, please.*♪

*What a coincidence.*

As time passed, my paranoia became worse. I'd close all the blinds in my room to hide so the people walking by on the street didn't take pictures of me. I felt like a celebrity every time I left the house, because people would point, talk, and laugh as I'd walk by. I continued to play poker and win, which was how I measured my success in life.

One morning, after the long walk back from the gym, I turned the corner in front of my apartment and saw an unlabeled brown package. A car zoomed by with guys laughing, knowing I'd take the bait. *Paparazzi.* I looked both ways, grabbed the package, and went to my room. *This is finally it. A message from something bigger than us. I was meant to have this package. Don't open it until after you tell her. This may bring you to them.* I called my mom. "Mom, I'm really stressed," I said, panting as I started to cry. "I don't think I'm ever going to see you again. This might be it for me." I felt like I had a greater purpose and she was too small to understand.

"Brett, I'm coming down there. Just wait for me."

"Okay."

I realized the package was actually labeled for one of my roommates, but it didn't matter. I got the message. I left it in the kitchen.

I shook off my weak moment and called my mom back. "Mom, you don't have to come. I'm fine."

"Brett, I'm already on my way. Just stay at your apartment." She sounded concerned.

I hung up, a bit frustrated, and took a walk up the street to get some food, defying her request.

"Brett, I'm outside of your apartment. Let me in."

"I'm walking back now. I got something to eat, so meet me on the corner." I started walking back and saw my mom standing all alone on the corner.

*Shit, she's in danger. I need to protect her.*

I walked into the street without looking to cross over. *I knew no cars would come.* Strange people were walking by her, talking under their breath about me. *Please don't let them get to her.* I finally made it to her safely and was relieved. I gave her a big hug, and when I pulled back, her face only had one eye. I blinked again and the second eye came back. *Stay away from her!* I locked the door behind us, and we safely made it to my apartment.

## Air Moccasins

"Brett, I think we should set up a time to see the doctor," she said.

This was a crushing blow. "Why? I'm totally fine." I settled down and went on my best behavior in fear of going back on medicine that made me lethargic or being blindsided and taken away into the hospital again.

"It doesn't mean anything. We just need to check in and make sure everything is okay."

"No!" I snapped back.

"Let's at least go back home and talk to Dad about it. He thinks you should, too."

"Why would I care what he thinks?"

"Brett! Get in the car."

"Fine."

We drove home.

*They have some nerve. How would they like to take pills because other people thought they should?*

We made it back to the house, where my dad was waiting in his car outside. We called the doctor on speakerphone.

"Hey, Brett."

"Hey, Dr. C."

"How are you feeling today?"

"I'm good but not sure why I'm talking to you."

"Can we schedule a meeting? It doesn't mean anything is going to happen. I just want to talk to you."

"No way."

My dad chimed in, "Brett, it's just a meeting."

"Yeah, honey, not a big deal," Mom added.

"Okay, then, why don't both of you go see a psychiatrist for no reason? It's no big deal." *My blood started to boil.* "Fine, but it better be quick." I hung up the phone and let into my mom. "Are you serious? I could punch you in the face right now!"

"Brett, don't talk like that to your mother."

"Oh, should I cheat on her instead?"

I ran upstairs to my room and found an old pair of moccasins and a hoodie. I slid into the footwear, threw the hoodie on, and charged down the steps to the front door. I yanked it open, walked out, and slammed the door behind me. Then, all was quiet. *Now this is nice.* It was a cool, peaceful evening. I walked down the front path to the street and started jogging. *I have to get away from these people.* I felt an overwhelming amount of energy and picked up the pace in my Nike Air moccasins. I made it to the main road, where cars sped by, frightening me, but I pressed on. *I'm not taking medicine again.* I looked up and saw a "Your Speed Limit" sign in the distance, tagging the speed of the passing cars. Next to it, a real speed limit sign read "Thirty-five miles per hour." A car sped by. "Your speed: 30." *Okay, I guess I need to run a bit faster.* I picked up the pace, approaching the signs more quickly. Another car sped by. "Your speed: 40." *Maybe I need to slow down a bit.* I slowed. Then the road became quiet and the sign went to 0. *You wanna see how fast I am? Watch this.* I engaged in an all-out sprint, waiting for the sign to tell me my speed. Just as I reached the finish line, where the sign was posted, a car sped by. "Your speed: 45." *That's what I thought.* I continued to jog with no final destination in mind. But I did know that I'd have to get through a tunnel in order to make it downtown. I thought about how I would swing through the ventilation pipes on the ceiling of the tunnel like monkey bars when I made it. I had run this very same trail hundreds of times in high school but always turned around at the library. I saw the library on the right and kept on going. *Breaking records.* At around the three-mile mark, I heard a voice calling my name from a car. "Brett! Stop running and get in the car!" I slowed down, exhausted, and let my parents take me home. I was frustrated and tired but still couldn't sleep. We had some leftover Ativan, a calming drug, from the last episode, and my mom grabbed it. They tried to get me to take the pill for the next hour or so, and finally, I gave in. The pill knocked me right out, and the next thing I knew, we were driving downtown for my doctor's visit the following morning.

## *Manic Rage*

We sat at a diner in the heart of the city about an hour before the appointment. I was so angry I could barely eat my food. My mom sat across me. As my buffalo chicken tenders arrived, it got worse. Like at the wellness center a few years earlier, everyone's voices started getting louder. *How could he treat his mother that way? I would never do that to my parents. Well, look, they are telling him he's sick when he's clearly not.* I felt more and more angry by the second. Finally, I stood up. *Fuck it, I'm getting the hell out of here! All these people are annoying.* I left the food on the table, my mom in her seat, and walked out of the diner. I was wearing nice jeans and shoes, a light-blue polo with a white undershirt, and a luxurious watch. I blended in with the college crowd and crossed the street. *I have to get out of here.* I noticed four bikes chained to a rail and aggressively tried to break one free. After three attempts, I moved on. I walked past the library, where I had studied for finals a short time ago. I found a bulletin board in close proximity to the library with student events, show-time for bands, and coupons for restaurants and ripped down all of them. A few students walked by quickly, saying nothing. *That's what I thought.* I strolled around to a building next to the library that had huge glass windows. I found a few rocks close by and fired them as hard as I could, hoping to shatter the glass. *How do you like that?* The glass held strong. My rage only got more intense. *You want to talk behind my back? You want to make me take medicine? I'm the crazy one? How successful have you been in your life? What were you like in high school? How much money have you made? All I hear is people complaining—fucking do something!*

I wandered across an open field, pumping myself up even more. I found a wooden park bench and saw blood. I had a brief flashback to basketball camp, attacking my weaker opponent. With all my strength, I ripped the bench out of the ground and threw it onto the field. A bus stopped a few feet ahead. I scurried on quickly, found a seat in the back, and hid on the floor, noticing people's shoes at eye level in the aisle. After a few blocks, I stood up and got off the bus, noticing that my hands were cut and bleeding from uprooting the bench. *All people suck. All people are lazy.* I walked down the sidewalk on the left side of the street, facing a line of parked cars. I punched out the side-view mirror on the first car and felt no pain. *All people suck.* I walked forward and punched out the next car's mirror. *All people are lazy.* The next one, punch. *All people suck.* Punch. *All people are lazy.* I looked to my left and saw an oversize Do Not Enter sign on one lane into a parking garage. I punched the sign with both hands rapidly. I had so much energy I felt like Mike Tyson. After about one hundred hits, I backed up and looked at the cars parked behind me. I sprinted up and jumped, landing with both feet on the front hood, making a dent. Feeling like a superhero, I ran over the front windshield over the top and slammed on the back hood. Then I jumped to the next car and repeated. I noticed my hand was covered in blood, and hopped off. I walked up to a homeless man and showed him my hand, asking where the hospital was. He looked at me blankly with no response.

A red Jeep pulled up behind me. "Hey! You think you can just jump on peoples' cars?"

"Fuck you!" I yelled back and kept walking.

No more than two minutes later, the flashing lights of a cop car pulled up next to me. Two men in blue jumped out and slammed me against the car, pulling my arms behind my lower back, where my back brace once protected, and cuffed me. They attempted to push my head into the back seat of the car, but I resisted hard. "Get the fuck off of me!" I wiggled and then felt the buzz of a Taser clicking, getting more intense. I pictured an old scientist turning up the voltage.

"You want to be tased?" roared the cop.

I stopped fighting for the moment as they pushed me into the back seat, knocking my head against the top of the car on the way in. *Smack!* They threw me in and slammed the door, hitting my outstretched foot. I grimaced in pain and pulled my leg back as they pushed the door shut. I lay down on the back seat and kicked the window as hard as I could, but it was no use. Three more cop cars arrived. I looked up, noticing a computer, beeping sounds, and other cops over the radio.

"He's going to steal the car!" the radio said. "Brett's going to steal the car!"

*I would if I could.*

I rolled over and looked up out of the rear windshield and saw a cross high in the sky on one of the campus churches. *At least God is watching.* An officer entered the vehicle, and the back seat window came down. A fat, bald, mustached cop with bad teeth stuck his head in. "Yeah, he's nuts, all right. Take him to the psych ward."

*Oh, no.*

The cop drove me five minutes up the road to the psychiatric hospital.

*No. No. No, not this again.*

Three cops yanked me out of the back seat. I tried to run them over and get away. They got more aggressive with me, took me inside, and put me in a padded room. "Get the fuck off me!" Two more officers came in and held all my limbs on the ground as I squirmed for dear life. "Get the fuck off me! I'm not going back in here!" I felt my head pressed against the ground as a woman in scrubs came in with a large needle. She applied alcohol to my left hamstring and stuck me. The next thing I knew, I was waking up in hell, again.

## Back in Hell

I was unsure exactly where I was the next morning, but it felt familiar, a window on my left, desk, chair, and bed across me. I rolled over and felt sore, like the day after a hard workout at the gym after not going for a while. I was wearing my street clothes, with a band around my right wrist. It had my name and a few random numbers and letters. I tried to sit up and felt pain in my lower back, wrists, and arms. I rolled my shirtsleeves up to my shoulder and noticed bruises all over my arm. I checked the other arm and found the same. I stood up and saw bruises on my legs. I limped out of my room, still gaining my bearings, and found a common area with middle-school-aged patients playing board games. A nurse with a warm smile saw me limping.

"Hey, Brett, how are you this morning?"

"Where am I?"

"You're at the hospital on the wrong floor right now. We needed a place to hold you while a patient was being discharged. After breakfast, you'll go upstairs."

*The hospital?*

I had a flashback of four grown police officers essentially beating the shit out of me as I yelled and resisted. I heard the kids chatting behind me. *OMG, he's here. He's actually here.* I became aware of the cameras on the ceilings. *I'm not a lab rat.* I grabbed a small box of Froot Loops and ate breakfast in my room, away from the groupies. Two security guards and a nurse entered my room.

"We're going to escort you to the adult floor. Stand up."

I felt strong and tough, like I had been through something with the cops as I entered the adult floor. *Don't fuck with me. I've done this already.* I don't need medicine; I had beaten this on my own last time. The floor had a similar layout as before, but the tenants were much different. I first noticed a five foot, petite, jittery blond woman bouncing around, talking one hundred miles per hour to herself. In the sixty seconds that it took me to walk down the hall and be escorted to my room, which was a single, thank God, she sat on every chair, had been in and out of her room three times, had spoken to four other patients, did a few cartwheels, and asked for the TV to be changed. *Restlessness sucks, doesn't it?* I sat on my bed and looked out of the window at my new view, which was a tall office building with square windows that I could spy on. *Or they can spy on me.*

The minute I had some privacy was the minute I started plotting my escape. I found a crack in the window like last time and gathered as much toothpaste and soap as I could. *I may be able to make a bomb with this and blow the wall down, but I'll need others' help this time.* I took a social approach to my grand escape in my older, more mature stage of life. *We'll all need to work together to get out of here.* I walked out to the main area, which, under different circumstances, would have looked like a library or community center with functioning members of society getting things done.

An attractive twenty-four-year-old woman with brunette hair, sweatpants, and her college-branded hoodie came out of her room.

"Can you all shut the fuck up?" Then she slammed her door close and went back to bed.

An attendant ran over. "You have to keep this door open."

"Fine, leave it open and fuck off!"

*She seems nice.* I walked to the next room like freshman year of college, getting to know everyone, and saw a skinny, good-looking young man with a baby face working on some assignments. His desk was perpendicular to the door, and he faced the wall, so I was only able to catch one side of him. "Hey, man, I'm Brett. You trying to get out of here?" He turned toward me and exposed the hidden side of his face and the third-degree burns that would be on it forever. I showed empathy. "I'm sorry, man, what happened?"

"I was in a fire and tried to kill myself when I realized I'd be like this forever. I may try to go to med school now."

"Good for you. Let's play Uno later."

He smiled and nodded, getting back to work.

I passed a locked bathroom. *Obviously.* As the hyper blond woman continued to run around in the main area, I walked past her room, which had original, beautiful artwork posted on the walls. *Interesting.* A man with curly hair, light beard, and blue sweater with long sleeves came out of his room. "Hey, I'm Brett. What are you in here for?"

He spoke perfect English with no accent, although he appeared to be of Middle Eastern descent. "Hey, Brett. Well, I'm a PhD student and wasn't making the cut. I didn't want to bring dishonor to my family by failing, so I worked and worked and worked, but I just wasn't getting it done. I couldn't do it." His eyes teared up. "The pressure got to me." He pulled up his sleeve, uncovering a train track of stitches riding up his arm. "So I tried to kill myself," he said matter-of-factly.

*Eh, I've seen worse. You'll bounce back, buddy.*

I kept moving and looked in on a black man about my age with tattoos covering his entire body, including teardrops on his face. I nodded. He nodded. The last roommate was a six foot four, strong-looking black man eating a candy bar, who seemed to be friendly with all the staff.

*The people here don't seem so bad, just a community of young adults working through some struggles.*

The lunch bell rang, and we were to have our first meal together. Only a few of us showed up, and I found myself sitting next to the gentleman with the teardrops on his face. He explained that each one represented a person he had killed. I had already known that. *Thank you, Lil Wayne.* We hit it off. He actually reminded me of some of my friends from home. Toward the end of the meal, he asked, "Brett, have you ever killed a man?"

"Uhhh, no, but I just got my ass kicked by a bunch of cops."

He laughed. "That's what's up." He slapped my hand, and we formed a bond. "You're going to be hungry later, B. Take this." He slipped a banana under the table, and I hid it in my hoodie.

"Thanks, man."

The six foot four man was in the middle of telling his story to the group. "I've been to prison. And this place is worse, man. They fuck with your mind in here. In jail, you just do your time and it's done. This place is a nightmare with mind tricks. It's hard to survive in here." He sat back in his chair and took a swig of his tiny paper-boxed apple juice for children. I laughed out loud.

*Yeah, it's real tough with you drinking your apple juice.*

He looked over at me with rage on his face. "What the fuck did you just say?"

"I just thought it was funny that you're drinking apple juice, talking about how hard life is."

"Oh, really?"

He stood up and took his shirt off, making a loud noise with the chair legs screeching on the floor, and the security guard became alert. He was huge.

"Do you still think that, little bitch?"

I planted my feet on the ground and had a clear path to the exit. I gave my new friend a look like, "Watch this." "Yes!" and I ran out of the dining room. He barged past the guard and chased me down the hall. I had plenty of room to run and was able to keep him away. If he got near, a quick shift got me passed him. Finally, a few guards pinned him against the wall and forced me to my room. It was exhilarating. I'm not sure what they did to him for the rest of the day, but the next time I saw him, it was like nothing had happened.

## Mind Games

I stubbornly held on to the idea that nothing was wrong with me. For the first two nights, I refused to take my medicine. This set off deeper hallucinations. If I stared at something long enough, it would start to form into whatever I wanted it to. I was breathing heavily in the middle of the night and stood up to look out of the window. I was directly across an office building with perfectly spaced windows, all the same size and design. I focused all my attention on the building, and in a magic-eye type of way, the windows became 3-D. Now I was holding 3-D windows in my mind. *Turn them on their side.* I tilted my head to one side and watched in amazement as the window cubes rotated. *Change the game.* I breathed on the glass, fogging it up and giving the 3-D windows a fuzzy, more circular look. *End the game.* I blinked hard three times, waxed off the fog with my hand, and everything went back to normal. *You may need to use these mind-control skills one day. Continue to practice.* I felt good and was able to sleep comfortably, seeing real evidence of the superpowers I possessed.

I tried everything to escape. I called Russell, telling him to raise an army to get me out of there; he sounded confused on the other end. I memorized the times of the day that the escape door was open for staff moving in and out; it was completely random. I even set up a staff member by lying faceup with my head near the door, so when he opened it, he would injure me. He lightly tapped my head and said, "Brett, please get up from there." I was looking everywhere I could to find holes in the system. A big rule on the floor was no shoelaces or sharp objects, two things that patients could use to harm themselves or others.

I had the bathroom to myself one morning. One towel, one shampoo bottle, and one soap bottle. The water pressure and heat on the shower/bath was surprisingly nice. I'd lean against it and let the water burn my back. I knew I was being watched by the scientists upstairs, so I had to let them know that this place was not helping and forcing me to burn myself. As I looked down to the drain, I noticed a small rip in the metal disc that held the switch to go from shower to bath. I kept the water on to buy some time and bent down. I pulled it with my hand and ripped off a makeshift razor. *Oh, this is good.* I placed it into the shampoo bottle and headed back to my room. I pushed down on the shampoo bottle, releasing the blade. I found an edge of the carpet that was raised and used the blade to cut more, then hid the blade under the carpet and threw my shorts on top.

*Not bad, Brett, not bad.*

I had no idea how or why I would use the razor, but it gave me some sort of power that I didn't have before, especially because no one knew I had it. I also realized that I'd left behind a sharp edge in the bathtub where I ripped the metal off. Anyone interested in killing himself had a way to do it in that bathroom. *Oops.*

In the very same bathroom a few days later, the Middle Eastern man was in the bathroom for much longer than usual. I had to pee really bad, which was the first thing on my mind. *Treat us like animals and we'll start to act like them.* I rolled up a towel in the corner of my room and peed on it, leaving the towel for someone else to clean up. The Middle Eastern man came out a few minutes later. I was relieved that I hadn't set him up for death.

Visiting hours were tough again, although this time I had money and a sense that I was independent and accomplished, so less to be embarrassed about. My dad smuggled candy in for me, and my mom brought new Tommy Hilfiger socks. I was embarrassed, as my roommates saw how spoiled I was. I had created a few games in my room to pass the time. I'd get a stack of paper from the recreation area and bring it back to my room. I had a piece of furniture with three cubbyholes. The top one was the easiest to make a shot, worth one point; then the middle, two points; then the bottom, three points. I'd stand in my room with the stack on my bed, take a piece, crumple, shoot, repeat. When my dad visited, we played, and it wasn't all that bad. I played Memory with my mom, and she told me, "Jessica and Jerry were on their honeymoon, and an Italian-looking man paid for their meal. Sounded like he may have been in the Mafia."

*OMG, they are after my family.*

"Uhh, that's weird. Are they okay?"

"Yeah, they're fine."

I'd created an intricate perspective of the way things were. Each area of society held another area accountable. The hospital represented science. They were allowed to experiment on us to a certain point, but if it got out of hand, then the police would get involved. The scientists would run tests on us. They'd make a wall crack, or plumbing run, or have the TV on a certain channel to test us. I'd be lying in bed. *How much longer do I have to stay in this place?* Then a light would flash out of the window. *Okay, someone knows that I want to get out of here.* Then I'd hear the wall crack. *Uh-oh, someone else wants to keep me in here.* Then an attendant would come in my room. "Are you going to take your meds tonight, Brett?" Then a siren would sound loudly, indicating that the hospital had gone too far, forcing me to take meds. "Sure." This would go on and on. Everything had a meaning. Every dot connected.

## Workout

I played what felt like seventy-two hours of Uno over the next two days. Blue, red, yellow, green, wild. The game was so easy by the end that I tried to trick myself into seeing different colors to make it more interesting. *Okay, for this round, blue is green, green is yellow, yellow is red, and red is blue.* My opponents couldn't tell the difference, and I might have won more this way. Like with poker, I was on autopilot while playing Uno. My mind would wander, wondering about how I had been free, going to basketball camps as a kid, then getting locked up, then free again, attending and graduating from the university, and now being locked up again. *How did this happen? How did this happen again?*

I looked up and saw a familiar face. A light-skinned black man with tattoos was telling other patients about his album. *No waaaay.* I pretended not to know him, and he walked right up to me. "Where do I know you from?"

"Ummm, West Side?"

"Oh, hell yeah. You bought my album." He gave me a hug. "Where do you live, man?"

"Uhhhh in the city somewhere." *Don't tell him where you are from.*

I realized that I had more than most of the people on the floor with me. There was a big Steelers versus Bengals game coming on in a few hours, and I wanted to do something special for the group. I took the package of expensive Tommy Hilfiger socks that my mom had brought and distributed them to the guys around the couch. *You need it more than I do.* The game started, and I took my seat, focused on willing the Steelers to victory. I created a scenario where I was the Steelers and all the players on the Steelers, and the hospital was the Bengals and all the players on the Bengals. "The Steelers really have a good shot of winning tonight, if they can play the full game."

*Good, I'm favored to win but must stay up for the whole game.*

"The Bengals have a few good weapons. Don't count them out."

*Fucking right they have weapons, a whole arsenal.*

The game started, and the announcers were not covering the game that night; they were covering my every move. I'd adjust my position in my chair. "He really needs to stay low there." *Get lower.* I'd get a little lower in my seat. "The Steelers' defense really takes orders well." *Keep doing what you are doing.* I'd stay in that position. One of my roommates would get up to use the bathroom, and I'd look over my shoulder. "Ben Roethlisberger needs to hold the defense off with his eyes if he wants to give his receiver the edge." *Come back and sit down.* I'd switch my seat to where he used to sit. "Ben Roethlisberger with the nice adjustment!" On and on, no matter what was said or who scored, it connected to this delusion.

Med time came right around halftime. I came back with every intention to watch the rest of the game but couldn't keep my eyes open with the heavy sedatives that I just took. I called it a night.

I patiently waited, day after day. Saw one doctor the first week, followed by a different doctor the next week, thinking they were using my body for their own research. Eventually, enough days passed that the discharge conversations began. I again thought I was getting out every night, only to be told that it was not scheduled for that day. I became restless again and started ripping magazines and letting the words fall on top of one another, looking for new words to form. Then I'd pour glue on the magazines, followed by soap and shampoo. I'd stick the entire collage on the wall, then rip it down, then rip the magazines even more, getting glue, shampoo, and soap all over my hands. I'd acknowledge that my hands were soiled and ask for a key to the bathroom to wash them. I'd wash my hands and look for another chain of events to pass the time.

The new adjustment to medicine made me extra hungry, again. I gained about ten pounds in ten days. After showering one day, I noticed my added weight. *You're disgusting, you fat fuck!* I went back to my room and mapped out a workout. Ten push-ups, jog around the floor, ten sit-ups, jog around the floor, repeat. *I wonder if the inventor of push-ups was trapped in a small room for a long period.* I did ten push-ups, jogged around with no problem, did ten sit-ups, jogged around, with a "Hey, Brett, take it easy" from the staff. Ten push-ups, jog around the floor, "Brett, stop running around," ten sit-ups, jog around the floor, "All right, that's enough, Brett, if you don't stop you know what happens." I slammed the door of my room. *Fuck!* As always, a staff member ran up and said, "You need to leave this door open." I said nothing and got in a push-up position. I started pumping out push-ups without counting, unleashing pent-up rage, for what felt like an hour. I felt my muscles ripping and went harder. Finally, I was spent and started crying alone, exhausted on the floor. I felt a bit better and realized I was really sweaty. There was nothing else to do but get the wet towel that I had just showered in and take another shower. Find activity, do activity, repeat. Finally, my discharge was scheduled.

## Locked-Up Funds

I was happy to be released from the hospital but was more confused than anything. *How could this have happened again?* I was aware that

127

a full recovery took about eighteen months last time, and I was in no place to be patient. That seemed like a lifetime away, but I happened to have an activity that had killed time and would kill more: poker. I stayed at my mom's house for about a month and then took on my recovery at my apartment in the West Side.

"Was I acting weird?" I asked my roommates.

"We didn't really notice anything, just that you kinda disappeared for a while."

I had it in my mind that I was running around like a lunatic. *Weird.* I tried to get back in my old routine right away, thinking about how I would play poker all day and regain my happiness that way.

"Good to see you again, Brett," said Dr. C.

"You too, Dr. C. Can you tell me why this happened again?"

He adjusted in his chair, and I had a flashback to my behavior when Ben Roethlisberger adjusted on the field. "Well, Brett, you were using marijuana, correct?"

"Yes."

"I believe that this was another substance-induced psychotic episode. I think that you still have psychotic disorder, NOS, but it was triggered by you smoking marijuana."

*Ugh, I did this to myself.*

"But, Brett, we saw how you came back last time, and we are hopeful that it will happen again. One thing that is supremely important, Brett: do not smoke any more marijuana. Marijuana will certainly put you back in the hospital."

"Okay, understood."

*All right, a little patience and no weed, and I'll be back, again.* The thought defeated me. *How did I let this happen again?* The medication plan was similar to the last time, the depression and anxiety were the same, but the guilt was much worse. *How could I have done this to myself? All I had to do was not smoke weed and this wouldn't have happened. The doctor confirmed that.* This time around, I wasn't worried about missing school or work. Everything was the same. I just didn't feel well. I was shy, vulnerable, scared, and trying to move forward quicker than I needed to. I attempted to play a full poker session, like before, and fell asleep halfway through, losing my entire $2,000 investment. I decided to play less tables on my laptop after that, allowing me to hang out with my roommates after work. I'd lie out on the couch, like I did on the floor last time, complaining that my life was over. Aaron would hit me with a pillow. He coined my sprawled-out position as the load position. One day, I won $30,000 in the load position and was completely indifferent. "You do realize that you made more money today than I did all of last year?" He hit me again with the pillow.

I could barely get out of bed each morning to brush my teeth, let alone work out. My old friend Tony, a personal trainer, called me every morning, forcing me to meet him at the gym so he could train me. I'd blow him off most of the time, but every so often he'd get me out and make me sweat, which was good for me. I was crippled, feeling restless, anxious, and depressed, but still able to do the same activities as before.

*How could I do this to myself? How could I let this happen? I can't believe this happened to me again!*

As I was finishing up a tournament one night, the poker birds were chirping. They were saying that all of online poker would be shut down immediately and to cash your money out as quickly as possible. I spoke to Jerry, my trusted news source for life, and he confirmed it. He also told me it was too late to take it off. I tried to log into my account and found that my money was tied up.

"How much did you have on there, Brett?"

"Ohhhh, eighty grand or so."

"Damn, you were really crushing it, huh?"

I had $80,000 locked up on the site that I had already paid taxes on. I reported $150,000 in income that year, paid $40,000 in taxes, but only received $30,000. My profit was $30,000 after all that, which was plenty, but I couldn't continue to play online poker. That was the hardest thing. I tried to convince myself that it would be a good thing, force me to learn more skills, and find something new. The problem was, I had no idea what that was. I had abandoned all other plans in order to play poker, and now I didn't have that. I started going to the casino every day while I figured it out, naturally.

"You should start learning how to code, Brett," Jerry said. "The people that know how to code in the future will be way ahead of everyone else." He was passionate about helping me get back on my feet. He had continued working on his fitness business while he worked full-time at another job. I went to the bookstore and followed his recommendations, not overly excited but willing to try. I kept the books in my room and did a few sections, but it wasn't clicking.

One day, my roommates approached me together and asked, "Are you up for moving? We want to get out of this shithole and move up in the world."

I was not thrilled about the actual move, but I smiled and replied, "I'm in."

## *Back to the Basics*

Month after month of sadness, anxiety, and vulnerability went by. I'd contemplated ending it all. *I've already experienced everything that's meaningful in life. What's the point of going on?* I had creative thoughts about suicide but never took it past a thought. I had unlimited time to do whatever I wanted but could not think of anything I wanted do. I read a few more books than I had previously, including *Fifty Shades of Grey*.

Jerry called me one day. "Brett, do you want to be an intern at my company? We can't pay you anything."

"What do I have to do?" I asked.

"We have a database of foods as part of our program that isn't accurate all the time. People e-mail us, wanting it to be updated, and I need you to update it."

"Okay."

For the next few weeks, I'd log in for a few hours each weekday and make sure that all e-mails were answered. The work was basic, but fulfilling. Jerry called me after a few weeks. "My partner, Stan, said he could use some help in sales. Want to help him? I still can't pay you anything."

"Okay."

I spoke with Stan a few times, which was a huge step for me, talking to a stranger and working toward a common goal. Stan had an arrogance about him that I'd never seen.

"Brett, go online and find as many gyms as you can. Call them all and try to sell our program to them. I'm much better at this than you, so don't get your hopes up. If you happen to sell something, then you probably got lucky."

*Thanks for the words of encouragement!*

My roommates would go to work in the morning, leaving me alone in the apartment. I wasn't running to the computer for poker; now I was hunched over on the couch, with my phone and laptop on the coffee table. "Hi, is this American Health and Fitness?" Hang up. "Hi, can I speak to the manager of Gladiator Gym?" Hang up. "Hi, may I speak with the owner of Joe's Gym?"

"Yes, this is Joe."

*Holy shit, now what do I do?*

"Uhhh, hi, uhhh, Joe, this is Brett with Systems Fit." Hang up.

I'd call and call. Finally, I got someone to set up a meeting with me, only to not show. *So this is the true nature of people, say one thing and not follow through.* A few weeks later, I was able to close a sale for $200/month. It felt amazing, and earning the $20 commission was more fulfilling that winning thousands playing online poker.

It became clear to me that I wasn't going to make a living working at Jerry's company at this stage. Both Jerry and Stan urged me to find a career in the fitness industry. "Let them pay to train you, then come back to us later," they would say. I still wasn't quite sure what I wanted to do. I looked into becoming a financial adviser but didn't want to take the Series 7. Finally, I decided to search online and find a random job that required no prior experience. The first company on the search was a marketing company. I called and asked how to apply for an interview. They replied, "How's tomorrow morning at 8:00 a.m.?"

"Okay."

I felt terrible when my alarm went off the following morning. I hadn't needed to be up for anything for the last two years! I dusted off an old suit in my closet, and it somehow still fit after the weight gain. Even after tapering off the medicine for this recovery, I'd kept some of the weight on. I drove to the interview, with both hands on the wheel and radio off. When I walked in, I saw about eight other candidates, all in suits, waiting to be interviewed. *No chance in hell I'm getting this job.* They called me in for the interview.

"Hi, Brett! Have a seat," a young woman with short black hair and white teeth said. I sat down. "So, Brett, tell me about yourself."

"Uhhh, well, I'm from the area and I enjoy chess and poker."

"Do you have any previous work experience?"

"Not particularly, although I was a professional poker player and have some sales experience."

"Interesting! I have a cousin that does that! What's the last book that you read?"

"Well, uhhh, *Fifty Shades of Grey.*" *Why in God's name would I say that?*

"I hear that's a good one, Brett." She winked. "Well, I think we are done here. Do you have any questions for me?"

"Yeah, what exactly do we do here?"

"Good question! We bring wholesale office supplies to the field at a cheaper price with more convenience for the customer."

"Okay."

"All right, Brett. Well, as you can see, I have more interviews. If you don't hear from us by tomorrow night, then unfortunately it wasn't a fit. Thanks for coming in today."

"Thank you." I walked out past the other candidates, who all looked more qualified than me. *No chance in hell I'm getting this job.*

## Sales

My phone rang with an unknown number the next day. "Hello?"

"Hey, Brett, this is Sandy with Marketing Solutions. I wanted to let you know that you got the job! Congratulations!"

"Great!"

"We'll see you at 8:00 a.m. tomorrow at the office." She hung up.

I felt a new kind of good, like there were opportunities ahead of me. I was anxious but decided to give it a shot. I let my family know about the good news, and everyone was impressed that I was digging out of this hole again, without leaning on poker.

I felt groggy when my alarm went off at six thirty the next morning. *Let's fucking go.* I was anxious but ready to get out there and see what I was made of. *If I fail, I fail. I've been through a lot.*

I arrived thirty minutes early and sat around awkwardly for twenty-five of them. Then we all stood in a circle on the carpet in a big room. "Good morning, everybody!" my manager yelled with a salesy energy. "Everybody, clap twice." The whole group except me clapped twice on command. I was a bit behind. I thought about basketball camp, clapping on the cement in between stretches. "Clap twice." This time, I joined in with the rest of the group. "Okay, everyone, we have a new rep today. Everybody, say hi to Brett."

"Hi, Brett!" the entire group pronounced all at once, like robots.

"Brett! Why don't you tell us a little bit about yourself?"

I had a flashback to the straitjacket and the padded room, the groups of people that I'd met who wanted to take their own lives, and my friend who had killed many people. *Stay away from those.*

"Hi! Well, my name is Brett, and I like to play chess and poker."

"My brother plays poker!" a fellow employee said.

"All right, guys, let's get into our morning routine."

I followed the guy next to me as the office broke into groups of four. The group of leaders drilled the rest of us on selling techniques, how to close, high-level strategies, and much more. *This is how much goes into selling a ream of paper?* They handed me a script and said, "Memorize that by tomorrow morning." They took me out on the road, the most successful reps driving practical cars. *I guess that's what I'm working to drive.* I thought about purchasing bottle service in Vegas, making $10,000 cash rain on my roommates, and earning $30,000 in one day.

"Every *no* will lead you to a *yes*. We're going to knock on as many doors as possible until someone shows interest. Once they show interest, we'll say the pitch. Once they want to buy, we'll rehash. Any questions?"

"Okay, no questions."

"Okay, then, tell me what *rehash* is?"

"Ummm, I don't know, sorry."

"Pay attention and ask questions. *Rehash* is when we sell them more than they wanted. When they say they want paper, we'll sell them paper and a bunch of other shit." I then followed him from door to door to door until finally a woman at a church opened.

"Hi, ma'am, how are you today?"

"I'm very well. How are you?"

"Great." He went right into pitch mode. "My name is Tom, and I'm with Box Office Products. We've been in business for over fifty years. Pretty long, right?" *A tie-down question; she has to say yes to it!*

"Yes," she said.

"Real quick." *Sense of urgency!* "Box Office Products are wholesale, which means they are much less expensive than the paper you are already using. How much do you pay for a ream of paper?"

"Well, around $50."

"Box is able to sell a ream for $29.99. Pretty significant difference, right?"

*There it is again.* I noticed her face change from skeptical to interested. "It is."

"What I do is take care of your order for the next ream right now to save you some money and make it more convenient. You're going to order more paper soon, anyway, right?" *He's still doing it.* "Okay, let's do it." He pulled out the order form with precision and reached into his backpack, finding a phone book size catalog. "While I fill this out, I want you to take a look through that." *Rehash.* "Toner is a big seller, and most of my clients like to fill up on their smaller items, like pens, pencils, sticky notes, etc."

Twenty minutes after we knocked on a stranger's door, we walked out with a $700 order, and Tom would make about $70 in commission. *That's a lot of work for $70.* Tom was pumped when we got in the car. "Let's fucking go, Brett! You get the next one." He sped to the next door, more fired up than ever.

"Hey, sir." *Greet the customer.*

"What are you trying to sell me?"

*Don't listen to people's bullshit. They don't know what they need.* "Me?" I looked around for effect. "Oh, I'm just here for the free coffee." I looked over his shoulder at the coffee maker behind his desk. He smirked. *Build rapport.* "How long have you been working here? It looks like you have a good handle on what's going on." *Find the decision maker.*

"Well, you are correct, I've been running this shop for over thirty years."

"I was negative seven years old back then."

He stared at me blankly. *Too much, too much.*

"Well, anyway, my name is Brett." I went hard into the pitch and came out with yet another sale.

I was killing it and working my way up as one of the top reps at the office. I didn't even notice my paychecks when depositing them, but it didn't matter. I was working on a tangible skill that had endless potential. It was more addicting than poker.

They sent us on a business trip to expand our territory. Three of us were to share a room, and one rep from Baltimore was going to meet us. Naturally, the other two reps with me shared a bed, and I was left with the other bed, waiting for my sleeping buddy to arrive. He knocked on the door, and I opened it, finding a six foot five eighteen-year-old beast. *Oh, this is my big spoon. This company spares no expense.* I had enough money to take a cab to downtown and stay at a luxury hotel but decided to stick it out. For the next five nights, I lay rigid on the edge of the bed, eyes wide-open, with a fidgety, snoring, huge stranger sleeping next to me. All I could think about was how much I'd rather have this bed than one at the hospital.

## Job Change

"And that's why Michael Jordan's championship runs were similar to us sticking to the pitch and breaking sales records."

The group of twenty reps cheered as I ended my morning speech, ready for another day in the field. The selling part of the job was great. Head out on the road all day, meet a bunch of people, enjoy the entertainment value of people who hate solicitors. The paperwork and long hours were draining. After a ten-hour day, I'd have to come home and handwrite thank-you notes for every sale that I had made. It became too much, and I decided to quit, without a real plan on what my next move would be. While looking for another job, I kept my head above water by playing poker. It was a much more balanced approach than previously, knowing that I was good at both poker and sales. I thought of Jerry during this time and knew that if I could get into the fitness industry, I could provide some real value later for his business. So I looked online at some of the largest gyms in my area. I submitted a résumé to the largest to start. After a week of not hearing back, I tried another gym, who called me within five minutes of applying.

"Can you come over here now?"

"Sure," I said.

I dressed business casual, found parking, and headed to the lobby, which was a new, clean, high-end gym. A middle-aged bald man with a swagger walked over to me. "Are you Brett?"

"Yes, sir."

"Hey, man, take a seat over here." He took me to a private area for the interview. We talked for a while, and then he asked, "So, Brett, any other hobbies outside of your sales job at Marketing Solutions?"

"Yeah, I was actually a professional poker player for a while." *Not sure I needed to say that.*

"Really? Isn't that illegal? Did you make any money? Why did you stop?"

"Well, yeah. I was in the top 1 percent on the biggest online sites. I stopped when it got shut down. Long story."

"So you're telling me that you could be sitting on your ass every day at the casino, making money, drinking beers, and you choose not to?"

"That's correct. I want to work."

"All right, Brett, I think we are done here. I'll call you if we think it's a fit."

He never called.

I went back to playing poker at the casino for another month while I looked for more job opportunities, and eventually, a family friend had a connection with the general manager at a large gym chain on the West Side. I was able to bypass some of the paperwork and go straight in for the interview. I grabbed the same outfit from the previous interview, which was hanging over my computer chair, and walked to the site, which was a few blocks away. I waited for about twenty minutes in the lobby until a short, older, muscular man put his hand out.

"Are you Brett?"

"Yes, sir."

"Follow me, Brett."

We went to his desk, and he asked the standard questions. For some reason, I still brought up the fact that I was a successful online poker player. "I know some people that count cards like that also," he replied, unaware that card-counting happens in blackjack, not poker. "Well, listen, Brett. I'd love to have you on my team, but I just don't have enough spots available. What I will do is call my friend Dave at the Oak Park location and see if he needs anyone." He picked up the phone and dialed. I could only hear one side of the conversation. "Hey, Dave! Yeah, yeah. Ha ha ha. Yeah, uh-huh, yeah. Hey, listen, I have a young man here that's interested in working. I'm full and thought you might want to have a look at him. Uh-huh, yeah, yeah. Ha ha ha ha. I doubt it. Oh, yeah, and he can count cards, so that should be useful. Ha ha ha ha. Okay, Dave. All right. You too. Bye-bye." He turned to me. "Can you head over to Oak Park and meet Dave?"

"Yes, sir, thank you so much."

Oak Park was close to my family home. On my drive over, I passed the high school where I had broken the basketball assist record, the trails that I had run miles on, the street signs that I thought were measuring my speed, and a whole bunch of other memories that reminded me that I was still close to home. It dawned on me that if I worked at this gym, then I'd see pretty much everyone that I had grown up with and their families. The paper job had given me a "fuck it" attitude that I took with me that day. I was still the person I'd always been. No one would understand why I was working an entry-level job at a gym up the street from where I grew up, and it didn't matter. I parked my car, prepared to make the most of whatever was in front of me, not realizing the radio was on a pop station playing "Starships" by Nicki Minaj.

*♪Starships were meant to fly, hands up and touch the sky, Can't stop 'cause we're so high, let's do this one more time.♪*

My mind started to connect some dots that shouldn't have been connected about starships, starting a new job, and me flying. *Starships, start-ships, starting—I was a star at my last job selling paper. Paper airplanes were meant to fly.* The chorus came around again.

*♪Starships were meant to fly...♪*

And then I turned the car off before the lyric could finish, silencing the song and my rapid thinking, fully aware of what was real and what was not. Proud that two episodes were behind me and I had a handle on how my mind operates, I took one deep breath and headed in for the interview. *Fuck it.*

## Stand Out

I walked through the doors of the gym with my head held high. I saw the most beautiful woman I'd ever seen in my life working behind the front desk. She had a hard face, however, and looked unapproachable. *Hi, my name is Brett with Box Office Products. Wrong job.* "Is Dave here?"

"Yep!" She smiled. "Dave is upstairs."

"Thanks." I walked up a staircase in the middle of the action and felt comfortable among the healthy people that surrounded me. I thought about all the burgers and fries that I'd eaten on the road selling paper. *Gross.*

I sat down with Dave and showed confidence that I could do the job. He hired me on the spot. "Your hours will be eight to six, Wednesday through Sunday. Will that be an issue?"

"Nope."

He then trained me on a few basic items, handled the paper-work, and closed with, "I'll be away tomorrow. I'll need you to run the gym."

"Okay," I said.

"Call me if you need anything."

I called Dave about twenty-seven times the next day but sold a few memberships and started to get the hang of things. Every once in a while, the big bad VP would come around and apply pressure on us to improve our sales numbers. I enjoyed it the most when I could get down to business on my own, with no interruptions. I liked that there was a system in place that could be repeated over and over: (1) Go out into the community and get leads. This was no problem. I'd just come out of a job where I had to sell something to strangers on the spot. All I had to do here was get a name, phone number, and e-mail in return for a free guest pass. We'd post signs at the local grocery store, mall, wherever. (2) Call them all and set up as many appointments as possible. I'd learned that people are full of shit. It was clear to me that no matter how many leads told me they were coming in, it was still unlikely to get a show. So I relentlessly called people, wasn't bothered by a no-show, and eventually had people coming to the front desk asking for me. (3) Give a great tour and price presentation. I'd come flying down the stairs with energy and really wanted to get to know the people who were coming in. They'd look at me skeptically, like a salesperson at first, but a few minutes later, I was able to create comfort. We'd make it to my office after the tour, and I'd explain to them the membership options and, most importantly, stay quiet as they made their decision. I'd drilled down a sales audio lesson by Tom Hopkins, who had sold the most houses in real estate history. "The one who speaks first owns the product," he said. Then, one of two things could happen. They'd either buy a membership, in which case I would ask for more referrals to save some of the legwork of getting new leads, or they would have objec-tions that must be overcome, the most common being, "I need to think about it." Ninety percent of objections had to do with price, but I learned a systematic process for overcoming these objections. (4) Overcome objections. "Brett, thanks for your time today. I need to think about it." *Line that gets us to the start.* "Obviously, you have a reason for saying that. Would you mind sharing it with me?" *Listen.* "Umm, yeah, it's too expensive." *Repeat.* "So it's too expensive?" "Yes." *Acknowledge.* "I get that. I have a bunch of bills also." *Isolate.* "Is there anything besides the price that's stopping you from starting today?" "Nope, just the price." *Question.* "What if I told you that $30/month is really only $1/day. Where do you drink your coffee?" "Starbucks." "Can you get your coffee at Dunkin' Donuts instead? It will cover the $1/day." "Maybe." *Answer.* "Well, it turns out the coffee is less expensive at Dunkin' Donuts." *Reclose.* "Let's get you started." "Well, all right."

I ran through these steps over and over and over, after "I don't want to start," "I don't have time," "It's not convenient." All the objections were overcome, and they were buying memberships.

One day, a woman came in and glanced around, walking out without speaking with anyone. I shot out of my office and found her in the parking lot. "Hi, ma'am! My name's Brett. Is there something I can help you with?"

"Don't worry about it. I was just looking at the pool."

We talked for a bit in the parking lot, and it was enough to get her back into the gym and buying a membership for no money down, $30 per month. But I didn't stop there. "Would you agree that once you start working out, you're going to want to keep working out?"

"Yes."

"Okay, the average member is with us for about three years. You seem like you may be a bit above average, but let's take a look at something. Well, $30 per month over a three-year period comes out to $1,080. We have an option to pay in full at $718 for three years instead. Which option makes more sense to you?"

"Uhh, well, I guess the three-year." She got out her credit card and paid $718 that day instead of going home with nothing. *Do you have any referrals?*

I was relentless day after day. It became a game to me, run through the process, repeat. Poker was the last thing on my mind, although my core strategy at selling memberships was just as effective as my poker tactics. After two and a half months, I was pro-moted to weekend general manager. My hours were now five to ten Wednesday, ten to eight Thursday, eight to six Friday, eight to eight Saturday and Sunday, ten to eight Monday, off Tuesday. I didn't care. I had a sense of purpose. After my great success in poker, the money from the gym still wasn't life-changing, but a general manager posi-tion would be, about $80,000 annually. As the weekend manager, I was a general manager in training, responsible for getting new hires up to speed and running the gym on the weekends. I liked training and managing even better than selling. My goal was to sit in my office and fill in the holes, while my sales team ran around, making all the commission. I had to give a speech in front of thirty salespeo-ple to help train.

I drew a water slide with a long straight ending on the white-board. "Selling a membership is like going down this slide." I high-lighted the long climb to get to the top. "The ladder represents all the legwork you do to get leads, and the end of the slide is a sale." I drew an arrow to the top of the slide. "This is your attempt to make the sale. When you skip steps and don't do a tour, give a lackluster price presentation, or don't build rapport, then you don't build the appropriate momentum to get to the end." I drew the arrow going down the slide and coming up short. "But when you follow all the steps, you are pushing yourself all the way to the end, every time. Remember that every person has a phone full of contacts that you want to join our gym." The crowd cheered, and I sat down feeling good. The next presenter pulled out a piece of scratch paper, and with his head down, he mumbled his words. I sat through the rest of the boring presentations and realized that I had something special. I was always afraid of public speaking, but not when I knew what I was talking about. I wanted others to learn what I knew. I was making a name for myself in this company, always on the leaderboard and hav-ing fun while doing it. My boss and others at the gym were hilarious people. I had carved out a place where I fit in and was good at what I did. *This is where I belong.*

## *Job Change*

"Brett, you're kicking ass. I'm making you a GM," said the VP one morning.

"Awesome!"

After nine months at the company, I was promoted to general manager. I'd run a twenty-thousand-square-foot beautiful facility with all the amenities: pool, sauna, hot tub, racquetball, and more. I showed up two hours early on my first day, ready to get leads. I couldn't believe that the company had the confidence in a twenty-six-year-old with nine months' experience to run this palace of a gym. "The last GM never showed up this early," the front desk girl said. I introduced myself to all the front desk staff, as they were the only others at the gym this early. Then I headed out in the community to get new leads. It was the only way I knew how to build business, and it worked.

When I got back to the gym, there were more cars in the parking lot. As I came through the doors, a six foot, mixed-skin muscular man with veins popping out jumped on my desk. "Hey, I'm Troy, and this is my gym."

"Ummm, okay."

He laughed and hopped down. "Nah, I'm just kidding. I'm the PT director. Nice to meet you."

I had a team of three sales associates to work with. The first one didn't speak any English; I found myself nodding to say hello. The second staff member was a woman about one hundred pounds overweight, with three Red Bulls on her desk. *Great way to promote health.* The last team member was a nice guy and was about to quit before they made me the GM. We hit it off. *Now this I can work with.* I was very serious about training and had high expectations for the team. This was my first experience with the company where I had full control.

I wasn't prepared for the issues that occurred at the gym outside sales. One day, a woman who had been coming to the gym for years wanted to bring her sixteen-year-old son and a friend in to work out. It was against company policy to allow a minor in without a membership or their legal guardian present. "Brett, can you come up here for a minute?" the front desk girl asked.

I came up. "Hey, guys, what's going on?"

"Hi, Brett," the mom said. "The last GM used to let us in, no questions. What's going on here? They're good kids."

"I can see that. Unfortunately, he can't come in without a membership or his parents present. If he gets hurt, it's the company's liability. I'm so sorry."

"Can't you just let us in? Do I have to call my husband, who's a lawyer?"

"Ma'am, you're welcome to do whatever you'd like, but he's not allowed into the gym. I'm sorry."

"Well, this is bullshit! You're just a new manager here. You'll be out of here like the rest of them."

I had brief flashback to being chased around at the hospital, the woman freaking out in a straitjacket, and of course, "Shooooooooot!" *Ha ha ha, it's hilarious how mad this soccer mom is getting.* I tried to hide the smirk on my face and replied, "I'm sorry about the rule."

She stormed out and, right as the door closed, yelled, "And the music sucks here, anyway!"

"Everybody good?" I asked the team. The full team replied yes. "Okay, back to work." I called her a few days later to apologize and smoothed things out. We ended on good terms.

Some of the team didn't make it, like the Red Bull queen and the non-English-speaking man, but Devin stuck with me and we brought in a few others. Cindy was a weekend general manager at another club, and they transferred her over to us. She was average at best, and I always knew that Devin would ultimately have the WGM spot.

On an extra busy day, I was up to my ears in work, and Cindy showed up an hour late. She walked in, went to the printer, got the printed document, and slammed it on my desk. "This is all the commission you stole from me!"

"Wait, what?"

"Yeah, look at this list of names. They were my leads, and you stole them from me."

"Cindy, sit down." I could feel the worst of my rage boiling up. "First of all, you are an hour late. Second, you come in here and accuse me of stealing forty dollars from you? Here." I grabbed two twenties from my pocket and threw them on the desk. "We're even. I'm busting my ass here all day by myself, and you show up an hour late with this bullshit? Really? Go home." She started crying. "Don't cry, just go home." She picked up her stuff and left. *Haven't felt that rage in a while.* I took a walk around the area to cool off and then went back to work.

A few months later, a woman walked up to the front desk and asked for Troy. "Is Troy here? He's training me today."

"Oh, no, ma'am," said the front-desk girl. "Troy is the one that sells you the training. Your trainer is someone different."

"Well, why did Troy ask me to send him naked pictures last night?" she said naively. She pulled out her phone and started scrolling through the naked pictures.

I hopped up. "Ma'am, I'm so sorry. There must be some misunderstanding."

Troy joined me and nervously came up with an excuse. We were able to tag-team the issue and resolve it. "Dude, you can't be doing that."

"It won't happen again."

A few weeks later, it happened again, and I had to report it. He flipped on me, but again, no worse than what happened in the hospital. "You're doing this because I'm black. You're racist!" I laughed it off. The VP didn't see any issue with her PT director manipulating women into sending him pictures, so the whole thing blew over. Troy and I didn't talk to each other after that.

I had Sundays off as a GM, and some of the online poker sites where coming back, so I was able to dabble. One Sunday, I won $30,000 online. *Still got it.* I went into work, entering at the same time that Troy did. I held the door for him, feeling a bit indifferent about our beef, especially after the big win last night, and it made it more comfortable.

On a different occasion, a man had a heart attack at the gym. Troy came to the rescue, which was huge, because I had no clue what I was doing.

It was amazing how many sketchy things were going on at the gym that were hidden. The old GM told a woman that he was her trainer and asked for her debit card password. She gave it to him, and every two weeks, he would go to an ATM and withdraw cash, and he'd pretend to be her trainer. He'd also have vodka in his water bottle, drinking all day. These things were as funny as they were terrible.

I had done things the right way and moved up quickly. My older brother's birthday was coming up, and we were going to surprise him. Unfortunately, I had a staff member quit the week that the trip was supposed to happen. My vacation had already been approved, and I had staff to cover. I got a call from my VP. "Brett, I see you have a vacation coming up, but I need you to skip it. We're behind on our numbers, and you are short-staffed."

"Ah, I'm sorry, but I can't."

"Well, I may have to let you go, then."

"What? You're going to fire me for going on a planned vacation?" I remembered a training where they said never to fire anyone, to make them quit on their own.

"No, I'm not firing you. I'm just saying you need to choose if you want to go on this vacation or not."

"Okay. Well, then, I guess you made your choice."

*What the fuck just happened?*

## Transition

I was in a bit of shock after the GM ride ended. Not only had I busted my ass, but I was also a top producer for them. I had poker to fall back on, but I had a taste of what it was like to be successful in the business world, and it was far better than sitting online all day, regardless of the money. *Maybe someday I can make more money in the business world than I ever could with poker.*

I made the trip for Jerry's birthday with my family. After all, I did get fired over it. Jerry and I got to talking, and the conversation led to where we both knew it would, with him offering me a job. "I can pay you $3,000 per month, but you'll cover all your own expenses. I know you have money from poker, so it's not a big deal. I'll be with the engineers here. You report to Stan in Texas."

*Thanks for telling me what is and is not a big deal to me.*

I agreed, with no pushback. Sure, I'd be making less than half of what I did at the gym, spend thousands on travel, apartment, and furniture, and be entering a new city with a friend or two, but it didn't matter. I had my confidence, poker as a backup money machine, and a fuck-it attitude.

I spent the next two months preparing for the trip and playing poker at night. I even found a World Series of Poker circuit event to play in Chicago, close to where my aunt and uncle lived during this period. I went deep in the main event and made it to the money. It was a great experience and showed that I could go deep in live tournaments as well, even as a hobbyist. A month before I left, I asked Stan, my new boss, if there was anything I should be doing to prepare for my new job. He told me to study the website of a competitor of ours. I didn't really see the point, but I did the best I could to get up to speed.

I took a quick trip with Jerry to find an apartment and meet the team, but I stayed quiet, knowing that we'd all be spending a lot of time with one another when I started in a few weeks. I didn't take the time to study the area; I could figure all that out when I got there. I noticed how hot it was.

The time came to make the three-day drive. My mom and I packed up the Civic and got rolling. We stayed overnight twice and had an easy time with the drive. When we were about two hours out of downtown, where my apartment was, we got caught in a snowstorm. We put the radio on, which I was hearing the same as my mom these days. "It hasn't snowed like this in decades." "Great!" we both said at the same time sarcastically. Trucks where flying by us, almost falling off the road. I had a flashback to taking my Civic into the ditch between highways two episodes ago. *Did that really happen? It feels like a dream.* That lead to me thinking about lying on the floor of a dirty bus and punching out side-view mirrors on parked cars. *I can't believe I did all that.* I'd had a few good years and came onto the business scene in a big way, using technique and psychology to excel in sales and management. The last two hours of the trip took seven, but we finally made it.

My mom went into cleaning mode, scrubbing random corners of my apartment, wiping down counters, setting up silverware. She even took me to Best Buy to get a big-screen TV, a housewarming gift. I looked at the operations of Best Buy completely different after working at the gym. *Ohhh, so he's the lead and has the authority to drop price. These people have to ask him for approval.* On and on. The world was making sense to me.

After a day of getting settled, my apartment looked great and it was time to say goodbye. "I'm here if you need me. You'll be great," she said as I dropped her off at the airport. On the fifteen-minute drive back to my new apartment, I had a familiar feeling of independence, like when Carter offered me that first beer at school. Speaking of beer, I'd been a casual drinker after episode number 2 and stayed miles away from marijuana. I had no interest in it anymore and was fully aware of the consequences of smoking. *I'm essentially committing suicide if I do.* I had a few days to relax before the first day of work. My friend Tony, who forced me to work out during my last recovery, had moved to Texas a year before I did. He was still a personal trainer and worked at the Four Seasons as a bartender. I'd hang out with him at the bar initially and used him as a personal trainer. The city was beautiful. My bedroom had doors that opened to the outside, and I'd often leave them open when I'd sleep. Overall, I was rolling. I had money, I could play poker if I needed to, I had a new job, new city, and most of all, my health issues were far behind me, with no signs of relapse.

## First Day of Work

A light gust of wind woke me up at 7:00 a.m. on the first Monday at Systems Fit. I stretched comfortably and found my way into the shower. I did my ritual of letting hot water burn my back and noticed the metal switch holder, with no sharp edges. After a quick flashback of the Middle Eastern man's stitched-up forearm, I turned the water off and got dressed in a T-shirt and casual jeans. I packed the laptop that I had purchased, ate a quick bowl of cereal, and took a coffee to-go. I used Google Maps to find the office, a large building with tinted windows. I found Systems Fit on the directory. I soon realized that we were two small offices in a shared office space in a five-thousand-square-foot space. I heard all types of buzz from the other companies as I walked through about how they were going to be the next Facebook, Twitter, whatever and not buying a single word of any of it. *How much money are you all making right now?*

I found Systems Fit in the back two rooms in the corner. Stan greeted me. "Hi, Jerry's little brother." *I already don't like this guy. Didn't like him before, don't like him now.* "I'll be busy closing sales all day with Ryan so we all have jobs tomorrow. Not that important, right?" He laughed at his own joke.

Ryan was a husky fellow, with a kind smile. When I came in, I noticed that he was shopping for a new truck on Craigslist and quickly went back to the Systems Fit website when he realized he was being watched by the CEO's younger brother.

"You'll be in the other office with the laymen, supporting my deals." He opened the door, and I heard loud typing from a hunched-over bearded man named Dave. He had a permanent look of stress on his face but shifted back to his Southern roots and welcomed me to the team. A red-haired woman, about thirty, was in the seat next to him. "Hi!" she said quickly and then got back to work.

"Okay, Brett," Stan continued, "you've settled in. I only have one rule: don't ask any questions. If you are asking me a question, it means you didn't try hard enough to find the answer yourself. If you've searched vigorously and still can't find the answer, then write it down, and not in a place where notes go to die."

"Got it," I said.

"Good luck, Sparky," Ryan chimed in, and they closed their door.

There was an unused desk and chair that was my new office. I looked around at Dave typing and Becky staring at her screen and realized that this was my new place of work. I thought about the energetic, beautiful, healthy people that I saw every day working at the gym. *What the hell did I get myself into?* I got set up and continued to read about our competitors; there was clearly no plan on what my job was or how I'd learn how to do it. We used G-chat, which opened the lines of communication. I had an incoming message from Jerry.

"How's it going down there, dude?"

"Not bad. Just getting started. Any suggestions on what I should do first?" I asked.

"Become a master at every aspect of the system."

"Roger that." I called over my shoulder to Becky. "Hey, Becky, would you mind helping me get into the system?"

"I'm not interested in helping you with anything at all," she replied.

Dave sighed and took a break from hacking away at his computer to help me out. "Whatchu need, mang?" He had a strong Southern accent.

"Just a little help getting set up."

"I gotchu."

When I finally got into the system, I realized we were sitting on a gold mine. I'm not sure Jerry had any clue how great his system really was. My previous company was the top gym in the country at that time, and their technology was light-years behind what Jerry and his team had created. Things that took six steps there took one step with Systems Fit. The speed at which features were released was mind-blowing. I observed Dave write a ticket for the engineering team about an issue, and five minutes later, it was resolved. *Holy shit! Jerry, you really got something here.* I was excited that I owned a little piece of this. I was clicking around with no supervision for the rest of the day, trying to teach myself as much as possible until five o'clock rolled around.

"All right, guys, thanks for all your help, I'll see you tomorrow," I said.

Stan stood up in the middle area between both offices. "Whoa, whoa, whoa, Brett, who said you could leave?"

"Uhhh, I just figured because it's five—"

He interrupted. "You leave when I say you can leave. And you check in with me before you leave, always."

"Uhh, okay. Am I good to go?" I asked.

He replied, "Brett. Do you have any allergies?

"Yeah, I'm allergic to cats. Why?"

"Ha, I figured. Studies show that people with allergies won't survive in the long run and can only handle a nine-to-five job. You can leave now."

I said goodbye, wondering what in God's name was wrong with this person. I walked outside and enjoyed the fifty-degree December weather and was onto the next thing. I drove back to my apartment and went for a peaceful jog by the lake. *I'll try again tomorrow.*

## No Training

A few days passed of me coming in early, reading about the system all day with no guidance, then doing the "leave at five dance" with Stan. One morning, I came in to the sight of an inspirational quote on the whiteboard that read, "We are here to serve the customers; they will tell us how well we are doing" (Chester Freehold, president of Boost Financial Services). *Hmm, isn't that obvious?* Stan barged into the room. "Boost Financial is a nine-hundred-plus-employee operation. They are our partner, and we are integrated with them through an API. Brett, do you know what an API is?"

"No."

"Amazing that you've been here this long and still don't know. An API stands for application program interface. It allows us to push and pull data from their system."

*He taught me something!* A few dots were connected.

"I've met Chester Freehold, and he bleeds customer service. Our process is similar to theirs. A customer signs up, we set them up, then we do an on-site visit. Then we work with them for ninety days until they are all stars with the system. Then we start billing and our customer support team takes over."

*That's a good idea, actually, minus the delayed billing.*

"Okay, Brett. Dave, come shadow this call that I have with a large group of trainers and the director at a fifty-location opportunity that we are currently piloting. We are currently piloting." *This is pretty cool, actually.* Dave and I took our laptops and set up behind Stan, who set up the video conference.

A shorter man, wearing a Z-sport-branded collared shirt, came onto the video conference call with a room full of trainers. "Guys, listen up. This is Stan with Systems Fit. He's going to teach us how to use the system today. Please give him your full attention."

"Thanks, Ron. Let me just start by saying that you are a lot shorter in real life than I pictured you on the phone." *OMG.* Dave and I made eye contact and couldn't help but laugh. "Anyways, when I created this entire system in my mind…" And then Stan went on with his sales routine that had been pretty effective after his opening insult.

Over the next few weeks, I stopped worrying about protocol and asked as many questions as I could. "Stan, I've looked for about thirty minutes and can't figure out how to put club-level scripts in for trainers using a system admin account. All I need to know is if this is possible, yes or no. I'll figure the rest out."

I knew he had the answer, but he said, "Go look it up again."
*Fucking damnit.*

One morning, after about six weeks on the job for me, he announced to the whole team that I wouldn't be useful to him for ninety full days, regardless of how hard I worked. By the two-month mark, it felt like he was intentionally trying to stunt my progress. Dave would console me, "Don't worry, B. He did the exact same thing to me a year ago."

One day, I received a random e-mail from the online poker site that had locked up $80,000 that I had already paid taxes on. "Your funds will be repaid soon. Please fill out this form." *Holy shit, yes!* I did the appropriate paperwork, and a few days later, I received, "Sorry for the delay, Bsteven$087, we've deposited $80,000 into your bank account. Congratulations!" I thought about Stan and the few poker sites that were back up and running and gave Jerry a call. "Jerry, I think I need to quit. It's brutal."

"Fuck," he said. "You're really screwing me here. I've wasted $9,000 on you. What are you going to do instead?"

"Well, uhh, I don't know. Maybe we could work on something together in the future."

"That's not how it works, Brett. I'm not sure I'd want to work with you again. I'll talk to Stan. Can you just stick it out for a few more months? Things change quickly around here."

"Can you tell me why you want me to stay so badly?"

He paused. "Because I can pay you less than other people that have the same skill set as you."

*Wow, worst possible answer.* I took a deep breath, not liking the idea that I was hurting my brother and putting him in a tough situation. "All right, I have three more months on my lease. I'll give it until then."

"Okay," he said.

I got used to working around Stan's bullshit and made some progress. Implementation was very interesting to me. How do we automate this process and still give a good experience? Why does it have to be ninety days? We want to be Boost Financial, but we aren't. Does spending the money to do an on-site every time even help? Do we have data to prove it? How do we measure progress? I'm able to run through this process with X number of customers; if we had more customers and more people, how many gyms can we do at once? How can we work better with sales upfront and customer service behind to smooth the process out?

I was proactive and created a step-by-step rollout process that could be fully executed from our home office over screen sharing instead of face-to-face. We had sold a single-location gym in California called Cowboy Gym. *This is the perfect opportunity to try my system.* Setup went perfectly, and I was going to have an initial call with the executive team. I decided to take the call from my apartment, in my pajamas. When the call started, I didn't realize I was on video, hair in a mess, apartment a mess behind me.

"Sorry, guys!" and I turned off video.

We had a laugh, and I pushed them through the once ninety-day process in seven days, gaining the revenue from the club upfront and securing their monthly billing. "This is big, Brett. Do you think they'll still use the system?" said Jerry.

"Yes," I said.

"Then sell as many gyms as possible!"

"I can handle it," I replied.

## *New Hires*

We started selling more, a lot more. A few months ago, a new deal would come in every few weeks and take ninety days minimum for billing. Now every other day we were bringing on a new club and billing immediately, turning them around in seven days. I had a step-by-step system from beginning to end that was working. Stan didn't like how fast we were moving. He thought we needed to slow down and be more like Boost Financial with support, but Jerry was all about the revenue. They had it out, and it led to Stan leaving the company. There were a few days of explaining to customers what had happened, but overall, not a huge deal. I was able to invest more and now owned more of the company. I saw the COO title and place in the company wide-open, and I wanted it. I told Jerry that if we hired one to two people, we'd make X amount more, assuming sales continued to roll in. "Start with 1," he said. Up to this point, I had needed to tap into a new skill set to become technologically savvy and provide overwhelmingly good support, but when I got the okay to hire, I felt extra comfortable. I interviewed a few people and hired a half-Filipino woman named Naomi. She was a bit shy, but very intelligent and good with computers. We got to work. I ran a morning meeting, showed her how everything was documented, and made myself available to her at all times. I worked alongside of her, and we were dangerously productive. She picked up my rollout system fast and even added to it to increase efficiency. Notes never went to die with her as Stan would have liked.

As growth continued, I was able to hire another person. Jerry visited for a weekend to check in and have bro time. We met up with my old friend Tony, who helped me in my recovery and hung out with me in Texas. I had spent a lot of time with Tony, and I'd often vent to him about Stan as we'd work out after work each day. I didn't see this job as a great fit for Tony. He had a big personality and great work ethic, but his strengths didn't lie in technology. Without my knowledge, he asked Jerry if he could work for Systems Fit. "Sure," Jerry said. "You can report to Brett." And that was that. I was very optimistic, as usual, and had it laid out for him, just like Naomi. I learned at my last job that everyone learns in their own way. Many of the things that came easy to Naomi were more of a struggle for Tony. After two short weeks, Jerry wanted to fire him. I thought about my close friendship with Tony and fought to keep him around. "No, Jerry. Let me work with him. He'll be fine." Tony got to a place where he was able to perform and be productive. *All I have to do is get him comfortable with a few things, and he'll crush it.*

More people were hired over the next few months. We experimented with different ways of achieving maximum efficiency. For a short time, we even trained all implementation staff on support, and all support staff on implementation. This showed huge savings on the budget sheet but lowered the quality of our service. We had to move back to the old way. Naomi was very good about implementing the newest technology on the market, which was a weakness of mine. When Naomi and Tony came on, I had the title of implementation manager, making $48,000 per year. But once Naomi got up and running, she became the implementation manager and I was promoted to manager of client services, now making $65,000. Still not close to what I made in poker, approaching a salary of GM. I had only been in Texas for one year.

Then we got some huge news that Fitness First, a three-thousand-location club, was interested using Systems Fit. "Brett, I need a rollout plan," Jerry would say. Strength 101, another beast in the industry, showed interest next. "Brett, I need a rollout plan." I created this and organized documents that made it look simple to roll out thousands of locations. We had done a twenty-location club, but not three thousand. Maybe I added a few extra time slots to make us look bigger than we were. Jerry presented the technology, which dazzled the CEOs of these monster companies, and then answered the question, "How the hell are you gonna roll all this out?" By presenting my rollout plan. "Looks good enough to me," the multimillionaire executives would say.

Jerry and I were on a business trip visiting a longtime customer, and he got an e-mail from the president of Fitness First. "We just got the deal," he said.

## Boost Financial Services

The stage was set. We had a deal with the largest gym in the world and were ready to take on the challenges that came with it. The deal was structured in such a way that we would only get paid after a location was activated. So although we had this big opportunity, we would not see the financial rewards until we started setting up and training locations. Part of our setup process required Boost Financial to be involved. Naturally, they would get a piece of every location that was rolled out as well. It was more crucial than ever that Systems Fit and Boost Financial were on the same page before looping in the Fitness First team.

Before plans were to move forward, Chester Freehold, Boost's president, invited me and a team member to see their office and learn about large-scale support. He and Jerry spoke regularly, but he wanted to see what Jerry's younger brother and manager of client services was all about. Did Jerry give him the job? Did he have any clue what he was doing? Was he a hard worker? Had he had to overcome any challenges in his life? Ciaran, a staff member who was rising fast in our implementation department, came with me to meet Chester Freehold and see the corporate operation.

When not helping customers day and night for Systems Fit, Ciaran was the lead singer in a heavy metal rock group. He was thirty-five, with long red hair, and a sword tattoo on his forearm, sometimes reminding me of the hospital. Not the most clean-cut person in the world, but great for Systems Fit at the time. Ciaran and I strolled through the airport with slacks and Systems Fit polos. "I'm not too sure who's picking us up, but I know the location," I said to Ciaran. He nodded. We found the meeting place, and an SUV pulled up.

"Brett, Ciaran, hop in. I'm Chester." *Holy shit, this is Chester Freehold.* He was a big guy with a jolly aura about him, very comforting. "You guys hungry?"

"Sure."

"All right, I'll take you to this great barbecue place."

His phone rang every other five minutes for the drive to the BBQ spot. During downtime, he spouted out helpful information. "Guys, the biggest mistake I see companies like yours make is that they don't know when to say no. You'll bring on a club because you get money, not realizing that you lose all that money if they are a pain in the ass! You guys at Systems Fit are smart, no doubt about that, but are you ready to roll out the eight-hundred-pound gorilla in the industry? How you gonna do that, Brett? Can the best high school player in the country play in the NFL? I'm not so sure, guys." He had a genuine, friendly tone in his voice and was being real with us.

*Chester, you've never seen a company like ours that works as hard as we do. We're going to blow your mind!*

We had a nice lunch, and Ciaran sat quietly while I asked Chester many questions about how his company ran. We talked about family and some rumors going around the industry before we headed to the corporate office. *I can't believe he's spending this much time with us.* He walked us around campus and shook hands with everyone, calling them by their first name. We passed a few employees taking a smoke break.

"That stuff will kill ya," he'd say with a smile.

Eventually, we made it back to his office. "The Systems Fit boys are in town!" he said with a jolly look on his face. He clapped and rubbed his hands together and took a seat. His desk was vast, and papers were everywhere. There were a few chairs along the wall and a massive whiteboard front and center across from Chester's desk. In the corner of the office was a circular table with a wooden chess set. *There it is.* He quieted the room. "Ciaran, you have a seat. Brett, take a marker to the whiteboard." I was so ready to have this conversation; I just couldn't believe it was with Chester Freehold, in a private meeting. "Now, Brett, I read over your rollout proposal. Very nice work, I must say. But can you actually do it? I've seen many Bretts, good-looking, smart, hardworking young men that say they can do a lot of things. So tell me, what's the org chart look like? Draw it up on the whiteboard."

*Good thing Jerry had made me write an org chart the day we hired Naomi.*

I drew squares and lines, speaking confidently about who did what and where we were going. I showed him how many hours it would take to roll out one location, how many employee hours were available, and how many locations we could do. On and on. What felt the best was that I had never done this before. The truth was that the second I started this job, every day required figuring out something new. By the end of our discussion, he had his concerns with our experience level but gave us his approval. I glanced over at the chess set. *I have to ask.* When the important stuff was over, I asked if he played chess. His eyes lit up.

"You play? No one in the entire company has beaten me. I don't think they're letting me win, if you know what I mean." Another big smile.

"Yeah, I play."

"Well, let's play!"

Ciaran gave me a look like, "What in the hell are you doing challenging this guy?" *I'm gaining respect.* Similar to poker, after the first few moves in chess, it was clear to me that I was a better player. When I checkmated him, he was a bit stunned.

"Well done, Brett. Let's play again." He started setting up the pieces, and I helped. Halfway through the second game, his secretary came in. "What? Can't you see we're busy?" He smiled.

"You have an appointment now."

"Make him wait."

She closed the door, and we played for another thirty minutes before I beat him again.

"Wow, I have a meeting. We'll play again later."

We spent the next few hours shadowing other departments, and then we were brought back to Chester's office. "Let's play again! I need to beat you." I made a mistake in this game, and we tied. He asked for one more game, and I beat him. A few other Boost staff were looking on, realizing their fearless leader was losing to me, in a David-versus-Goliath way. *Maybe I'm Goliath when it comes to chess.* We closed the day with a full team meeting that Chester led. He looked a bit disoriented as he started the meeting.

"Team, Systems Fit is here. This is Ciaran, and Brett. Brett just whooped me in chess all afternoon, and I'm in a bit of shock, but the world must continue turning." He gave me a wink and got into the meeting.

We gained respect that trip, proving that we belonged in this arena. When we made it back to home base, Ciaran told the story and my team looked at me in awe. Over the next few weeks, I worked with a lot of Boost staff to prepare for the Fitness First rollout. Most conversations started with, "I heard you beat Mr. Freehold in chess. Is that true?"

## *Best Man Again*

Using the balance of my systems background from poker, my fuck-it attitude from Marketing Solutions, and my sales persistence and management experience from the gym, things were going great at Systems Fit. I spent all my time thinking about work. I made myself available for work at any day or time of the week. I talked about work when I would go on dates. Jerry and I would talk for hours after work about work. Work was my entire world, and I was unaware of it. On Monday mornings, I'd pop out of bed and be ready to roll. I'd be antsy driving home on a Friday, knowing that the action would slow down all weekend. The weekends were hard for me. I wasn't feeling depressed, but I couldn't find anything that I wanted to do. I'd go to the gym and swim laps, read by the lake, or get a fancy lunch, but I spent most of my time alone. I decided to reach out to a therapist to help keep an eye on myself. We spoke once per week.

"Brett, I'm getting married, and you and Jerry are my best men!" Russell said, very excited. "Let's go!" I had finally found something to put my energy into that wasn't work, Russell's bachelor party. Jerry thought about work exponentially more than I did, so I took responsibility for planning. *Is there a number higher than infinity for hours thinking about work?*

"All right, Russ, send me a list of all your friends that you want to invite to this thing. Oh, and where do you want to have—"

"Vegas," he answered before I could finish asking.

He sent me a list of twenty-five names, and I got to work. I planned a pool party that would be epic and broke out the cost for the twenty-one guests that RSVP'd yes. The next few months consisted of work (*Yay!*), lonely weekends, and smart-ass e-mails circulating to the group about Russell's big party.

I showed up to the hotel and was almost tackled in the lobby by Russell's old high school friend who had been partying all day. "Brett! Vegas! Russell! Wedding!" His eyes were crossed.

I patted him on the back and said, "Remember the three goals of this trip: (1) Make it here, good job on that; (2) show up to the pool party tomorrow; (3) leave."

He lost focus after number one, and I made my way up to the room.

That night, we got a little rowdy and headed out to a club. *Isn't it amazing that I was at this very same club a few years ago?* I had three quick flashbacks, playing at the featured table, playing in the underground game at home, and playing Uno in the hospital. I took a small sip of my drink and was able to enjoy the loud music and bright lights. The next morning, I led a pack of twenty-one wolves to the pool, where the partying continued. One of the guys in our group shut down the place by rocking a speedo with a bow tie and buttons down the front of it. On and on, drink after drink. It was a day to remember. All of us made it home on Sunday, I think.

I felt great after getting away for a weekend, but continued to feel lonely at home outside work. I signed up for an online dating site and went on a few interesting dates, mostly women who didn't represent themselves very accurately online. But I did find someone who looked the same in real life as she did in her profile. We had a good first date and met a few times after. Eventually, we both decided not to date other people, and we became very close. After three months of us dating, her lease was up where she was staying, and I asked her to move in. *This will solve all my loneliness issues.* Having her around filled the void, but new challenges arose. After a long week of work, I'd be so excited that she'd be around when I got home. When I'd get home and get a work call, I'd struggle balancing my attention and often missed an important call or took a call and upset her. We moved really fast and took it one step further by getting a puppy.

I wasn't sleeping well. At night, I'd hear a dog pattering around in his crate, and in the morning, I'd hear the dog whimpering. I'd start my day at 5:00 a.m. to walk him. I'd have two cups of coffee instead of one. In my mind, I was perfectly balanced, great job, great girlfriend, a dog, but in reality, I was managing large amounts of stress on very little sleep. Our office continued to expand—more space, more people. The managers that I had trained were now training other managers who had lower-level staff to train. Staff would straighten up as I walked past them. I had a young confidence with a wise attitude about how far we'd come. Most problems had been solved with some brainstorming and effort, until the Fitness First tsunami hit us.

## *Rollout Disaster*

With the recent raise in pay and poker money coming in, I felt it necessary to upgrade my car. I traded in the Civic, which helped me through ups and downs from college, to the West Side, and to Texas, for a brand-new Audi A4, black on black. I'm not really a car guy, but this thing was a beast. The speaker system was thunderous, and accelerating felt like being shot out of a cannon. I'd ride up the most popular street in the city with my music bumpin' and eat at the finest restaurants in town—East Grand Café for gourmet, the Scorching Taco for Mexican, and Slice Pizza for pizza. I'd ride up the highway to work and zip through traffic on the way home. I was really falling into this role as an executive at a fast-growing company.

We attended a Fitness First conference that gave us a platform to sign up as many locations as we could to get on Systems Fit. The line was out of the door, and we realized how big things were about to get. We had about fifteen support staff in Texas at this time, which by my calculations meant we could roll out about seventy-five locations per month. We had one hundred sign-ups at the conference, so it seemed manageable. It wasn't until after the conference that we were informed on how the customized Fitness First software was going to work. So we had a room full of staff with no clue how to implement the thing. We held on to the agreements for a few days before doing anything, and then our phones started ringing off the hook. "When is the rollout? Why did you bill me? Is the software even ready? I thought it would work a different way." On and on. Not to mention that another beast of a gym was coming on board at the same time.

The Fitness First corporate team was disappointed in how we, or in their minds, how I, handled the rollout and the quality of our customer support in general. The president of Fitness First asked that I be removed from my seat, due to lack of experience and poor leadership ability. Jerry defended me. "With all due respect, I fully disagree," he said. "Brett has figured everything out up to this point and will figure this out too." This bought me some time, but the Fitness First corporate troops were already on their way to snoop in on my operation.

We had six small offices at this point, which we were proud of. We'd figured out how to implement software cheaply, efficiently, and remotely. We had a growing team; I had trained a few managers in different departments, and they had trained experts on their respective teams. *Not bad for a guy wearing a straitjacket five years ago, with zero executive experience.* A few Fitness First staff showed up, and one Boost Financial team member was there to soften the blow and ensure everyone kept their cool. "Welcome to Texas, everyone!" The Fitness First team looked at me like I was less than garbage.

"I'm surprised you guys are working. It's, like, 4:00 p.m. on a Friday," they said.

I had a flashback to the endless hours, 24-7 commitment, and dedicating my entire life to this place for the last two years. "Yeah, we have a lot of fun," I replied. I showed them around, and they pointed out the half-broken desk chairs we used and the dirty sink, things that they didn't have to deal with at the corporate office. Then they got their hands on our entire operation, asking questions like "Why don't you guys just hire, like, ten more people?" and statements like, "If I was running this office, I would do it this way, then there would be no problems at all." They worked with us for a few days, and we progressed slightly on getting organized, with plenty of work still to do. "Brett, Charles has asked you to come to a meeting in Minnesota and present your plan to clean up this mess. Justin and I will meet you in Dallas beforehand to look it over." Charles was the president of Fitness First. I was a bit overwhelmed and spent that entire weekend developing a custom rollout for this customer. My girlfriend was not pleased.

I had a draft, went to Dallas, and finalized it. Took a 5:00 a.m. flight to Minnesota and met Jerry for the big meeting. We pulled up to an isolated mansion of an office, made it past security, and sat around a twenty-foot oval wooden conference table. Chester Freehold was there with his Boost Financial crew and a big smile on his face, easing the tension, as always. "Hey, Brett! Charles, let me tell you, this kid is an excellent chess player."

Charles gave me a half-smile, fully aware that I was the source of his recent headaches. The meeting began with a few opening remarks, and then he got into it. "Guys, we need to move as fast as possible and get Systems Fit into all the clubs. What is the big hold up?"

I answered confidently, "Charles, we apologize for the stress of this rollout. We're happy to go at whatever pace you'd like to go, within reason. The issue is that when we teach software to leaders in this industry, there is a steep learning curve. It's not something that you look at once and then master. The more locations we roll out, the lower the quality of the learning, and vice versa. Does that make sense?"

"Yes, Brett." His glare eased a bit after realizing I wasn't afraid of him. "So what's the maximum number of locations you can do?" he asked.

I flashed back to my last job training at the gym, where they taught "porcupines," answering a question with a question. What do you do when someone throws a porcupine at you? You throw it back. "Are you interested in the highest-quality rollouts?" I asked. *This will get a yes.*

"Yes," he said.

"Knowing that rollouts will be high quality, is thirty per month reasonable?" I continued.

"Yes. All right, so we'll go for thirty, and if you need additional resources, we're happy to provide them to you."

I sat back, and we moved to the next topic. *Thank you, Marketing Solutions, old gym job, and Tom Hopkins!*

## Blowup

"Brett, you're kicking ass. I can't give you a raise, but I want to make you the director of operations."

"Sounds good to me, Jerry. Don't worry about the raise."

And just like that, I had an executive title. With my amount of ownership, I realized that arguing about a raise now and creating tension with Jerry would not help the company. Everything was about helping the company.

After the initial hiccup, we found a groove on the Fitness First rollout. I asked for as many employees as possible, showing the long-term value after each was trained and ready to roll. We upgraded our office in a big way. The five-thousand-square-foot shared office space that I had walked through two and a half years earlier was now all ours. We had ten offices, a conference room, break area, and a massive call center. The Systems Fit logo was professionally painted on the wall. We looked like a real company. At Jerry's office, they were making the same growth progress with about fifteen staff. We had thirty-five. It was fulfilling to see the initial group of staff that had worked in tiny closets now working out of big offices and leading large teams. I'd created four layers of management and had the final say on any big issues. Jerry asked me to be on the board of directors. Our staff consisted of Muslims, Sikhs, blacks, whites, gays, Hispanics, and more. If you were willing to work hard, then you were allowed on the team.

At home, I was getting less and less sleep with the puppy. I'd vent to my therapist that I was having issues and would open up about past hospital experiences. I was in a place where work was more important than my relationship, so I ended it. I didn't feel the effects of the breakup until about three months later, when I felt very lonely and bored at home. Russell's wedding was coming up, where I had to give a speech in front of about three hundred people. Again, I performed well, this time with no health issues. I felt okay. My loneliness in Texas was balanced by overwhelming excitement at work. I joined a chess club on Sundays to kill some time and would search for activities to do. Unfortunately, I had to fire Tony after months of trying to keep him on board. This put a dent in our friendship, and I could no longer reach out to him. I was left with a few new friends that I barely knew and a group of work people that I liked, but also I was their boss. I planned a trip for Thanksgiving and was looking forward to some family time with my mom, Russell, and his wife's family.

"Brett, I have a girl that you might want to meet when you get here," Russell's wife said.

"Cool." I friended her on Facebook, and we chatted back and forth for a while before the trip.

When I arrived, she said, "Brett, you should text her!"

"Nah, I wasn't that close with her. I may just pass, but thanks."

"No, Brett, we have plans to go bowling with her later tonight. You should text her."

"Oh, thanks for setting that up. I don't really think I want to text her."

"Brett, you're always saying how lonely you are. We're trying to help you out here."

"I'm not interested! If she wants to come, then she can come. I'm not texting her," I reacted strongly.

A few hours later, her friend texted her that she was sick and wasn't going to meet us. We had an awkward afternoon and evening but still bowled and had a good time.

After the long weekend, Russell drove my mom and me back to the airport, going in different directions but close to the same departure time. I sat shotgun, with my mom in the back seat. "So, Russell, why was your wife asking me to text that girl so many times? I felt uncomfortable."

"She loves you! She wasn't trying to make you feel uncomfortable. We just know that you're always complaining about being alone, so we tried to set you up."

"And how is setting me up with someone here going to help with that?"

"We did it for you, Brett."

"Well, I didn't ask you to do anything! Just let me figure this out on my own from now on."

"Fine! We won't ever set you up with anyone again."

I could feel my blood boil. "I just think it's a little fake, that's all."

"Fake?"

"Yeah, you guys just assume that I'm going to like someone that you choose for me. I don't even live here."

"Wow, you think I'm fake."

I flipped a switch. "Yeah, I do, so leave me the fuck alone and stop telling me who to text and when."

My mom straightened up in the back seat. "Brett, he was just trying to help. I can see both sides here."

"I don't need either of you. I live all alone in a city and go about my days without you. No one is ever there, and I'm fine on my own. I don't need any fake help."

Russell got riled up. "Fake? Dude, shut up! We're just trying to help you. You always call me whining about being alone."

"Dude, you aren't helping. Everything you do is fake."

He was ready to pull the car over and fight me. We yelled back and forth all the way to the airport, me breathing hard and getting angrier, him tearing up, realizing something was wrong with me.

"Well, I guess I have to drop you off like this."

I grabbed my bag and walked out, not saying a word. Mom jumped out of the car and asked me to say goodbye to him. "I'm not going to console him while he cries like you do." I walked alone into the terminal.

## *Big Goals*

"Russell! I'm really sorry for everything that happened last week," I said with full energy at 6:00 a.m. the following Tuesday.

"It's fine."

"So what are you up to?"

"I'm just getting ready for work. Let's talk later."

"All right, love you."

For most of my time in Texas, I'd sleep until about seven thirty and run through my morning routine of hard-boiled eggs and coffee. These days, I was getting up closer to five thirty; there was just so much to do and not enough hours in the day. Of all thirty-five staff members, I was typically the first one in the office. I had a core group of three senior managers that represented different departments of the support team. They all had managers and lower-level staff under them. This was the team that I'd give direct orders to and use reporting to hold them accountable. I'd taught them every possible thing that I read about and learned in sales and management, and I had their respect. Two of them had tripled their salary after being with the company for about two years. The walls between offices were thin, and oftentimes I could hear a call or a training happening in a room next door. I paid no attention usually. As the tasks became bigger and my word would be passed down the chain, I began to double-check what I had said against what I could hear through the walls.

"John, I need you to create a report that uses variables of your choosing to give a customer health score. We'll use this to understand which customers need more proactive support versus ones that are doing just fine."

"Yes, sir."

He'd call two of his staff members into his office, and I'd go into mine. "Guys, Brett needs a report that uses variables of our choosing to give a customer health score. We'll use this to understand which customers need more proactive support versus ones that are doing just fine."

*Attaboy, John.*

I'd walk out into the main area and observe John's managers tell their teams about the variables that needed to be figured out. "Brett and John need us to find variables that will help us give a customer health score. I'm not sure how they will use them, but we have to find them." Then the staff went to work on the assignment. Hour after hour, day after day. "Brett told us to do this, Brett told us to do that." *I'm really making an impact here.*

We had an amazing year. I was to be promoted to VP of client services, with a six-figure salary, effective January 1. Jerry found room in the budget for an all-team visit to Texas. His fifteen engineers and a few other staff would join our team of thirty-five for food, Topgolf, zip-lining, and a few drinks. I was to give opening remarks to the full company upon arrival. As the team poured in and staff greeted one another, I felt pure joy. I thought about the two offices where this all started for me. I thought about the endless time and energy that I had committed to the projects. I remembered my experiences with big-time executives in the industry. I had a quick flashback to where I was five years ago at this time, the speeches I'd give at my brother's weddings and as GM, preparing me for this moment. I quieted the crowd and got up to the podium with only a few notes. Looking out at a sea of men and women of all shapes, sizes, backgrounds, and ages.

"Welcome to Texas. This company is like no other company." I had the full attention of the room. "We've built software and service from the ground up. We've had opportunities to slow down but said, 'Bring them on.' We've learned and evolved at a rapid rate and understood more than anyone that change is constant. I've personally seen staff come in with no background and grow into company leaders, passing on our values to all that came after them. All that aside, I've learned that communication is key. I've followed messages like a game of phone tag and have seen how, if slightly off, that can shift our entire organization. So I ask you to have an amazing time this weekend. Get to know team members outside of your cities and departments, and most of all, never forget that you are an integral part of Systems Fit. You are what makes this company special."

I got a loud round of applause. It was exhilarating. I had an image of doing this next year with twice the staff. *If we double in staff every year for the next ten years, we'll have 25,600 staff. I have a new goal.*

## *Ramp Up*

"Honestly, Brett, I wouldn't want to work with anyone else. You and your team rock."

I smiled and hung up the phone. *Third call of the day like that.* I was juggling so many things at once, but it felt easy. I'd even be bored at work sometimes, reading management books in my office. We had enough staff to do almost all the work. I was truly an overseer. I saw my therapist and was particularly excited. We had our usual meeting. *His job is to know what I know and then use that to help him know what I should know.* "So when I give an order, I can kind of hear people talking about me through the wall. Is it real or fake? Sometimes I don't know," I asked.

"It's irrelevant," he replied. "Err on the side of realizing that it doesn't matter."

"Fair enough."

I drove home and got to bed early that evening.

My eyes shot open the next morning. I rolled over and saw 5:00 a.m. on my phone. The alarm was set for seven, but what the heck? I got up. Took a hot shower, made eggs and coffee, and headed into the office two hours early. I had my usual rap music bumpin' in the Audi as I drove through the quiet city and off to work. Machine Gun Kelly's "Hold On" played.

> ♪*Now hold on, shut up, who remembers my come up?*
> *Who remembers my broke ass when I had no food for my stomach?*
> *Who remembers my haters when I was keepin' it G?*
> *'Cause I don't remember them bitches but them hoes remember me.*♪

I set up in my office and looked at e-mails and reports until other staff started to show. Two staff came in, and I could hear them talking through the walls.

"He said I should start going to the gym," one person said.

"Wow, that's aggressive," replied the other.

*I never told anyone they should start going to the gym. Since when am I aggressive? Oh, wait, they aren't talking about you. Err on the side of realizing that it doesn't matter.* More staff came in, including my senior team of three. I gave them assignments. I sat in my office and listened.

"He wants us to finish this by end of day." *Me.* "He made me dinner last night." *Not me.* "He had a question for me." *Me.* "He wants me to come with him and his family on vacation." *Not me.* I had it all sorted out, no issues. I came out of my office to a full team working, loud noises all around. *Brett can't handle this job. Brett is too young. Everything Brett got in life, he was given. He thinks we're talking about him. He's lost it, again.* I then heard the Weeknd's "Starboy" come on the radio.

♪*I'm a motherfuckin' starboy.*♪

*Shit, the radio is even talking about me.* I went back to my office and sat down, once again thinking it was all real, thinking that the world was watching me, with no awareness that this was a three-peat. I messaged Jerry. "Jerry, I'm not feeling well today. Cool if I take the rest of the day off?"

"Umm, yeah, feel better."

I felt at ease. The voices quieted and I decided to go for a walk, with no destination in mind. I saw cars flying by on the highway. *There's no way all those cars are following the speed limit. Why is the system set up that way? Why are you allowed to go over and it's acceptable? There should be a sign that has the max speed limit and if you go over, you're speeding. End of story.* I took out my phone and jotted down "Speed Limit Issue" in the Notes app.

My train of thought was interrupted by a bird chirping. It was leading me somewhere. I followed the sound for a few minutes and noticed a bird land in a tree in the residential neighborhood. When I saw the house, it all made sense. There was a blue-and-gold sign in the lawn with the number 12 on it and a basketball, my high school colors and number. *This can't be a coincidence.* I almost walked up to the door and knocked, but the bird flew away and the wind blew hard. *Something isn't right about this.* I headed back to my car and to the office and thought about what had just happened. *Signs are fake, like the one in the grass. But birds and wind are natural and real. It's time to start focusing on nature and not fake signs.* I made it back to my car and thought about how much pollution I was putting into the air. *All right, it would be ridiculous to walk all the way home, so I'll have to drive.* I got in the car and push-started the engine. The radio blasted loudly after I had not turned it down on the way in; I guess I didn't realize how loud it was. Kanye West's "I Am a God" was playing.

♪*I am a God. Even though I'm a man of God.*
*My whole life in the hands of God. So y'all*
*better quit playing with God.*♪

*That can't be a coincidence.* I glanced to the sky and saw faces in the clouds. *That can't be a coincidence. All right, Brett, this is your new spaceship. Take it for a spin.* I put all the windows down and turned the radio even louder, booming, as loud as it went, feeling each thump of the beat. I zoomed out of the parking lot and made it to the highway, speed limit, fifty-five. I put the car in cruise control on fifty-five. *I'm setting a good example for the rest of them.* The cars in front of me formed a puzzle. I wasn't going to speed up or slow down for anyone. I'd change lanes if I got too close to a car in front, and I'd flash them if I had nowhere to go. *Live game of Tetris.* Then I remembered. *Man-made signs are fake. None of this is real.* I floored it, breaking the rule of the man-made speed limit sign and found some open road, approaching 90 in a few seconds, then 100, then 110. *Cops are the only thing that can stop you.* I slowed down, realizing that I needed to stay patient, for now. I made it back to my apartment and zoomed into the parking garage, seeing it in a new way, the possibilities were endless.

## *Bridge*

I unlocked the door to my apartment and pulled the key out, walked in, and let the door close behind me. I stood in my Systems Fit polo and khaki pants, scanning the room like I was in it for the first time. I drew outlines of the shapes that I saw in my mind: Countertop, L-shaped. Light fixture, circle. TV, rectangle. I was able to use my mind and draw on the canvas of my apartment. *I have a great idea!* I saw the remote and grabbed it, walking back to the original point of entry. I turned the TV on. "This is the best pillow you've ever seen!" An older man with black hair, a mustache, and a blue shirt was promoting his invention. I used the same mind trick on the TV, only with moving objects on the screen. *Cool!* I kept my focus on the moving shapes on the TV but held the previous shapes from before. I walked slowly to my couch, noticing the position of all my mental lines moving. *Whoa!* I stood up on my couch for an aerial view, then jumped a few times, shaking the entire system. I decided to power down the trick and take a walk. It wouldn't pollute the environment.

I changed into comfortable clothing and thought about the human race as a whole. *How can I help them if I don't know them?* I started walking outside on a path. I noticed a woman walking. "Excuse me, miss," I asked.

She smiled warmly. "Yes?"

"I'm doing a survey. What do you think is the single most important thing that we could be doing better as a society?"

She answered right away. "We need to treat one another with more respect."

"Thanks!"

She kept walking.

I asked a few more people, and they had similar answers. I was getting deeper into the trail and saw a biker walking his bike. "Sir."

"Not interested," he said.

"But, sir—"

Leave me alone."

He hopped on and started pedaling. I chased him for a bit, and he left me in the dust. *You won't be able to help them all.* I decided to take a break in the middle of the trail, lying down and completely extending, blocking half of the trail. I was at peace, hearing bikes and feet and animals go by. I got up about an hour later. It was still sunny, but approaching late afternoon. I continued my quest and noticed three women sitting at a table, drinking wine out of cups that hid the open beverage.

"Hey, ladies, mind if I join you?"

"Not at all. Have a seat. What's your name?"

"Brett."

"Hey, Brett." They introduced themselves.

"So what are you guys talking about?" I was enamored by an enormous Ferris wheel through the trees. One of the women started answering, and I zoned out. *OMG the entire city is my playground. These three women must be angels.* "Well, we aren't from around here, Brett." They looked at one another with a special secret. *They are from another planet. They've come to help me get to heaven. I'm the youngest person to ever figure this out.* "Thinking like that won't get you anywhere, Brett."

"How do I make it to heaven?" I asked.

They looked at one another, confused. "What are you talking about?"

"If you don't want me to rat you out for the wine, tell me," I said.

Their faces turned negative. "You need to leave," one woman replied.

"I'm not leaving until you tell me."

The three of them got up, and I followed them through down the path. Other people were walking in both directions. "Hey, listen, I'm sorry," I said.

"Leave us alone!"

I sparked up conversation with a random person walking by. "Hey, if I follow those women, am I likely to be arrested?"

"Yes," he said. "You should probably turn around, buddy."

*Another angel saving me.* I took a leisurely walk back and approached a relatively wide bridge, about fifty feet from the water below, with a No Diving sign on it. *If signs are fake, it means I need to jump off this bridge.* I leaned over the bridge, ready to jump. I glanced back at the sign, and it had disappeared. I blinked a few times, and it felt like I was waking up for the first time and the entire world had changed. I needed to regroup at home base, so I started sprinting home. I made it back to my apartment and decided that I no longer needed food or sleep to recharge, just TV. I turned all the lights off and lay on the couch, anxious to see what the world had thought about my journey today. "I see what he's getting at, but did he really need to be so aggressive with those women? And the way he figured out that he was supposed to jump off the bridge but then had the logic to not do it, amazing! He's also already aware that the world is small and the entire city is his own amusement park."

I rested for a few hours, knowing that I had a big night out ahead of me.

## Luxury Hotel

*What is the point of ever wearing something that isn't comfortable?* I rose off the couch and threw on my gray sweatpants and university hoodie. It was dark outside, but I hadn't slept or even come close to napping. My afternoon was spent remotely controlling the messages that were being subliminally sent through the TV, all with the push of a button. *So that's why they call it a remote control.* I thought about the bare essentials, keys, cell phone, wallet, and threw them into a small backpack. I slipped on my shoes and headed out for the night. All five of my senses were hyperalert as I began the ten-minute walk over the bridge to downtown. Lights were extra bright. I could hear everything. The smell of tacos was strong even though there wasn't a food truck for miles. My own saliva tasted like bottled water. The warm air gave me goose bumps. *This city is filled with rotten people and disease.* A man wearing a hoodie walked past me with his eyes straight forward. *He knows I'm here to clean up the city tonight. Rid the city of all of them.* I made it across the bridge, admiring the lighted buildings. Then I zoomed out and saw a picture of the entire planet, zoomed in a bit and saw Texas, zoomed in more and saw the city. The lights on one of the buildings started flashing. I stood up tall, with my thumb and middle finger surrounding the building in the distance, then turned my hand and saw the building turn on its side. I lost my balance, and it felt like I was turning the whole world. I broke my focus and fell back. *Learn how to use these powers slowly.* I walked around with swagger; after all, I had just turned a building on its side, disrupting the entire rotation of the planet. I approached a luxurious hotel where crowds of rich men and women were not pleased to see me.

"I thought he was supposed to stay in tonight! I took a bet that Brett would remain locked in his cage. Now he's out?"

*Keeping me caged, huh?*

I took a deep breath and approached the hotel, knowing I would be surrounded by the enemy. I walked right into the fancy cocktail lounge and heard the entire place talking about me, like I was an A-list celebrity. *Autographs later, guys.* I was underdressed, to say the least, but I found a comfortable white couch that no one was using. I lay down on it with my shoes on, like it was the couch at my apartment. I overheard a younger gentleman talking about his experience in the tech industry, using my every movement as research that he could funnel back to the tech world to gain an edge over more traditional industries like food or car sales.

"Who lies on the couch like that in a place like this? This kid is on the next level!"

I turned to my left and noticed an older couple staring at me and shaking their heads. Then I heard them praying to God that I would be okay. *You're the ones that want to keep me caged in!* Security for the hotel came over.

"Sir, we need you to take your shoes off."

I kicked them off, and they went a few feet in the other direction.

"Sir, we're going to have to ask you to leave."

I got smart with them. "Are you sure? Who told you that?"

Like the cops in my previous episode, more security came. I had learned my lesson last time and darted out before anyone knew

I was gone. I found my way into another crowded place, the Steak House. I sat at the bar and asked the waitress if she could turn the music down. She looked at me funny and said, "There's no music on." Then a man far away turned to his friend and laughed.

*He's laughing at me.*

"What's your problem?" I yelled across the bar.

He asked me if I was all right and wanted a drink. I got up and left. I found a quiet intersection in the middle of the city and sat down, waiting. Waiting for some greater power to show up. Waiting to get my next task. The entire city went silent. No people, no traffic, just streetlights changing from green to yellow to red. I got up and walked home, feeling a bit out of sorts. I slammed my feet with each step, feeling the entire planet wobble back and forth based on the force of my steps. I managed to get back to my apartment in one piece. I lay down on the floor with my head facing the ceiling.

*Dear, world, I think it's time I told you a little about who I am. I was born in 1987. I have two brothers and a great mom. I've done great things in basketball, poker, and work, and I'm going to represent all the people on this planet well.*

I knew that the entire world heard me. I had insight in that I knew there was something big happening.

It was now one o'clock in the morning, and I hadn't eaten since breakfast. Not hungry, not tired, and with all the power in the world at my fingertips. I turned on the TV and plopped on the couch for some rest.

## Late-Night Drive

*It's time to take a drive.* At 3:00 a.m., I saw a car commercial, which tipped me off that I needed to get in my car. Still wearing the gray sweats and university hoodie, I left my apartment for a night ride. I laughed to myself. *Night ride, what Russell and I used to call our late-night runs.* I thought about my late-night run in my Nike Air moccasins, my run home from the bridge yesterday, and connected this to a car running. *So many dots connecting.* I made it to my car and pushed to start it. Again, the radio came blasting on with Lil Wayne's "John."

*♪Four Four bulldog my motherfuckin' pet, I point
it at you and tell that montherfucka' fetch.♪*

*Let's go all natural. Remember that signs are fake and nature is real.
Technically,* the radio can be seen as a fake sign. I turned the radio off
and put all the windows down, including the sunroof. I drove nice
and easy out of the apartment garage and made a right turn over the
bridge leading to the city, the same bridge that I had crossed a few
hours earlier after making my mark on the luxury hotel, the Steak
House, and the entire city. I hadn't slept or eaten for almost a full day
but had more energy than I'd ever had in my entire life. *I don't need
food or sleep. I'm not like everyone else.* The cool air felt nice as I entered
the heart of the city, with no plan or purpose. Then a light turned
red, forcing me to stop. It felt like I was punched in the gut. No one
was around, so I went right through. The city was quiet. *Can't stop
me.* I saw a green light in the distance and sped up to make the light.
I did. My head was on a swivel, looking for green lights to make. At
every intersection I'd see green, red, or yellow and make my turns
based on the roads that would lead me to green. *Get ten greens in the
next five minutes.* I looked at my clock, which read 4:10 a.m. *Okay,
by 4:15 a.m., I need to get ten greens.* It was exhilarating. *I'm running
sprints with my car.* I spent the next five minutes stopping and going,
counting every move through a green light, going through red lights,
and subtracting those until I finally got all ten greens. My clock read
4:14. I was proud of myself. It was a big accomplishment. I headed
back to my parking garage and parked with precision. I went back
inside my apartment and stared at the clock, waiting for the sun to
rise. I was so restless it hurt. I decided that taking a shower would
help.
    I closed all the doors in the bathroom and turned the water on
as hot as it could go. While I waited, I stared at myself in the mirror.
My eyes looked heavy. *You don't need sleep.* I splashed water on my
face and then aggressively splashed it all over the huge mirror in the
bathroom. I started counting the beads of water from left to right,
starting from the top left. *One, two, three, four, five, six, seven, eight,
nine, ten, eleven, twelve.* At twelve, I noticed a bead dripping down

the mirror. *Twelve. Basketball number, 12. Water number. Nothing but net, nothing but wet, swoosh, splash.* At this point, the bathroom was full of steam and beads were falling all over the mirror, drawing natural pictures of faces, letters, numbers, all adding up and clearly connecting for me. *Face, two eyeballs, one mouth, one nose. Face has four letters. Two eyes plus one mouth plus one nose equals four. Face equals two eyes, one mouth, one nose.* Eventually, the cloud of steam blinded the entire mirror. I stripped down and used the wall to find my way in. The water burned me, but I did not react. *Learn how to accept the pain.*

I worked my way under the water and got comfortable. I had a couple of shampoo bottles, bodywash, and soap in the corner and was attracted to them. I opened all the bottles at once and dumped them on my head. As the soap trickled down my face, I opened my eyes on purpose but soon realized I would need my vision. The sound of the water hitting the bottles was like music. I picked one up and knocked it against the wall. *I'm a musician.* I knocked it harder, grabbed a bottle of a different size, and noticed the difference in sound. I experimented with every combination of bottles and sound and finally started hitting the bottles against the wall as hard as I could like a drum set, denting them severely and making loud noises. I lay on my back and let the water from the shower hit me directly in the face. I closed my eyes for a few minutes and woke up to the shower water in my mouth. I sat up and turned the shower off, leaving the bottles in disarray on the floor of the tub. I grabbed my toothbrush because it was convenient and walked around my apartment a few times, brushing my teeth without toothpaste. I lay in my bed and stared at the fire sprinkler on the wall. A small ghost appeared, looking like Boo from Mario. I blinked, and he would disappear. I'd stare again, and Boo would appear again. I stared at him in amazement, forcing myself not to blink. He flew all around my room. Finally, the sun shined through my window, and that was the end of Boo. I knew if I stared at the fire sprinkler, he'd come back.

I decided there needed to be some balance of signs and nature and didn't want to fully watch TV. I put a chair halfway between the sliding door to the outside patio and turned the TV on. This way, I could hear birds and see natural signs on my left, while also hearing the TV and fake signs on my right. I sat, content, having a front-row seat to the battle of the century. Man versus nature.

## Homeless

I must have dozed off for a bit but was awakened by my phone. "Brett, it's nine o'clock. Why aren't you at work?

"Oh, hey, Jerry. I don't think I'm going in today."

"Why?"

"I'm just not feeling that well."

"Well, all right, it's just not like you to do this."

"Yeah, I'm just not feeling well."

"Okay."

*Another day off!* Another beautiful day, birds chirping. I called Tony and asked if he wanted to go to lunch; we had rekindled our friendship a few months back. Lunch was light-years away, but I had big plans. Actually, it was high hopes, no plans. I threw on a new outfit of shorts, shirt, and shoes, grabbed the essentials, and began my walk over the bridge and into downtown. The cars shooting by were extra loud. I found an intersection and noticed something hanging over a tree branch. *This is a test. The older gods are watching me figure it out.* I thought of twenty old men sitting around a table in the sky, looking down on me. On the branch there was a green cord, with a plug on the end of it. *Okay, once I get this thing, what do I do with it?* I saw an outlet next to a bench nearby. *Bingo.* I jumped as high as I could but wasn't even close. I tried again and realized that cars and buses were zooming by close to where I was landing. I got smart and broke a smaller branch off the bottom of the tree, then used it to shake the higher branch, releasing the green cord. It fell on the ground.

"Sir, can I help you with something?" a pretty woman working in the massage parlor in the building behind me, with big windows, looking out, asked.

*She's trying to stall me.* "Yeah, actually. What would be the best way I can clean up the city today?"

"Huh?"

*She doesn't want me to get the elders in the sky's respect.*

"Like, if I wanted to show off to my boss in the sky, if you know what I mean?"

"Huh? Well, there are a lot of cigarette butts everywhere. I'm sure you could clean those up."

*Maybe she's on my side.* "Thank you!"

I sprinted back to the green cord and plugged it into the outlet. I looked up the sidewalk and noticed thousands of cigarette butts blinking for me to pick up. I walked with my head down, picking butts off the street for about ten minutes. Then I found a piece of candy with ants running all over it, connecting it to my previous visions. *This can't be a coincidence.* Then I found a perfectly wrapped piece of candy. I picked it up and looked around. *Am I supposed to eat this?* A light turned red, so I put it down and went back to cigarette butts, walking by a homeless man. *It's important that I understand how every person lives, including him.* There was a nearby garbage can. *No man has ever had this level of insight.* I heard the elders impressed by where my head was. I reached in and found an old Burger King bag. *Keep going.* I went into the bag and found a half-eaten pickle with mustard and ketchup all over it. With no hesitation, I ate the pickle and threw the bag back into the garbage. *The elders cheered. Mission complete.* I walked back the same way I had come in, and the streets were free of cigarette butts. When I made it to the bridge, however, there were thousands more. I still wanted to impress the higher-ups, so I started picking them up.

A young woman walked by. "Ma'am, we're cleaning up the city. Would you like to help?"

"Sure!" She got next to me and started picking up the litter.

Another man walked by, and he helped also. Even an elderly woman with one arm bent over and joined the cause. I had started a chain of soldiers, helping them and myself.

It was almost time for lunch, so I said goodbye and the crowd dispersed. I found my ride and made it to Tony's place with no red lights stopping me. *That can't be a coincidence.* I barged into his place. "Dude, I just helped an army of people clean up the city."

He didn't question it. "That's sweet, dude." He laughed.

"No, like all types of cool shit is happening. I'm seeing ghosts and shit."

His face changed. "You tell your doctor about any of this stuff?"

"Doctor? Why?"

"I don't know, man. That would probably be a good idea."

"Yeah, whatever. Let's go eat."

We were on a mission. The elders had sent Tony to protect me. He had already been to heaven and was going to show me the ropes. "Follow me, dude," he said. I stayed close behind him as we walked on a sidewalk downtown. Everyone was looking at us and talking about us. *There he is. He's not afraid. Wow!* Tony snapped a photo of the two of us.

"Why'd you do that?"

"Ummm, why not?"

We found a crowded restaurant and sat at the bar. The entire restaurant pretended not to notice us, but their eyes said different.

"What would you like to drink, sir?" the bartender asked.

I turned to Tony. "Should I have a drink or not?"

"Uhhh, I don't know, man, whatever you want."

As I turned to look at him, his face remained the same, but the backdrop was a blue sky and clouds, no restaurant. He smiled at me. "Can you believe how cool this place is?" *Is Tony talking about heaven?*

"Sir, what would you like?"

"Whatever he's having."

I had a beer and took a few bites of the sandwich I had ordered. After lunch, I asked if he wanted to take a ride in my car. "I've been flying around in this thing. You gotta see it."

He declined. "Be careful out there, B. Call me if you need anything."

"All right, sir."

We made eye contact before he left. *You're close to making it, man. Keep going.*

## *Treadmill*

After having something to eat and sipping on a cold beer, I headed back to my apartment and felt tired, finally. As soon as I hit the couch, I dozed off in peaceful silence, even though it was still sunny and midafternoon. It had been about thirty-six hours with no real sleep and barely any food. I had dreams of saving the planet and moving on to whatever the next phase of life was for me.

I woke up gently and decided that another shower was in order. Showers always woke me up before work, although now it was dark and much later in the day. I had another play session, bottles crashing, water burning, lying on my back, letting the water hit my face. Then I messed with the steam on the mirror and brushed my teeth—with toothpaste this time. I felt like working out and it was too dark outside, so I went to the community gym in my building. *What's the big deal if I work out after I shower?* It was completely empty and quiet. *Ah, that feels nice.* I scanned the gym and noticed a treadmill with a blinking light, signaling me to get on it. It faced a window to the outside street. I walked over in a cutoff shirt, shorts, low-cut socks, and my real Nike running shoes—the moccasins stayed upstairs. I got on without starting the belt and took inventory of my surroundings. I'm standing on the treadmill, with all its controls facing me. There was a Hooters restaurant across the street, a blinking crosswalk sign that counted down when it was time to walk across, and a streetlight in my upper right view, managing the traffic. The sky was dark, making the traffic lights and signs even more bright. The regular bright lights were on inside the gym, causing a reflection off the window back into the gym, allowing me to see behind me, although everything was backward. The back wall of the gym, which I could now see from the reflection on the window, had a large mirror with a TV mounted on the top. I had a fuzzy view of what was behind me from the mirror and a clear view of the TV by looking to my upper left, although, again, backward. The TV had an NFL game on with closed captioning.

I adjusted my posture and took a deep breath, with the whole room under my watch, traffic and streetlights outside, control at my fingertips, backward TV and gym in the reflection. I started to walk, putting the speed at 0.5, the minimum. I got a feel for the pattern of the traffic light. *Red light, one one thousand, two one thousand, three one thousand, four one thousand, five one thousand.* I started walking to the count. *Six one thousand, seven one thousand, eight one thousand, nine one thousand, ten one thousand.* All the way up to twenty. The light changed to green, and I put the speed up to 9.0 and sprinted for about twenty seconds until the light turned to yellow, when I put my arms on the railings of the treadmill and did dips while the belt ran under me, counting in the same manner for a few seconds until the light turned red. Then I put the speed back to 0.5 and repeated. I was counting in my head but then realized that the Walk sign could do the counting for me. After a few cycles, I had the timing down.

*Light changes to red. Walk sign counts down with white hand symbol. Walk sign changes to flashing red hand. Light changes to green. Walk sign changes to red. Light changes to yellow. And walk sign stays solid on the red hand. Light changes to red. Walk sign counts down with white hand symbol. Repeat.*

While this system was running, I was using the timer on the treadmill to ensure the seconds on the treadmill matched the seconds on the Walk sign. It did. I was really working the treadmill, going from 0.5 to 9.0, hanging from the rails, repeating. But it was too easy. I glanced up at the backward TV and read the closed caption in reverse to decipher. "He needs to work much harder than that if he wants to win this game." With the timing memorized, I turned around on the treadmill and started back-pedaling to the same count, seeing myself in the mirror, seeing the TV regular view, pivoting for a few seconds to change the speed on every cycle.

"Look at that!" I read on the TV backward.

But I still wasn't getting tired, even after sixty minutes. I turned around, facing forward, saw the green light, looked up at the TV, and read in reverse, "What's he gonna do next?" I walked at 0.5 as I raised the elevation to the max, then I pressed on the speed button to the max. I was in an all-out sprint on the max settings, slamming my feet on the belt with every stride, feeling free. Sweat was pouring off me onto the belt, making it slippery and harder to navigate. I wasn't going to stop, no matter what. I slammed my feet on the belt harder, stared at all the lights on the street, counters on the treadmill, TV, reflections, and finally the belt slowed down.

*What the fuck?* I had overworked the treadmill, causing the plug to pull out of the wall. The symbolism was crystal clear. *When you put a cord into an outlet, like earlier today, you must also pull a cord out of an outlet. Everything must balance.* When I got off the machine, I was having trouble deciding which way to look at the TV, backward or forward. I decided backward, because it was the secret way. When I glanced up, the closed caption read, "!ɴᴡᴏᴅʜᴄᴜᴏᴛ."

## East Grand Café

The sunlight woke me up in my bed the next morning. I turned over, and my clock read 7:00 a.m. *Another beautiful day!* I'd convinced Jerry that I was still sick, so my schedule was wide-open. I was so used to being a celebrity that people talking about me and taking pictures was no longer an issue. TV and radio were the same. I thought I was hungry and decided to drive to East Grand Café, a place I had been about one hundred times over the three years I'd been in Texas. I roared up the Audi and blasted 50 Cent's "In Da Club."

♪*You can find me in the club, bottle full of bub.*♪

*Maybe I'll get a club sandwich with a bottle full of bub.* I imprinted the word *bub* on my windshield and let the arms of the letter *b*'s fall down, turning them into letter *p*'s. *Pup.* I drove out of the parking garage and saw a puppy being walked on the street. *That can't be a coincidence.* I zoomed up the road, windows open, music blasting, with the whole street watching me in awe. I wasn't just looking at the traffic light in front of me anymore—that would be too basic. I was able to see the light in front of me and the four lights ahead of it for the upcoming intersections. I started to figure out patterns and how the lights worked with one another. *Light 3 turns red after Light 1 turns yellow after—*

*Beeeeeep!*

The car behind me broke my train of thought. *He's jealous.* I zoomed into the garage and intentionally parked between two spots to test the waters. The music was so loud that when I turned the car off, it felt like I warped into another, more peaceful dimension. I strolled into East Grand Café, sunglasses on, khaki shorts and T-shirt. Just what I expected. The entire restaurant shut down and turned when I walked in.

"Table for one, please." I looked at the hostess like, "Can you believe this?"

She smiled back. "Right this way."

I saw my empty booth in the back corner of the restaurant and walked by haters in the other booths against the wall and haters at tables in the middle of the restaurant. It was really loud.

*OMG, that's him! He's in the same restaurant as me! I thought he'd be taller. I don't like him. He's ugly. He's hot. I hope he fails. I hope he makes it.*

I'd grown accustomed to this type of talk over the last week, and it didn't bother me. What did bother me was the old man in the booth across me and the group of four in the booth directly in front of me. I could hear the old man's thoughts as he turned toward me, then back, then poured a cup of coffee.

*Who the fuck do you think you are, kid? You're nothing. I've been at this much longer than you have, and you think you'll get it all? Fuck off.*

This made me angry, and I replied, still sitting quietly in my seat. *Well, let me tell you something, you old piece of shit. You know nothing about me, you don't know what I've been through, and you aren't like me, so why don't you just shut the fuck up?*

Then the table of four in front of me had an opinion on our telepathic argument. A hipster, wearing a beanie, was the leader. *I just think it's so messed up how he goes after old people. Also homeless people. Did you guys see what he did yesterday with the pickle?* They all nodded in agreement. *Just go home, Brett. Go home.*

We made eye contact, and I replied without saying a thing. *Wow, of all people, you're the one that's going to talk shit on me? Look at you, dude. You're a loser. Hit the gym or something.* I saw his eyes tear up. *Are you crying? Take off that stupid hat. You're a fucking joke.* He put his hand on his head and adjusted his hat. *That's right, I'm in your head, you'll do whatever I want you to do, bitch.*

I saw my waiter coming over. "Hi, sir! What will you have to drink?"

"Water is fine, thanks so much."

I heard a waitress a few tables up. "Well, you know." She laughed. "Everybody celebrates Christmas."

"No, they don't!" I yelled from three tables back.

"Excuse me?" she said.

"Not everybody celebrates Christmas. You said everyone does, and you were wrong."

"Well, I wasn't talking to you, sir."

"Well, maybe you should be more aware of your surroundings."

She apologized, and by the time my waiter got back, I had gotten up and left. I put on the most spacy Lil Wayne song I could find, called "I Feel Like Dying," and put it on full blast back in my car in the garage. *You know what? Fuck this.* I swung out and decided I wasn't going to leave through the exit; I was going to go out the in. I flew around and faced the incoming traffic head-on, putting my car in park. I put my seat back and lounged, enjoying the mix of frustrated people honking at me and Lil Wayne playing on the radio at hyper volume.

♪ *Only once the drugs are done that I feel like dying...*
*I feel like dying.* ♪

"Move your car, asshole!" yelled a pissed-off person unable to get into the garage.

♪ *I'm sittin' on the clouds, I got smoke comin' from my seat,*
*I can play basketball with the moon, I got the whole world at my feet.* ♪

"What are you doing? Get out of the way!" another person called out.

Finally, the attendant came up to me, totally confused, and asked me to leave.

"Why?"

"Sir, if you don't leave, I'm going to have to call the cops."

I thought about my head smashing against the cop car a few years ago and said, "Thank you." I spun around fast and took off through the exit, zooming around on small streets to get back to my apartment, raging a bit. When I made it back to my apartment, I scanned the room. *This place isn't me. Time for renovation.*

## Renovation

Once again, I'm standing, looking around at my apartment. *I don't like this view.* I used the couch to hoist myself up to the kitchen counter, where I leaned against the wall with the cabinets nearby. *A true bird's-eye view. This must be what it's like.* Things were too clear. I needed to make it more interesting. I reached down near the sink and found a large bottle of dish soap, then got back into place, scanning the room from up above. I squeezed the soap all over the counter, admiring the way the colors shone and bubbled up. I took a step forward and almost slipped to a dangerous fall. I held my balance and torpedoed off the counter and onto the gray Ikea couch that I'd built with my girlfriend about eighteen months ago, forcing one of the seat pillows to become undone from the rest of the couch. I felt rage and tried to rip the pillow in half—it would not tear. I pushed it back into its place aggressively and looked around for more.

I decided music would be the perfect addition to my mood. I put on my favorite playlist on Spotify and turned it all the way up, starting with Rae Sremmurd's "Look Alive."

♪*I'm so far out of sight, yeah that sounds about right.*
*Kill this cup, not my vibe, be the highlight of my night.*♪

*Now this is a party.* I found old pictures in an envelope of my brothers and took them to the kitchen. *Just let it flow, let your body do the work. Don't fight it.* I'd lost all sense of reality as the music blasted, looking at my soaped kitchen counter, holding pictures from my childhood, ready to use the soap as glue.

*♪Look alive, look alive. We can start with something
light. I can get you so right, I just need an invite.♪*

I meticulously built a collage of pictures on the counter, perfectly organized, every angle sharp, like Dexter cleaning up after a
kill. Eminem's "Brainless" came on next, and I heard a line that I'd
memorized.

*♪Still in my skulls a vacant, empty void. Been
using it more as a bin for storage.
Take some inventory in this gourd, there's a Ford engine, door
hinge, syringe, an orange, an extension cord, and a Ninja sword.
Not to mention four lynch pins and a stringent stored, ironing
board, a bench a wench, an oru winch, an attention whore.
Everything but a brain.♪*

An engine, door hinge, syringe, orange, extension cord, Ninja
sword, four lynch pins, ironing board, and a bench flashed in front
of me. This got me more fired up. I couldn't even stand still, jumping
up and down to release some energy. I went to the kitchen cabinets
and decided that I didn't like cleaning, didn't like keeping things
organized. *This is my fucking house, right? I pay rent, right?* I crashed
plates, bowls, glasses all over the floor of the kitchen.

*♪Mama always said, if you had a brain you'd be
dangerous, a brain you'd be dangerous.
Imma prove ya wrong, Mama, I'm gonna grow one
day to be famous, one day to be famous.♪*

With both hands, I cleared the drawers, silverware, and everything else. *This will be my new wasteland. When I don't care about
something, I'll throw it here.* I noticed my foot had a cut from broken
glass as I carefully stepped out of the kitchen landfill. It hurt, and I
was pissed off. I ripped open the door to the closet in the hallway
off the kitchen. There was a large cardboard box that had held my
TV, and I started punching it aggressively. I ripped my shirt off and

punched harder, faster. There were some wipes that I kept in storage in a plastic container, and I threw them over the wasteland, shattering the glass on my oven. *Good, the glass is supposed to go there.* I realized that I'd need a place to sleep that night, so I designated the couch area as a safe place. I moved my pillows and blankets from my bed to the couch, made a little walkway to the door, and kept that space organized. Then I cleared off all counters in the bathroom and let the water run, closing the doors behind me. *This will be my steam room.* At this point, the kitchen was a garbage dump, the bathroom was a steam room, and the TV area was my bedroom. The only room left was my previous bedroom. The song had changed to Drake's "6 Man."

♪*I just got the new deal. I am in the Matrix,*
*and I just took the blue pill.*♪

I rocked my head after hearing "I am in the Matrix." I kicked my mattress with all my might. Then I emptied my dresser, tossing clothes everywhere.

♪*I don't need no fuckin' body, I run my own shit.*♪

One of my shirts got stuck on the ceiling fan and looked like a real ghost. *Ha! This is what people are afraid of. Afraid of fake ghosts! I've seen a real ghost.* I was drawn to the camera on my twenty-seven-inch Mac PC, the one that I'd bought with my poker money. *Someone is watching me.* I thought about scientists using the camera to study my every move. Then I pulled up Photobooth so I had an unrecorded video of myself. *I'll give you a show!* I turned all the lights off and put on a bright-orange Systems Fit shirt. The screen only picked up the orange shirt, making me look like a ghost. *Who's the ghost now?* I jumped around aggressively, trying to scare them. *This must be how horror movies are made!* I kept jumping up and down, shirt flying around with the ceiling fan, shower steaming up the bathroom, a mess of broken glass and plastic in the kitchen. I kicked a tin of Altoids on the ground, spraying little white pills everywhere, followed by throwing the pack of condoms that I had in the air. I yelled at the top of my lungs, "Is this what you want?" alone in my apartment. My veins were popping out of my skin as I screamed in rage again.

*♪I knew it would end up like this.*
*I'm fucking psychic, young, but I'm makin'*
*millions to work the night shift.♪*

I walked right up to my computer and threw it as hard as I could against the wall, shattering parts of the screen and denting the wall, which forced the plug out of the outlet, like the treadmill. The music stopped, and my automatic breathing kicked in. I noticed the pills and condoms. *The dark side of me.* I went into the bathroom and shut off the shower. *The part of me that likes to relax.* I went to the kitchen. *The lazy side of me.* I looked at the counter full of pictures. *My past.* I grabbed the bottle of dish soap that still had some left in it and walked to the last section, which was perfectly organized. *Me.* I pressed the soap out and did my best to draw a woman on the right side of the couch. *My girlfriend.*

## I Feel Like Dying

I was exhausted. Still low on fuel and sleep from the chaos of the last few days, I took a seat on the couch. It was dark outside. My mind slowed down, very few thoughts, and vision blurred. I lay on the couch and rested my focus on the wooden floor underneath the TV. I heard a crack in the wall. *That's them trying to get me to do something.* I heard a voice outside. *That's paparazzi.* I heard a motorcycle roar. *That's the danger in the world.* I heard a police siren. *That's the protection in the world.* I heard an ambulance siren. *I'm not sick!* Round after round, every sound meant something. I kept staring at the wooden floor, not letting the cracks and sounds distract me.

*He's doing it. He's really doing it!* I heard someone say outside.

Then, like a miracle, I started to see something form in the wood. *He's starting the process!* All of a sudden, three tiny wooden logs came out of the ground and set themselves on fire. *Holy shit! I've never seen anything like this. What does it mean?* I heard a crack, then voices. *This is the beginning of the end of your life.* It didn't bother me. I was so exhausted and didn't have anything left in the tank. I started to become aware of my automatic breathing system. Breathe in. Breathe out. Breathe in. Breathe out. And eventually saliva would form and I'd swallow automatically. *My saliva represents all the poison in the world. When I swallow, I'm helping cure cancer and AIDS. When I spit, I'm making it worse.*

After this thought, the fire grew larger and something exceptional happened. A small pig wiggled its way out from the flame. The fire was still burning, and now a pig was moving across my wooden floor. *He's made it to level 2!* I was sold on the idea that these were the steps everyone takes when they are about to move to the afterlife. I had accepted my fate. Then the pig stood up, transforming into a dinosaur. *They are showing me the history of the Earth.* Then the logs spread, working their way up the walls. I was frightened and blinked, erasing the entire scene altogether. The wall cracked, a siren rang, and I tried again. Every time I got to the logs spreading, the story would end. My breathing slowed and I closed my eyes. Hearing every breath and swallow. Then a white circle formed with my eyes closed. It was spinning. *I guess this is it, the light at the end of the tunnel that everyone talks about.* I was approaching the light. *All he has to do is stop the breathing cycle and he'll make it!* I was waiting for my breath to stop, but it never did. The entire world was waiting for my breath to stop, but I was someone special. *Well, I've just experienced what it feels like to die. Where the fuck is everyone that loves me? Why am I all alone?* My mind had had enough for this round and would live to fight another day.

The next morning, I called my mom. "I changed my room to fit my personality! Oh, and I'm not coming home for the holidays," I said.

She started crying hysterically. "Brett? Something's going on."

I hung up on her, and then Jerry called. "Brett, what are you doing? Mom is crying and you're missing work again."

"Yeah, I don't know why she's crying. I'm still not feeling well."

I was able to hold it together on the phone with Jerry and hang up without any huge argument. I couldn't help but think about my spit. *When I spit it out, I'm hurting the world and helping myself. When I swallow it, I'm helping the world and hurting myself.*

I was hungry and wanted to get a slice of pizza. It was a ten-minute walk. For the first five minutes, I was swallowing all my spit. Then I became angry, not willing to take on the pain of the entire world. *Why the fuck do I care about them?* I started spitting on the ground. I made it to the crowded pizza shop and sat at the bar. I ordered a slice and spit all over the pizza. *Take that.* The entire restaurant was talking about me, betting on me, commentating on last night's hallucination. It was overwhelming. Then I heard a voice.

"Brett, this is the one who's been testing you. You are a man now."

*God?* I saw an image of an atom, then a cell, then cells dividing, then a tadpole, then a frog, a bird, a dog, a wolf, a gorilla, and a human. I felt a surge of energy like no other.

"Brett, show them how far you've come to be who you are. Take control!" The voices got louder and louder, irritating me more and more. "Right now. Do it, Brett!"

I stood and turned around. "Everybody shut the fuck up! I've had enough of you all talking behind my back!" I screamed, looking out at the crowd. "Shut the fuck up!" I yelled even louder, as loud as I could. The place went silent, except for Twenty One Pilots' "Heathens" playing on the pop station in the background.

*♪Please don't make any sudden moves*
*You don't know the half of the abused♪*

I looked around and saw nervous college students, fathers ready to protect their wives and young children, and restaurant staff looking for the closest phone to call 911. I took a deep breath, enjoying the peace and quiet that hadn't existed in my world for the last week. A beam of sunshine shed through the window, landing directly into my eyes. *I've served you well, haven't I, God?* Then a brave man, about my height, chubby, and friendly, joined me in the spotlight.

"Hey, man, you all right? Let's take a walk outside." He represented everything I was going to change about the world, this fat, fake world. Then his face transformed, teeth growing into fangs, eyes widening, voice deepening. All the spectators disappeared. He put his hand on my shoulder and, in a deep voice, belted out, "Come on, **man**. There are kids **here**." I felt his internal poison being transferred to my shoulder and saw his words floating in front of me. Come on, man, there are kids here. I pulled the letters that I needed to unscramble, and the words hear me lit up in the sky. This is your world, Brett. You are my son. Now, go take it. Then I was back in the pizza place, with the crowd of insignificant mortals. I looked at the man's hand on my shoulder and thrust my arms forward, with perfectly utilized force, knocking him back over the table behind him. A chair shifted, and silverware dinged on the floor. A woman shrieked. Kids cried. Now, about thirty men stood up, ready to physically remove me from the premises, fifteen of them standing in front of the exit. God showed me an image of myself as a high school basketball player running sprint after sprint to motivate me to escape. I got low and charged forward toward the door, like the crowd wasn't even there. I was met by punches, name-calling, "Kick his ass!" and the loud rip of my shirt. We were all looking for the same result, getting me out of the restaurant. Eventually, our combined force knocked me out of the front door and onto the street.

## Capture

*What's everyone so upset about?* I had moved on quickly from the incident at the pizza place. What God had in store next was bigger. *The world is much bigger than that place. Show the whole world who you are.* I walked into the middle of the street and took my shirt off, catching everyone's attention, like I had wanted. Then I did my signature car-jump move, landing on the hood of a parked car on the most popular street in the city. A crowd of people came over, and I got scared, so I jumped down.

*Time to go home.*

I started walking back to my apartment after using my ninth life and realized that I had no shirt on. I turned around and saw it lying in the middle of the road up the street. I got my shirt and put it back on. *Man, I'm thirsty.* I saw East Grand Café and started walking in that direction. Then two police cars pulled up next to me.

"Sir, put your arms behind your back and get against the wall."

They were not aggressive, not condescending, so I didn't resist. *Yet another test.* They walked me to the back of the cop car and guided me in. I heard the same beeps and similar communication sitting in the back of the cop car as last time. I closed my eyes and listened to the patterns of the beeps and the cops talking about what to do with me over the radio. "We have another incident up North. Do you copy?"

The Systems Fit office was North. *Oh, no! They are going after the whole office.*

I sat helpless, not able to protect my employees from the SWAT team heading their way.

Finally, an officer came to the window. "Name?"

"Brett Stevens."

"Address?"

"Ah, 402 East Kindlesburg Drive."

"Phone number?"

"Ah, 555-371-1942."

He looked back to one of the officers. "He's pretty coherent, guys." *That's because I'm a spy.* "Where are you employed?"

"It's called Systems Fit."

"What do you do for them?"

"I'm the director of operations, responsible for thirty-five people. I'm also on the board of directors and own some of the company."

"Wow," he said.

We had a few more words, and I was crystal clear on my answers. I'd need to be to escape this one. As we were talking, the fiery Texas sun glared in the background. The officer was directly in line, eclipsing the sun. I could no longer hear what he was saying. His arms were relaxed and leaning over the car door as he spoke. *He's confessing. I'm his priest.* He kept talking, and then another cop leaned over, talking as well. They were lining up to confess their sins to me. I nodded and smiled. I saw an ambulance pull up. *This is it, the balance of security and science.*

"Okay, Brett, we're going to help you out of the car."

As I got out, a whirlwind of panic hit me. I was dehydrated and could barely stand up. A paramedic wheeled a chair over to me, and I found my seat. *That feels better.* I looked up and noticed hundreds of people watching. I guess my stunt in the middle of the most crowded street in the city got their attention. They were too far away from me to hear them talking about my every move.

"All right, Brett. Well, we aren't going to arrest you."

"Awesome! So I'll just go home, then."

"Well, no. We're going to have to take you to the hospital. You answered all our questions, but you can't be threatening people and jumping on cars." He was not smiling or laughing about it. He was genuine.

*Nooooo, it happened again.*

I had an awareness of what would happen next. They wheeled me to the ambulance and laid me on my back. There was a man in uniform ready, waiting to check my vitals, sparking conversation so I didn't pass out from dehydration. The siren went off, and we moved fast toward the hospital. I had a view of the cars behind us and was in a time warp.

"Brett, what's going on?" the paramedic asked.

"I'm just so tired."

"What are you tired of."

"I just think the entire world needs to change."

The back window was now blurry and moving at light speed like a spaceship in Star Wars.

"That's very good, Brett." He gave me a smirk, and then I knew that he was God, giving me the power to change the world. "What would you want to change it to?"

"I'd like to see less complaining, more hard work, more respect, more accountability."

The ambulance stopped, and we came out of the time warp. "A world like this?" he said, implying that he had just changed the entire world based on my answer. Then he went back into paramedic mode, got me out of the ambulance, and wheeled me into the emergency room. A team of four strapped me down on a table and set me up with needles. This was the first chance I had to look at my body in a long time, battered, bruised, and bloody. A nurse came in and dispassionately pulled my pants down and stuck me with a catheter up my urethra. I winced but did not yell. Then all the staff left, leaving me alone, cuffed to the table, hooked up to machines and needles. I lay back on the table and looked straight up, seeing my reflection in a square window on the ceiling. I thought about Mel Gibson being tortured at the end of *Braveheart* with only the shot of his head and the audience imagining the torture happening below. I couldn't fight anymore. I wasn't angry. My thoughts stopped altogether. I rested my eyes and had a pleasant dream about playing 33 with my brothers.

## *Survival*

An attendant's footsteps woke me up. He was carrying a tray of food and had a warm smile. He let my arms out of the cuffs, raised my bed to an appropriate angle, and handed it to me. "Eat up," he said. It was a reminder that I needed to eat. I was starving. I shoveled in the food and chugged my drink, and he took the tray. "Wait here. We'll be getting you soon."

My therapist showed up about an hour later, looking shocked. He was comforting and then went on his way.

After about three hours, I was escorted up an elevator to a lobby, where Russell and my mom were waiting. I smirked at Russell. *What the hell did I get into this time?* He smiled back.

"How are you?" he said.

"I'm fine. It's amazing that you guys flew here, same day."

We waited another thirty minutes, and then I was handed a packet of paperwork to fill out by a staff member. I rushed through the stack of paper, signing things, unsure what it all meant. "Can you imagine someone filling all this out with no one here to help them?" my mom said.

When I was finished, my mom and I got into the back of a cop car, who escorted us to the hospital area that I'd be staying in. Russell followed in a cab. We said our goodbyes, and once again, I was handing in my shoelaces, wallet, phone, keys. I was left wearing shoes without laces, low-cut socks, blue shorts, and my T-shirt that was ripped at the neck, thrown into the middle of the street, and somehow managed its way back onto my body. I was still exhausted, having gotten only sporadic sleep for the last seven days. I was walked to my room and saw a college-aged kid already asleep, my bed catty corner to his, and a few multilevel cubbies. I fell asleep immediately, no shower, no toothbrush.

I woke up to the sound of beeping. A young half-Asian woman took my arm and wrapped the strap around to get my blood pressure for morning vitals. She reminded me of my ex-girlfriend. I had about an hour before breakfast and meds, so I took a shower. My roommate was still fast asleep. *What do they have him on?* The bathrooms did not have doors or locks but were private inside the rooms. There were also public bathrooms in the hall, an upgrade from the last hospital. The sink was outside with a mirror, and then a curtain separated the sink from the shower and toilet. Another curtain separated the shower from the toilet. *Up close and personal.* I grabbed the soap and shampoo that I received upon entering, stripped down, and turned the shower on, letting it heat up. I got in and leaned against the wall. The hot water felt great against my back. Then I heard my roommate peeing.

"What's up, dude? I'm Chris," he said.

"Brett," I replied.

*I've never met anyone under these circumstances before.* He flushed the toilet, and it roared, scaring me. He left the room. Then I leaned forward onto my forearms and closed my eyes. *You fucked up, Brett. You fucked it all up.* The water got slightly colder. It felt like something evil was inside me. I opened my mouth, letting the water pour around my lips, eyes still closed, trying to breathe it out. I made a moaning sound. "Ahhhhh," like the doctor tells you. "Say, ah." My legs felt weak. I bent down and sat with my back against the wall, water still crashing down. *Locked up again, Brett. You fucked up, Brett.* I stopped fighting it altogether, allowing my body to let gravity take over. I toppled against the wall, knocking my head, water still running, arms sprawled out, like a dead body. I moaned again. "Ahhhhhh!" Water was hitting directly into my ear now, making a pattering sound and fogging out my ability to hear. Finally, I laid my head on the floor of the shower, feeling officially dead. *This is your lowest point. You must die to truly feel alive.*

"Brett!" shouted a staff member. "You okay in there, Brett?"

"Yeah, I'm fine!" I belted out.

Next thing I knew, there was a staff member in my room with ten towels, cleaning up the flood that I had created, looking at me naked on the ground like it was just another day at the office.

"Brett, we have to make sure that when we shower, we put a towel down and don't flood the room. Does that make sense, Brett?"

"Noooo, I've never showered before," I said sarcastically.

"Brett, there are a lot of floors in this place. You happen to be on an easy one. Don't make me put you on the floor where people go away for a very, very long time. Remember, I'm the one that controls your medicine." Her wink and smile told a story of power and control.

"My apologies."

"I'm glad we have an understanding."

*No fucking way I'm staying here longer than I have to.*

## New Roommates

"Here are your meds, Brett," said the same woman who had just threatened me an hour earlier.

*If I don't take the pill, then things will escalate.* I swallowed the pill and started walking down the long hallway toward my room. *Enjoy your meds, Brett.* I saw the woman's face in front of me with an evil smile. Then my right foot felt heavy, heavy like the night I moved the entire planet with it downtown. When I took the step, the hallway rotated to the right; when I stepped with my left, the halfway rotated to the left. I got very anxious and scared, tiptoeing down the center of the hallway. Eventually, I got on my knees and crawled back to my room, where I was able to climb into bed. I must have looked foolish to anyone watching, crawling down the hallway. I thought about the idea that the entire world was spinning at this very moment. I felt more anxiety and panic. I couldn't stop it. I settled a bit, hungry for breakfast, and used the wall for support to get out of my room and all the way back up the hall. The feeling of the world spinning past, and a new hallucination began.

I was standing, holding my food tray in the community room, with a TV on my left. *Welcome back, Brett! We're excited to share this holiday season with you.* There were a few tables with chairs, board games, larger chairs facing the TV, and a whiteboard on the right. I saw a memory of myself standing in front of my managers, using a whiteboard to cover a topic. There was a piano and windows with shutters. I found an outlet behind the TV and instantly saw a face coming out of it. *Most outlets do look like faces, don't they? Backs of cars do as well, now that I think about it.* I found a spot in the back left corner of the room where I could sit with no one behind me.

A short woman with black hair, glasses, and a pink hospital gown was talking on the community payphone behind me in the lobby, loudly. "I'm going to fucking cut you when I get home! You beat the shit out of me, and now I'm going to kill you!" She slammed the phone down and stormed off to her room.

ESPN was talking about an old friend of mine, Darrelle Revis. *He's only a football player. I'm changing the world.* I scoffed. The woman came back out of her room, talking to everyone, loudly. She grabbed her tray and set it right in front of my view of the TV. *What the fuck.* I didn't say anything for a few minutes, letting her rant, but eventually, I got sick of it.

"Hey, would you mind moving out of my way?" I asked politely.

She stood up and flipped her tray. Staff came running in. "You and all men need to stop telling me what to do! I'll fucking kill you all." The staff surrounded her and took her away. I never saw her again.

"Yo, you just fucked with her mind," chimed in a Hispanic-looking kid my age wearing a green hoodie covering up tattoos. *He's wearing green, the color of poison. This guy represents toxicity. I'm talking with the source of all disease and nuclear chemicals in the world.* He walked over to the piano and started playing. I pictured disease spreading around the world with every note. *Stay the fuck away from that guy.* I threw my garbage out.

"Hey, man, you wanna play chess?" said a kid that looked like me.

"Sure."

The sounds on the TV and piano played as we set up the game on one of the tables. I beat him fast the first game. *He's your brain, only one step behind. He'll never catch up.* The next game started with him making the exact same move that I made last game. It all made sense. *I'm beating my own mind in chess.* After I beat him, he sat in the back corner of the room where I had just come from. *Yep, tracing my steps.* The green-hooded demon got up from the keyboard and went back to his room, leaving the piano wide-open. I needed a way to clean up the abstract, poison mess that was made on the piano. I brought the chess set over to the piano and went into a focus stronger than I needed playing twelve tables of online poker. I gently put the white pieces on the white keys and the black pieces on the black keys. I strolled over to the play area and grabbed a deck of cards, standing the kings on the kings and the queens on the queens. I laid out numbers 2–10 on the keys. Then I grabbed a checkerboard and built a castle on the top of the piano. I noticed a deck of Uno cards and laid them out in a color-coordinated manner on the top of the piano. It was beautiful. I sat down and remembered where I was. *Why am I here for the third fucking time?* I slammed on the keys, ruining my masterpiece. Then I saw faces wherever I looked. Two dots and a line jumped out at me. I stood up fast and felt anxiety. The whole world was shaking again, and I could feel it spinning rapidly. I tried to take a few steps but fell over. I made it to one of the chairs that was facing the TV, Darrelle Revis's name still showing. *Full circle.* My body's breathing systems kicked in, and I settled down. I got up slow, toed the line back to my room, and used the bathroom with no door to throw up.

## *Panic Attack*

I was sitting in a group, feeling alert as ever. Everything the social worker was saying was applying to me, as usual. "We need to be more like him, the staff too. He's living in real time, so when I say to breathe in, he's breathing in as I say it."

I was bored with all this. I hunched over in my seat with my mouth in my hands, staring at my feet. My shoes had no laces, and I had been wobbly since I got here. *Test your balance.* I pulled my heels back and touched my toes together, creating a Nike teepee, and carefully slipped my feet out, leaving the shoes standing like a teepee. I felt proud. Then I kept the shoes as is, putting my socks and feet on both sides of the teepee and mouth back on my hands. *Put all your focus on one thing. Test out your mind.* I tightened my forehead and stared at my shoes like a magician trying to lift an object with their mind. It looked like this from the outside, but internally, I was raging. Large blue crystals started forming in the ground. I moved my head up, and they were all over the floor, getting larger. In the middle of the upside-down earthquake, a blue figure started to appear. *Mega Man!* I had created the main character in my favorite video game from the ground up. I thought about John and his mission to beat every level of every Mega Man game in one semester; he would have been proud.

*Keep pushing. Keep pushing.*

I was practically shaking, and my face was red as crystals started coming out of the walls and ceiling. *Pull back, pull back.* Something told me to harness my energy and learn to control it. The figures faded away.

I looked up and saw my mom and dad in the lobby. *How?* Visiting hours. I hadn't had any good contact with my dad in a very long time. He said hello like we were meeting for dinner. I was walking slow and a bit dizzy from the Mega Man trick. There was a side area near the lobby that had a few chairs and a counter. I hopped up onto the counter, my mom sat on my right, and my dad stood on my left. I started feeling really woozy. *Maybe I pushed it too far?* I tried to breathe slow.

"Brett, you all right?" my dad asked.

"No, I'm not doing all right. I feel like I'm going to die."

"You're not going to die, Brett."

My breathing got heavier, and I started to slouch. There were doctors on the floor that all charged up to me at once to help. This was overwhelming and sent me into a panic. *I can't breathe, the walls are closing in, I see the white light, and I can't move my arm!* A woman came rushing in and pushed the doctors out of the way. She helped me off the counter and put me in a chair, giving me a squeeze ball in my paralyzed hand. She looked me directly in the eyes.

"Brett! You are having a panic attack. Nothing bad is going to happen."

*I'm going to die, I'm going to die, I'm going to die.*

My heart was falling out of my chest. "I can't move my fucking hand!" I yelled.

"Squeeze the ball and breathe." She started breathing, and I mimicked her. I slowly gained back the ability to move my hand, squeezing the ball harder and harder with each breath. She gave me an opened orange juice container like my mom had during my asthma attack in Little League. It tasted the same. "Sip this. You just had your first panic attack."

*Holy fuck, I used to think that was all bullshit.*

I regained my wits, and everyone left, except my mom and dad. I was so angry. "Well, here we are again, everybody!" I looked at my mom. "Are you clueless? I've been talking to you on the phone for the past month, telling you about wearing half-broken sunglasses, speed limits, and pollution, and you have no clue!" I sighed. "And you." I looked at my dad. "You've been nowhere! You were in Texas last week and didn't call me. Just leave, get the fuck out of here! Fucking leave!" I pointed to the exit. He started walking. "I'm almost dying everywhere I go, and no one is here to help me!" In the midst of my panic attack, someone called an ambulance. I was fine at this point but had to go through the motions of getting on another stretcher, being escorted to the ambulance, getting in the ambulance, and transported to the emergency room. They stuck more needles in my arm to get me hydrated, and we sat for about an hour. Afterward, I was brought back to my unit where the panic attack had originally occurred.

"You all right, man?" my roommate said.

"Yeah, just frustrated."

## Christmas

I'm lying in bed, alone, staring up and frightened. Two large eyeballs and a creepy mouth formed on the dull white ceiling. I tried to look away, but the face followed me wherever my eyes went. I closed my eyes, expecting it to go away, but there it was, showing up in the darkness.

*This must be the devil. This must be what hell is like.*

I tried to get out of bed, but my step rocked the entire planet. I was left stagnant, unable to escape this nightmare. I tiptoed carefully to view what time it was: 4:00 p.m. *All right, thirty minutes until group.* I attended all the groups because it was a great way to show that I could follow a schedule, something that doctors liked to see before discharging patients. Also, the good instructors kept my attention and helped me come back to earth. I waited patiently in the group room until about four forty-five and became angry. I walked up to the front desk.

"Ummm, there's supposed to be a group right now. Why hasn't it started?" I asked.

"Group starts at four thirty," he said with a smirk.

"Look at the clock behind you. It says four forty-five."

"Oh, yeah, those clocks aren't right. It's actually three forty-five."

*The scientists are intentionally changing the clocks on us! I wonder how many years I've been in here.*

I checked my skin to make sure it had not become wrinkled over time. "Well, uh, you should really get that fixed. You know why? Because I can barely walk down the hallway, and the devil is chasing me, you fucking moron. This would never fly at my company. All meetings start exactly when they are supposed to."

The evil woman that handled my meds came over. "If you want to know the time, then why don't you get a damn watch? Look, I have one."

I looked up and down her black scrubs. *This woman works for the devil.* "And how would I do that?"

"Call your mommy, figure it out." And she walked away.

I got really anxious trying to figure out all the steps involved with going to the front desk, finding my mom's number, asking for a watch, planning on when she could bring it in. *Fuck all that.*

I found a room where my peers were talking about all the drugs they took. "Can you believe the fucking clocks in this place are all wrong? It's like they are trying to mind-fuck us."

They all looked at me and had a moment of silence. Then they all agreed. "Yes, fuck those clocks," one guy said. I held out until group began, an hour late. The group was called animal therapy. An older woman and her husband had a dog on a leash at the front of the room. *These assholes, that dog represents me, these are the elders!* They warmly said hello.

"Hi, we're just here to let this little boy walk around. Feel free to pet him, hug him, do whatever you like with him." This made me furious. *Yeah, do whatever you want with me.* When the couple reached me, they asked, "Would you like to pet him?"

I stood up. "No, I don't want to pet your fucking dog. How dare you taunt me like this?" The old man looked scared. "How about I pet both of you instead. How about you're the animal in the cage and I'm your master?"

They started backing up slowly. I saw security on its way and knew it was time to settle down. Not worth it.

I spent Christmas in the hospital that year, making collages, doing third-grade crossword puzzles, and being asked if I wanted a piece of candy for coloring in between the lines. I participated because I knew it was my fastest way out. I finally did get the call that my mom and Jerry were coming to pick me up. They had both come to visiting hours a few days ago, where Jerry and I had our third hospital chess match. I thought I might be assassinated by a sniper on my first walk outside. I needed help to stand up straight.

"So am I going back to work tomorrow, guys?"

"Brett, you and I are going to fly back home tonight and get organized."

I accepted this idea. I had Ativan on hand during the nighttime flight. The lights looked beautiful from the plane, forming into all sorts of intense 3-D figures. I was in awe and enjoyed the bird's-eye view. We made it back home, and I was to see a psychiatrist first thing in the morning. I was disoriented, moving in and out of confusion, anger, anxiety, restlessness, and other emotional states rapidly. The hallucinations did not slow down at home—outlets and backs of cars looking like faces, conversations in the nearby room were still about me, and I couldn't turn on the TV. I was glad to at least have the option. I was still under the impression that I had a short stay at home and then it was back to Texas for me, managing my team of thirty-five. I thought everything that had happened made me tougher, stronger.

"Are you still thinking that people are talking about you?" my mom asked.

"Yes, it's a test. One day they really will be talking about me. This is how I'm being groomed!"

I was still unwell, but at least I was home and safe.

## *Diagnosis*

*Where the hell am I?* I adjusted myself on the futon in the guest room at my mom's place. I saw a dresser with a TV on my left and noticed a closet behind me. The window straight ahead gave sight to a small forest behind the house, where snow-covered trees swayed back and forth. *Ugh, I'm back at home again.* The anxiety was strong and kept me glued to the bed, trying to fall back asleep and wake up in my downtown Texas apartment, where I had awakened last month at this time. *I don't know what's ahead of me, but I'll make the most of it.* I got up and made it downstairs, where my mom had my meds laid out. I had no sense of what I was supposed to be taking, when or how I was going to get to where I needed to be. *Well, the only place I need to be is at the doctors.*

"Don't worry about a thing," she said. "Your father is going to swing by and drive us downtown to see Dr. D." *So this is the guy that will be able to help everyone understand why I needed to do what I did.*

My dad drove on the thirty-minute ride to the doctor's while I was in the front seat and my mom was in the back. When I buckled up, I had a sense of what this drive would be like. After all, this was my third time confronting a situation like this. We kept the radio down, and I cracked my window to remind myself what the cold felt like. We drove along Main Street, where I relived my Air moccasin route once again, passing the speed limit sign, the library, and of course, making it through the tunnel that I had failed to reach. We made it to a modest building and sat in the waiting room.

A tall man with a thick gray beard came out. "Brett?" All three of us stood up. "Hi, Brett. Are you comfortable talking without your parents at first?"

*I'm twenty-nine.* "Yes," I said, realizing how dependent I had become over the last seventy-two hours. I followed him to his office, where he invited me to sit down. The room was big, with large windows on my left and behind his head. His desk was bare except for a blank white sheet of printer paper with a pen perfectly straight next to it. While he sat down, I heard cars flying by on the street below with a loud *VROOOOOM!* Out of the corner of my eye, I noticed the operation of a gas station, cars pulling in, people pumping, cars pulling out. *Cars are like people. Water is like fuel.* I became dehydrated and felt a bit of panic, similar to the panic at the hospital, where I lost the use of my left hand. This thought made the panic worse. I must have been noticeably frightened.

"Brett, do you want some water?" Dr. D asked.

"Yes, please." He hopped out and came back with cold water. I took a sip. "Thanks." I felt better.

"So tell me why you are here."

"Well, I was working in Texas."

"Texas?" he interrupted.

"Yeah," I answered.

"Such a nice place. I'm sorry, continue."

"I was working in Texas, and my thoughts started getting a little out of hand. *And still are.* In my worst moments, I almost jumped off a bridge, destroyed my apartment, and held a pizza shop hostage. This is the third time in my life I've had something like this happen. I wasn't doing any drugs and was drinking casually."

"Do you have a family history of mental illness?" he asked.

"Yes, my dad and my aunt, his sister, had something like this happen to them. I don't have details."

"Were you extra free with money?"

"No."

"Are you on any medications?"

"Yes. They gave me Zyprexa at the hospital, but they made it as needed for a few days, so I was only taking a multivitamin."

He scoffed. He sat back in his chair, and I focused on his face intensely as the cars and gas station were distracting. I had another moment of dehydration and a panicked look on my face. "Did you eat anything today, Brett?"

"Uh, no, I forgot."

He pulled out grapes and nuts and told me to eat. "Brett, it's very important that you eat when you take your meds, got it?"

"Yes."

"Okay, Brett, can we ask your parents to come in?"

"Sure."

My parents came in with a concerned look. I felt defeated because I still needed my parents to help me, even at age twenty-nine.

"So what's going on, Doc?" my dad said.

"Well, I believe Brett has Bipolar I." *What the fuck does that mean?* "It's associated with having multiple manic episodes."

"What do I have to do to get better?"

"Well, I'm going to prescribe lithium, the gold standard for treating bipolar disorder."

*Fuck more meds.* "Well, how does it work?" I asked.

"We actually don't know. It was discovered by mistake but proves to be the best form of treatment."

*So you're telling me that I have to take a drug and you don't know how it works?* "Are there any side effects?"

"Yes. You'll experience some stiffness and possibly achy muscles. Your kidneys will be strongly affected by this, so you'll have to get blood work done to ensure your levels are where they need to be. You also may experience some shakiness and have to pee more than usual. Headaches and nausea may also occur."

*Ugh, this is going to suck for a while, but then I'll be off the meds and back to normal.* "So you'll wean me off the meds over time?"

"No, Brett. Bipolar is a chronic illness. It means that you will have to take these drugs indefinitely to decrease your chances of having another dangerous manic episode."

*No fucking way! I'll find a way to get off this shit.*

"So, Brett, you'll take Ativan in the morning, afternoon, and evening. You'll take lithium and the Zyprexa in the evening as well. I'll see you back here in one week, and we'll see how you are doing. Any drugs, alcohol, caffeine, lack of sleep, and extra stress are triggers here, Brett."

I looked over and saw my mom writing notes like there was no tomorrow.

## Rough Night

Naturally, I had a rough time sleeping at night, even with the Ativan. I was defenseless against my own mind in the darkness. *Look at you, lying here at your mom's house while your brothers and friends are out doing something with themselves, married, starting families. You've lost it all. Your leadership is weak, and you'll never be successful at anything ever again.* I tried so hard to push back. *Wait a minute, I was successful at other things. I have been through this before.* The "chronic" factor took over. *You heard the doctor. You'll be on medicine the rest of your life. Your body isn't able to make it on its own. You're crippled. Can't even have a beer.* After my own mind had beaten the shit out of me, I'd toss and turn with worry. *What if I forget to take my meds? What if I take the wrong meds? What if my kidneys stop working? What the hell am I going to do tomorrow? What if I have another manic episode?* Then the old delusions would kick in.

I looked up and saw a gorilla with my face on the ceiling fighting a wolf. I tried to close my eyes, but the battle was still front and center in the darkness. The wolf ripped my head off and chewed on it. I swallowed with fear. I turned to my side and saw a small orange light on the wall. Moments later, a flame was floating around in my room. I worried that my room would burn. I sat up in bed and went to my mom's room, waking her up, telling her about what I saw, knowing that none of it was real but reacting like it was. I was so tired but could not sleep. I sat next to her in bed and stared at the ceiling fan because there was no other place to look. A root formed and a tree started growing from her ceiling. I was afraid and went back to my room, tried to sleep again without success, and then woke my mom up, again.

"Let's find a board game to pass some time," she said at three in the morning. We found an unopened game of Stratego. I taught her how to set up the game and play. We played for about an hour. "We're going to remember these days, Brett. Hang in there."

At around five in the morning, I tried to sleep again in my room. My mind was still on, running through clichés that I'd heard my whole life. *Everything happens for a reason. Yeah, well, I sure as hell can't see one. You're meant to be where you are. Yeah? I'm meant to be living in my mom's house, really? It could be worse. Yeah? It could also be better.* At some point, I felt a few minutes of normal, feeling humble, still thinking, however. *It really could be worse. What I experienced tonight is what a blind person experiences every day. Eyes closed, not sleeping. It really could be worse. Maybe things do happen for a reason. I don't know what's ahead of me, but I'll make the most of it.* I actually chuckled about the mess I was in and sneaked a few positive thoughts into the mix.

I felt terrible the next morning and worried that if I didn't get enough sleep, that could trigger another manic episode that day. I just didn't understand how any of this worked, how sensitive I was, or what would cause a relapse. I choked down my pills and sat, not sure what to do. *I could go for a run!* I put on a hoodie and sweatpants, laced up my shoes, and headed out for a long run through the snowy neighborhood. Or so I thought. I took about ten strides and quit, immediately. *This is stupid.* I went back in and turned on the TV.

"Well, that was a weak attempt to run!" said the newscaster. I turned off the TV immediately, scared that I was aware it was not real but dealing with the real feelings. *I'll go get some food! Oh, wait, I can't drive.* "Mom, can we get some food?" I asked.

"Sure, Brett," she said. "But would you rather I make you something?"

"No, I need to get the fuck out of this house."

"Okay."

She drove us to a nearby diner, where everyone was looking and talking about me. *It's not real. It's not real. It's not real. They are just eating. Nobody cares what you are doing. It's not real.* I willed myself to come back to reality and deal with the annoying distractions.

"What will you have to drink?" said the friendly waitress. I was nervous to order.

My mom went first. "I'll have a coffee and a water."

"And you, sir?"

*She knows! She knows I'm crazy. She knows I'm bipolar!* "Ughhh," I stumbled over my words. "I…I'll have a coffee and a water also." She wrote it down, and I yelled, "And can you make it decaf?" I was not used to ordering decaf or emphasizing that it had to be decaf.

"Sure, honey," she said.

*Great, I'm being treated like a child again.*

## Stepper

Like with the last two episodes, the meds made me really hungry, which led to weight gain. I'd often think about the character Fat Bastard from *Austin Powers* and laugh at myself while eating a bowl of ice cream. *I eat because I'm unhappy, and I'm unhappy because I eat.*

I was lying on the couch one afternoon, attempting to read *Siddhartha* by Hermann Hesse, and I got sidetracked. *I should really get off my ass and work out.* Then I went back to trying to read without success. *I literally can't retain any of this.* I rested the book on my fat stomach and felt anxiety about not being able to work out or read.

*I lost all my discipline. In the past, I would have been able to get myself to do anything I wanted. Now I'm useless and helpless.* Then I tried to take a stance against my depression. *You know what? Fuck this! I'm going to get off my ass and go do something. I can do whatever I want.* I put the book down with determination but felt anxious the second I stood up. *What's the point? Why are you even trying? It's only one workout. You're never going to stick with it. Maybe try again later.* I went right back to the couch and try to read the book again.

One morning, I woke up and I couldn't take it anymore, realizing that if I continued to give in to my thoughts, I would never get out. I realized that the longer I waited, the harder it would be. I was a member at a gym in Texas, and there happened to be a location close by. *Don't go. There will be people there who will laugh at you.* I took a deep breath and started tying my running shoes. *They are going to know that you are bipolar.* I stood up and asked my mom to drop me off at the gym. "Wow," she said. *Aww, your mommy is proud that her twenty-nine-year-old son is trying to get out of the house.* We got in the car and made it to the gym. "I'll be right here when you are done," she said. *Be careful, Brett, we all remember what happened in Texas when you were around a big crowd of people.* I took a deep breath, noticing that when I didn't talk back or fight the thoughts, they passed. I walked in.

The front-desk woman looked at me, confused. *She can tell.* Then she smiled. "How are you?" she said.

"Good," I said in a low voice.

"What? I can't hear you."

"Good!" I said, louder.

I took my card back and began the walk past the crowded cardio area. *I'm having an issue with the volume of my voice, apparently.* Cardio equipment was on my right, and TVs and free weights on my left. It was the most stimulation I'd had in a while. I breathed slowly and observed the false connections my mind was making. *Woman on the treadmill is wearing blue pants. Man using the free weights is wearing a blue shirt. The letters in* blue *spell* lube *when rearranged. Man on the cross trainer is lubed in sweat.* I kept breathing and was almost to the locker room. *Sweat is mainly made up of water.* I took a sip of water from the fountain. I looked up and saw a commercial with water in the background. I made it to the locker room, where sinks, toilets, and showers were running. Two men were talking.

"Have you seen the movie *Waterworld* with Kevin Costner?"

"No. Let me guess, there's a lot of water in it?"

They both laughed.

*There's no way that's a coincidence. Yes, it is!* I took another deep breath and put my stuff in a locker. I walked out with my head down and found an open stepper in the back right corner of the gym. *Perfect!* I couldn't help but think about the treadmill that I worked to exhaustion in Texas. This time I was looking out at an entire gym of stimulation. Eight TVs, fifty people, weights crashing, and so much more. *This will be fun! No. Do your thirty minutes on the stepper and get the fuck out of here.* I looked out at the gym and was overwhelmed. *Eight TVs, four are on commercial break, two commercials are targeting the same market, ten people are watching TV. Stop!* I started walking slowly on the stepper and let my head hang in my arms, which were supported by the rails, limiting my view to my feet and the steps moving only. I focused on trying to breathe with each step. *Right foot, breathe in. Left foot, breathe out. Repeat.* I didn't look up for the next ten minutes. All of a sudden, I started to feel hot, so I looked up and took a deep breath before going back to my head-in-arms position. Another five minutes passed. *Halfway, I'm doing it! Right foot, breathe in. Left foot, breathe out. Repeat.* Then I started to sweat. Each bead dripped on the steps themselves, and I couldn't help but notice the small puddle that it made.

I became fixated on my own sweat and lost track of my breathing and steps for about five minutes. I was in a trance. Five minutes later, the beads were a vibrant green color. It was beautiful. I lost track of time, and the stepper beeped, halting the system. *Mission accomplished.* I pulled my head up from the facedown position it had been in for about the last thirty minutes and was frightened. The entire room had turned green! I blinked a few times, and it stayed green. *Uh-oh, did I just make myself color-blind?* A few seconds later, color came back to my world and I felt confused, but relieved.

I made it back to the car, where my mom was waiting. "What the fuck is wrong with me?" I yelled.

"What's wrong? What happened?" she replied.

"The whole gym just turned green. Everything."

"Wow, Brett. I can't imagine what that would be like. Try to relax. We can call the doctor and tell him about it."

"This is fucking bullshit! I can't escape this. It's inside of me, forever."

She put her hand on my back and drove home.

## Blood Work

I had to get blood work done a number of times, but there was one particular time when I had to fast the night before. No food or water after dinner, no breakfast in the morning, and then straight to the clinic. I was eating lunch the day before when it hit me. *Whoa, whoa, whoa. I'm supposed to eat when I take my medicine, but I can't eat tonight after dinner or tomorrow morning when I take my medicine.* I felt a little sick thinking about the potential nausea from not eating with my meds. I followed instructions and felt fine that night. When I woke up, I was very aware that I hadn't eaten last night and that I wouldn't be eating this morning either. I still felt okay as we headed to the clinic.

On the drive over, I tried to understand how I felt. *Remember when I could just wake up and eat whatever I wanted, whenever I wanted it? That was nice. When I wouldn't eat until noon in the past until I felt hungry, then I got something to eat, no big deal. I wonder if what I'm feeling really isn't a big deal, just new.*

I still wasn't convinced and got panicky as I walked in to get my blood drawn.

"Brett?" the phlebotomist said.

"Yep, that's me." I stood up and followed her to the room. I sat down.

"Brett, what's your address?"

*Uhh, 402 East Kindlesburg Drive, Texas.* "Ummm, I may have to check on that."

"Okay, we can grab your mom and fill this out after," she said. *I'm so not an independent person!* "Before we get started, do you get woozy around needles?"

I thought about the catheter up my urethra and IVs in my arms recently. "Well, I should be fine, but I haven't eaten anything, and I feel a bit light-headed."

"Well, I don't know, Brett. I've seen people pass out from that. Do you want me to take you to a more comfortable room?"

I thought about the panic attack and decided I just needed to get this over with. "No, let's just do it."

"Which arm, right or left?"

*Why does it matter, lady?* "Umm, right." *It's closer to her.*

She took out a small alcohol wipe and dressed the area between my forearm and bicep where she would be drawing the blood. The alcohol felt cold on my skin. It felt the same as the alcohol that was used on my hamstring before the sedative was administered during my second manic episode. "Little pinch, Brett." I watched the needle go in. It wasn't painful. I watched as my blood flowed out of my arm and into the tube. I took a few breaths and noticed that the tube was almost full. *Almost done! And isn't it weird that if you replace the t with an l in tube, then you get blue or lube?* I was excited to be almost done. Then she took the first tube out and replaced it with a second. *Interesting.* I looked up on the counter and noticed that there were six more empty tubes waiting. *Oh, shit.* I started to panic a bit. *Well, I haven't had any food, any water, and now I'm losing blood.*

"How you doing over there, Brett?"

"Oh, I'm fine," I said. I kept breathing, feeling more and more light-headed as tube 6 filled, then tube 7. Finally, she pulled the needle out and covered the area with a Band-Aid.

"All done."

*Thank God.* My mom helped with some of the paperwork, and we left.

It was not until we were halfway home that I realized that I had no clue what would happen next. *Do I go back to the clinic to get my results and then bring them to Dr. D? Do they e-mail them to me so I can print or forward them to Dr. D? Do they send them directly to Dr. D?*

The answer was not a hard one to find, but the thinking and uncertainty that came with going through this process for the first time was a big deal. It was frustrating to not have the proactive instruction of what would happen next and what I had to do. *Can you imagine what people with zero family support and less resources go through?*

On the next visit to Dr. D's office, he informed me that my results were good, everything in the range that it needed to be in. "Now, Brett, this stuff can fluctuate all the time, so I'm going to ask you to do this about once per month while we figure out the correct level of lithium in your blood, okay?"

"Yes, sir, I'll do whatever I have to do," I said with a defeated tone.

"Brett, I had a patient years back who was bipolar I. He would drag himself into my office in the winter, depressed as ever. But one thing he would always say was that in six months he would be manic, excited, and loving life. Sure enough, when summer came, he'd strut into my office wearing an expensive suit. He asked me to look out into the parking lot, where he had purchased a new BMW. The reason I'm telling you this is that you will get better, Brett. You will achieve great things in your life. Keep doing what you are doing."

I left his office with a small sense of hope that things might get better for me.

## *Therapy*

"I know it's hard, but you're lucky, Brett. You have a roof over your head, a family that loves you, and no pressure to get back to work. When I was diagnosed, I had to go straight back to work. It could definitely be worse," my aunt preached.

"Yes, I am lucky. Oh, wow, you had to go straight back to work?" I replied.

I had been a pleaser my whole life, telling people what they wanted to hear and pretending to not need anything from anyone. I didn't know it yet, but in order to fully accept that I had a chronic illness, I wouldn't be able to operate in this manner anymore. I wouldn't be able to suppress my real thoughts and feelings. *I've always had a roof over my head and a family that loves me. I've always liked to work. I don't feel lucky.* Then I'd get deeply involved in the back-and-forth of what was fair. *Some people don't have roofs over their heads, don't have families that love them, can't get a job. Am I lucky to have all four of my limbs? To have been born in the first place?*

I'd been in and out of therapy for the past decade, and part of my recovery would require not only a psychiatrist to prescribe and monitor medication but also a therapist to "talk it out." Dr. D recommended Dr. E, whose office was about an hour away from my mom's house, where I was staying. I didn't have a car at this point and wasn't comfortable driving on my own, so my mom rode shotgun as I timidly manned the one-hour trip. I believed in therapy and agreed that it was time well spent, although I hated the circumstances I was in during it. Rarely did I make a choice to be in therapy; it was always required as a part of recovery.

♪ *That's life (that's life). That's what all the people say.*
*You're riding high in April, shot down in May.*
*But I know I'm gonna change that tune, when*
*I'm back on top, back on top in June.*♪

Frank Sinatra played on the drive into the parking lot.
"Brett?"
*Here we go again. Another mental health professional that I have to spout out my story to.* "Yeah, that's me."
"Come on in. Sit wherever you like."
My mom stayed in the lobby, and Dad showed up for support. My meds were still being adjusted at this point, and I was still hypersensitive, having psychotic thoughts at times. There were two chairs facing each other and an old-fashioned, maroon-colored couch against the wall. *He's already evaluating my behavior. If I sit in his chair, then he'll see me as dominant, always having to be in control. If I sit in the other chair, he'll think I'm trying to work on his level, as an associate. If I sit on the couch, then we'll have a mutual understanding that I'm the patient and he's the professional.*

I sat on the couch to make things easier. He sat down and grabbed a notebook and pen. *So tell me why you are here, Brett.* "So tell me why you are here, Brett."

The next five minutes were filled with phrases like "Two previous episodes," "Dad left," "Everything was connecting," "They are telling me I'm Bipolar I," "I can handle all this no problem." Dr. E took notes ferociously and then put his pen and pad down. *I believe I can help you, Brett.* "I believe I can help you, Brett." *Can we bring your parents in?* "Can we bring your parents in?"

"Sure," I replied.

Mom sat on the couch with me, and Dad sat on the chair. *I believe Brett is bipolar I.* "I agree with Dr. D that Brett is bipolar." *Okay, can we schedule our next appointment and all go home now?* "I think it would be wise to confirm that there is nothing else going on. We should set up an appointment for him to see a neurologist."

*Neurologist? What's a* neurologist? *Do I have brain cancer? What are they going to do to me? Will I survive? What will happen?*

"Brett, do you have any questions? We'll pick up therapy next week."

"Nope."

I spent the next few days convincing myself that if I had brain cancer, then I would deal with it. "It's probably nothing," my dad said. We walked through the cancer section of the hospital to get to the neurologist's office. I observed very sick people walking around with concerned family members supporting them. *I'm a bad person for thinking that I'm owed anything. I am lucky.* I thought about how that could be me if the results of this test were unfavorable. *How could my life have spiraled out of control so fast?* We made it to the waiting room, and my name was called. I thought about how I was able to answer the cop's questions in Texas, which boosted my confidence.

"Brett, are you on any medications?" asked the nurse.

I flashed back to the many doctor's appointments during my upbringing where I'd scoff and be able to answer "No." "Yes," I said.

"Okay. What are they, how much do you take, and what are they for?"

I got nervous because I wasn't an expert on all this yet. "Uhhh, well, lithium. I think it's 1,350 milligrams. It's for my bipolar." *My bipolar…the bipolar that I have?*

"Any others?"

"Risperdal, not sure of the dosage. I take it at night. It's for psychotic thoughts."

"Any others?"

"I just started on Lexapro, but I'm not really sure how much or what it does. I just know that I take it twice per day."

"Okay. Any others?"

"Yes, I take Ativan for anxiety, as needed."

She put all this information into her computer, while I got anxious if it was accurate or not.

The doctor came in and performed a basic examination, making me touch my nose, bend over, and reach over my head. He told me that I was fine and no further testing was needed. I felt good that I hadn't been given more bad news and was dropped into a deeper ditch than I was already in. After all, I was battling hard just to be even.

## *Outpatient*

Our family had not been a cohesive unit for eleven years since my dad left, and that did not change when I came home from Texas. I was seeing Dr. D once per week and Dr. E twice per week, but I was still heavily depressed and unsure what to do with my time. My mom was hoping for more guidance from the professionals, so she put it out there that I might need more help. She asked my dad and Russell if they had any ideas on what else could be done, because they were both doctors.

"Brett, I'm setting up a meeting with a connection of mine at another hospital," my dad said. "Brett, I'm setting you up at the intensive outpatient program at the university hospital," Russell said. *Do I get any say in what I do? I'm fine with Dr. D and Dr. E. I'm not up for a change.* My dad and Russell were not on the same page, both thinking that one would be better than the other. I ended up meeting my dad's connection first.

"So, Brett, tell me what happened in Texas," the new doctor said. Fast-forward ten minutes, and he confirmed that I had Bipolar I. He explained that there are two types of bipolar. Bipolar I, associated with mania, deep depression, and psychosis. Bipolar II, associated with a less severe form of mania, hypomania, and also associated with depression. He seemed wise but didn't do enough to justify my changing to him. He introduced me to Kay Jameson's book *The Unquiet Mind*, the most popular book on bipolar disorder that exists to date. The intensive outpatient program seemed like a major upgrade, where I'd be among others who had recent episodes. They'd teach me tangible skills that I could use to manage bipolar. The program was near the university hospital, where I had been hospitalized on two separate occasions.

I was sitting shotgun as my mom rode us through the main street on campus. I read "Pink, 'Just Give Me a Reason'" on the satellite radio and looked out of the window.

*♪Just give me a reason, just a little bit's enough,*
*Just a second, we're not broken, just bent,*
*And we can learn to love again. ♪*

I looked out and saw the library and large glass window that I had tried to throw a rock through. *Not broken, just bent.* Next, I saw the park bench that I tore out was replaced. *Not broken, just bent.* We made a left turn up the street where I had memories of studying for exams and spending time with my college friends. I thought about myself. *Not broken, just bent.* She parked the car, and we headed into the lobby. My heart sank from seeing the same patterns on the floor that I saw on the floor at the hospital. All three episodes blended together. Screaming in a straitjacket. Eating a pickle out of the trash. Pulling the handle off the shower of the bathtub to use as a blade. I lost track of what had happened where, but this floor brought it all back.

*Just make it to the front counter and sign in.*

"You okay, Brett?" my mom asked, focused on how to get me registered.

"Yeah, I'm fine. Why?" *Can she tell I'm having a mini breakdown over here?*

"Just asking," she said.

*So I may appear fine on the outside even though I'm about to lose it on the inside. Noted.*

We went up an elevator, and I looked at my mom skeptically. *Tell me you aren't putting me back in the hospital. What is this place? How could you?* I felt betrayed and unsure what I was walking into. I thought about how I'd looked back at my mom from a locked room during the first episode, with no awareness of what was happening. We made it upstairs and waited for about an hour. Finally, a tall, curvy woman with red hair came out.

"Brett?"

"Yep," I said, so used to the question.

"Follow me, dear." I followed her to a room, and we both sat down. "So, Brett, tell me what happened in Texas."

*Will this ever end?* I told my story again.

Next came a new question. "Have you had any thoughts about harming yourself?"

*Well, isn't that an interesting question? I just had one now after you asked.* "No," I said.

"Have you had any thoughts about harming others?"

*This is an easy one.* "No."

She had a few more questions and informed me that class would start soon and I was good to go.

I sat closest to the door in case I needed to escape the classroom, which had a chalkboard and desks. I was the first one there and read on the board, "Breathe in, breathe out." I took a deep breath, feeling panicky and anxious. I hadn't been around a group of people in months. A man my age, with gray sweatpants and a red T-shirt, came in first, sitting right next to me. *Fuck, please don't say hi, please don't say hi.*

"Hi!" he said. "What's your name?"

I turned to my right. "Brett." That was as far as the conversation went. *I wonder what this guy did to be in here.*

An overweight teenager was next, then a skinny older woman, then a few others that were different ages and backgrounds, then a girl who was "hot," as we would have said in middle school. *Maybe this won't be so bad after all.*

It was bad, very bad.

I couldn't keep my attention on anything and felt the room spinning. I watched the instructor go around the room and ask each attendee if they completed their homework of things like getting out of bed, going for a walk, or baking apple pie. *Lame, lame, and lame.* We got a fifteen-minute break, where I watched everyone my age get in a circle to smoke, including the hot one. I was turned off and didn't fit in. I made it through the three-hour class, got picked up, and headed home. I had a day to look at assignments before heading back. I drove myself this time.

I got into the elevator and looked around for the second class, not having to be dependent on anyone. *I can do this.* I found my desk and was asked to see the doctor, who saw each patient once per week to measure progress.

"Brett?" There were two of them. An older man with black hair, glasses, and a white coat, and a younger resident with a notepad and clean face.

"Brett," the older doctor said, "do you mind if I allow Tim to shadow us today?"

"Not at all," I replied.

We sat down in his office, me on one side and the two of them on the other. "So, Brett, tell me what happened in Texas." When I was done explaining again, the doctor smiled and asked the resident to leave. "Brett, I know exactly what you have, but I'm going to test the resident." He smiled like this was some game that they were playing. He called the resident back in, where he guessed what I had incorrectly, and then finally the doctor said bipolar. "So what I'm going to do is pump you with as much lithium as you can handle. You have to cancel with your other doctors in order to allow me to treat you."

*No way in hell that's happening.*
I showed good face for the rest of the meeting and then went straight to my car and drove home, leaving all my class materials behind. No way in hell was I going back to that place.

## *Mourning Texas*

Weeks of doctor's visits and attempts to work out went by. I was getting the hang of driving again and was offered my stepmom's car, which I was grateful for. The car had over one hundred thousand miles on it and an old speaker system. I had a lot of time on my hands to think and feel bad for myself. My eyes opened. *Ugh, I'm at my mom's house.* I'd often walk through an entire day in my life in Texas versus now. I thought about waking up in my new, downtown apartment. *My life was perfect.* I walked to the bathroom at my mom's house and found my morning pills. *Fuck my life.* I thought about Texas and not having to take any pills at all. *My life was so easy.* I walked downstairs and put a decaf K-Cup into the Keurig. *I wish I could have caffeine.* I thought about the amazing coffee in Texas that got me revved up for the day. *I'll never experience that feeling again.* I drank my decaf, and I was dumbfounded about how I would spend my time. *Why is this so hard?* I thought about the excitement of working at Systems Fit and being a boss. *I had no issues back then.* I looked in the mirror and forced myself to get in the car and go to the gym. *I'm fat, and it's only getting worse.* I thought about how proud I was of my physical appearance in Texas. *Why was it so easy?* I got in an old Honda and drove to the gym. *This car represents my life right now.* I fantasized about the Audi A4. *I was so much cooler back then.* I made it home to a quiet house, searching for my next activity. *I'm so bored.* I thought about going out in downtown Texas with a drink in my hand, having a blast. *That will never happen again.*

My depression wasn't really about the diagnosis or the lifestyle changes that I had to make, but the life that I had lost. *So I work really hard in basketball and get a concussion in the biggest game of my life. I try to enjoy my college experience and I lose it all. I become a professional poker player only to lose that too. Then I build a company from the ground up and get ripped away from that. What's the point of trying at anything?* My life had become a journey of the highest of highs and the lowest of lows. I was not equipped with the proper tools to understand that my life was not so perfect before and after my episodes.

I tried a support group. It was pouring rain on the fifty-minute drive to the community library for the group that Thursday night; it was as hard as the day I was dropped off at basketball camp, where I'd meet Michael Jordan. *Breathe in, breathe out.* My hands were not steady as I parallel-parked on the tight street and walked in.

"Is there a group here tonight?" I asked the front desk.

"A group for what?" she replied.

*A group for all the other nutjobs like me.* I stumbled over my words. "Umm, just a support group, I think?"

She checked the schedule. "Oh, yeah, it's upstairs."

I said my thank-you and walked up. I saw a room full of adults in the back and felt my heart pound as I took my seat in the circle. My mouth was dry. *I knew I should have brought a water like the doctor said.* The next two hours were spent with each individual sharing how their week went. I heard stories about how some partied hard the previous weekend as they explained how they could handle alcohol on top of their meds. Others talked about how their sons and daughters were wrong for not understanding their illness, an excuse for not keeping in touch. Many explained how they had been depressed for most of their lives. In most stories, I found a choice or decision made by the individual that was their fault.

*You complain about your meds being off, but you drink all the time. You blame your kids for not understanding, but you've made no effort to talk to them. You've been depressed most of your life? Well, that just sucks.*

I made a vow that I would stay the course and do exactly what I was told by the professionals, even with no guarantees it would prevent another manic episode. Finally, it was my turn.

"Hey, my name is Brett." *This is kind of what I made new employees do at work.* "I was in Texas, and I had my third manic episode. I was diagnosed Bipolar I recently, and I'm afraid. I've always thought

I could control everything in my life, and now I know that I can't. Thank you."

A man raised his hand in the back and started speaking. "Brett, let me tell you, it will get better."

A girl with tattoos down her arm chimed in, "Yeah, Brett, I felt the same way you did. It will get better."

The entire room showed support. At home, my stories were taken in with amazement, but here, my stories were common. The group uncovered a part of me that needed work, being comfortable with uncertainty and vulnerability.

## *Solutions*

But I wasn't comfortable with uncertainty and vulnerability. I'd spent most of my life preparing for what was ahead of me and working hard to get there, ultimately achieving success. I had confidence and was capable. Now I was unsure and scared. Dr. D recommended I see a good friend of his, a rabbi. He could serve as a spiritual adviser in my uncertain world and be another activity on my calendar each week. I was raised Jewish but never took religion too seriously. I believed in evolution and science, finding it hard to put faith into something I could not see with my own two eyes. During my episodes, God played a major role, which was confusing to me.

I pulled up to our meeting place and noticed the sun get brighter as I walked to the door. *Maybe God does exist.* A bearded man my height opened the door and gave me a warm welcome. We sat in his office, and he made it very clear that he wasn't trying to sway me one way or another, only to have an open discussion. We got right into it. "Well, I'm not so sure I believe in God. I'm more of a logic person," I said.

"We have plans and designs for everything around us. Is it not logical to think that there was a plan for the world?" he replied.

*Hmmm.* "What is the soul?" I asked.

"The soul is our inner essence. You must nurture it like a garden. Seeds are planted by doing good deeds. Your traits are the gardening tools," he answered. This made me feel good; it gave me back some control. We'd spend about an hour per week discussing similar topics, and I'd always feel a bit better when I left.

I'd have similar conversations with my therapist, but he would provide a much different type of support. My eyes shot open. *Ugh, another day. I feel like shit. I can't do it. What's the point of all this?* I dragged myself to therapy and plopped down in the chair. "So, Brett, what's going on?" Dr. E asked.

"I feel like shit. I'm bored. I lost my old life, and I'm a loser, living at home with my mom." *Ah, feels good to say it out loud.*

"And...," he replied.

*Huh?* "And I'll never get the things I want in life."

"And what do you want in life?" he asked.

"I want to like my job, have a family, and be comfortable."

"So tell me more about why you think you won't have what you want in life."

"I just can't get myself to do anything. I have to do something!"

"Brett, you are doing something. You take your meds, you show up to therapy, you've cut out caffeine, alcohol, and drugs. You are learning that life is not all about work. How long has it been?"

I laughed. "About three months."

"Just because you don't have these tangible things laid out for you does not mean you can't be happy."

*He's right.* "But I don't feel happy. These meds are throwing me off-balance."

"When you were running sprints in basketball practice, how did it feel?"

"Terrible."

"So why did you do it?"

"Because I wanted to be a starter, and I knew the conditioning would be good for me in the long run."

"Exactly!"

I thought about the pain associated with running sprints. *That's not worse than this.* My perspective shifted a bit. "So I can view this whole thing like a sprint and know that I'll reach the finish line if I do everything I'm supposed to do, as fast as possible?"

"That's close. This is a marathon. There will be ups and downs. You will pace yourself and build off what you've already learned. You won't always be at your best or 100 percent sure of everything, but who really is? You can have bipolar and live a rewarding life."

*I can have bipolar and live a rewarding life. It will take discipline, patience, self-awareness, and hard work, but I'll do it. I always have.*

"Times up!" he said with a smile. *Can we keep talking? Please?* "All right, I'll see you next week."

The buzz from therapy would fade a couple of hours after the session, but I always paid close attention to the new insights that I had learned. The "running sprints" analogy was very helpful.

Dr. D's office was about an hour away from where I lived, and I was only seeing him about once per month. He was managing my medication but leaving the rest of my recovery up to the rabbi and Dr. E. My mom did intense research to find a psychiatrist that was a bit more hands-on. She found Dr. F and begged me to meet with her. I was okay with the team that I already had and resisted the idea of changing at first. Finally, I gave in. Dr. F's office was only a five-minute drive from my mom's house. It was not until I walked into the building that I realized it was the same office that I'd been brought to for evaluation after coming home from down South during my first episode, before going to the university hospital. I walked in and felt anxious sitting on the same couch and listening to the same music that I had ten years ago. I was slightly better now than when I had come home, but I was still anxious, confused, depressed, and unsure how to manage all this.

*Back to square one, again. Where did my twenties go?*

I didn't know what to expect. The door opened. Dr. F called me into her office.

## Improvement

Dr. F had a plan. After a few meetings, she'd determined that I was highly competitive and motivated by reward. *So that explains why I feel the need to please others, work hard, and prove myself over and over. So that's where my anxiety comes from.*

"Brett, I want you to think of your life like a pie chart." I held an image of a blank circle in my mind. "From what I can see, for most of your life, you've put about 90 percent of your energy into work, leaving family and hobbies to share the last 10 percent." I filled in the pie chart with these percentages. "This has been a very successful model for you, becoming the starting point guard on your basketball team, rising to the top of online poker, and building an office of thirty-five at Systems Fit, but it has come at a huge cost, intense stress and lack of sleep." *Oh, so stress is the new weed.* "Brett, our goal here is to balance out the pie chart. You've been able to be successful as a 90 percent guy, but can you do it as a 50 percent guy?"

I evened out the sections of the pie chart, and it started to make sense. "How do I do this?" I asked.

"You make sure that you are never wondering what you should be doing. You become the master of your own time, realizing what you spend your time on."

*Oh my god, I've been so deep into work that I haven't been able to stay balanced. There's an entire side of life that I've been overlooking. What should I fill my schedule with?* Dr. F helped me with that too.

"We're going to work together over time and tweak your routine as you go, as you build your life back." *This is like the first day at a new job, the job of my entire life.* "You will always take your medication when you are supposed to. You take lithium at night now, and I'm going to add a drug called Lamictal to supplement lithium. The dose of Lamictal must be raised over time. If you take too much at once, it can lead to a serious skin condition." *Oh, damn.* "It will stabilize your mood, and you'll take it twice per day. You will also take omega-3 fish oils three times per day to help with your mood. The lithium may cause issues with your thyroid, in which case we'll put you on a drug called Synthroid to manage that. You cannot eat an hour before or after you take Synthroid. The medication is important, but without a healthy lifestyle, you will be at a higher risk of another episode. Make sure to get plenty of sleep, eat healthy foods, work out, and I'll work with you to find activities, like volunteering, to keep you structured. Also, I want to teach you a breathing exercise right now. It's the equivalent of taking an antianxiety medication.

Breathe in for four seconds, hold for four seconds, breathe out for four seconds, don't breathe for four seconds. Repeat four times. Do this three times per day. Raise the cycles weekly until you are doing eight seconds and eight reps. I'd also like to see you meditate each morning." I had a lot of questions, and she answered them all.

Wake up. *Synthroid, have to kill an hour.* Brush teeth, shower, breathing exercise number 1, meditate, eat breakfast, *fish oil number 1, Lamictal number 1.* Morning activity, eat lunch. *Breathing exercise number 2, fish oil number 2.* Afternoon activity, eat dinner, evening activity. *Breathing exercise number 3, fish oil number 3, Lamictal number 2, lithium.* Sleep. One side effect of lithium was that it made me pee throughout the night, which hurt my ability to get a good night's sleep. This was an ongoing issue.

It took some time to nail down this routine, but it became second nature. I found that I could do my breathing exercises in the car on the way to activities and kept an afternoon fish oil on me at all times. I had to fill in my activities. While I was in a manic episode, my perception of everything was skewed, all five senses unclear, thinking delusional thoughts, making false connections. While I was recovering from a manic episode, the same was true, everything dull, lack of confidence, unsure of my own body. I had to consciously push through my own insecurities to show up for volunteering. I overcame my fear of social interaction and volunteered for a few months, organizing boxes in a warehouse for an organization that sent medical supplies to countries in need across the globe. Our organization helped thousands of people in third world countries get supplies that they would not have had otherwise, like wheelchairs, crutches, bandages, and more. While I was using the volunteer opportunity to test my own ability to get out of the house and manage anxiety, helping out others in a big way was consistent with my life goals. Moving boxes around in a quiet warehouse was a reminder of how far I'd fallen in my career, however. I pushed through these thoughts and showed up consistently, boosting my capacity for what I could handle. I was never too good for any task.

Over time, I started reading and was able to concentrate more. I had considerable time on my hands and worked with my old friend

John on a poker blog. I'd write an article covering the poker hand of the week, he would edit, I'd update, and he would post. I liked writing and looked forward to the articles coming out each week. I didn't want to play poker during this time, but I dabbled when I was bored. I wanted to teach others how to play and formed a small training business. I also joined a chess club, which served as a scheduled activity twice per week.

After understanding my daily routine and having enough activities to fill up my week, I had to think about what type of work would be good. I was anxious about starting out in a new job at the ground level. Dr. F recommended some sort of educational or training program to get my brain back in gear before getting a job. I decided to try real estate, because I'd have a flexible schedule and it required an educational program beforehand. I worked really hard for two months of real estate classes, studying, giving presentations, interacting, staying out past 10:00 p.m. for class, and retraining my brain. I passed the course, studied hard for the licensing exam, and I am now a licensed real estate agent.

Later that year, Systems Fit sold for an eight-figure amount, leaving me to collect a seven-figure amount. It felt nice to see the money in my account, but the buzz faded quickly.

"Is this Mr. Thomas?"

"Yes, who is this?"

"Hi, my name is Brett Stevens, and I was wondering if I could come in and affiliate with your real estate company today?"

"Sure! I'll be here all day."

Here I am, clean-shaven, new haircut, in shape, wearing nice pants, shoes, and shirt, driving up the road to officially become a realtor, and I'm content. A car zooms by, followed by a flashback to my picking up Russell down South, and then it passes. The fluffy clouds shift and appear to be looking at me. I breathe, and it passes. Kanye West's "I Am a God" plays on the radio.

*♪I am a God.♪*

It reminds me of the madness. I breathe, and it passes. I'm stopped at a red light. *That's just a red light.* I find the building and park my car, wondering if my anxiety is from trauma or a new job interview. *New job interview.* I walk in, and Mr. Thomas is waiting with a smile. "Hey, Brett! Welcome." We go into his office, and I have a seat, feeling good. Proud of what I've survived to get to this moment, wondering what the next chapter will bring. Mr. Thomas sits back in his chair and says, "So, Brett, tell me a little bit about yourself."

## Hope

My experience with Bipolar I disorder has been tough. I wasn't born with it, although I may have inherited the tendency from my family. Then one or more factors, like concussions, substance use, or stressful events had to happen in order for it to be expressed. It is such a deep, personal, and mysterious disorder that no one can relate to except others who have been there. It comes with a stigma, that I am crazy and can't be trusted because I might "blow up" again. There's no cure, and I have no guarantees on my long-term health. I'm constantly wondering what will happen to me if I screw up my routine, forget to take my meds, or take the wrong meds. The hardest thing for me is that it affects all five senses. I can't run away from it. Any sort of stimulation can remind me of something terrible from past episodes.

I've learned through basketball that no matter how undersized or physically inferior, mental toughness can win. I can work harder, spend more time, and want it more than anyone else. Even though I'm now aware of my chronic brain disorder, my mantra does not change. I feel like it is manageable. I feel like I am the same person right now that I used to be. I feel confident that I can be successful in anything that I take on. I feel that someone will love me for who I am and find my experience with bipolar to be interesting, deep, and complex. I see it as something special, as something that I can reflect on and always work on to improve. With my doctors' help, I have been able to take my recovery into my own hands, not only with medication, but by staying disciplined and balancing my career, social life, hobbies, and health.

It takes time to learn how to talk about bipolar disorder with anyone outside mental health professionals. My family thinks checking in and seeing how I am is really helping, and I don't blame them for it. Often, it's confusing because explaining how I am is such a complex answer when I'm depressed, coming down from a manic episode, dealing with new meds, or feeling lonely. My friends and family want to see me for who I have always been, but my lifestyle has changed. I don't order regular coffee anymore. I don't go to the bar and buy shots for everyone. I don't stay out all night.

I get asked, Why do I live at home? *Because I went crazy again and had nowhere else to go.* I live at home because Systems Fit sold and I wanted to figure out my next move. What am I doing with my life? *I'm figuring out how to deal with my chronic illness.* I'm starting a business and a new career in real estate. Why don't I work nine to five? *Because I'm finding balance and need to be available during the week for doctors' appointments.* I have my hands in a lot of things and would prefer to have a balanced life. I have scripts for these answers that make it less heavy.

I've learned that explaining to new friends why I don't drink is not as easy as it seems. If I say that I used to drink and don't now, I'm tagged as an ex-alcoholic. If I say that I can't drink because of my mental illness, then I'm heavily judged. I've found that saying "I take a pill that doesn't mix well with alcohol" is most effective.

I cannot speak for all mental illnesses. I cannot even speak for all people who have bipolar disorder. But I can speak for myself. My issue is hidden and abstract. It feels like I know something that others don't. It feels like I have to hide it for my own safety, not because I'm worried that I'm not in control, but because it's easier. When a person is in a wheelchair, you hold the door for them. You are extra nice. We build ramps and we offer special parking, all of which is totally great and needed. I have less rights. I can't join the military or purchase a firearm. I'd never want to do either of those things, but the fact that I can't, feels like a violation. When I turned eighteen, my mental health issue was not yet diagnosed, and I could have done those things. But today I feel as healthy as I did back then.

Fifteen percent of people with bipolar disorder commit suicide. I can see clearly how one would want to. I hope to be in the 85 percent that battle every day. I hope to do the best that I can and capitalize on the unique, rare, dazzling perspective that I have of the world because of my illness. The thought of the mentally ill running large companies, rising to the top of the entertainment industry, creating artwork so beautiful that it makes one question what was going through the artist's mind when creating it, and living happy, peaceful lives makes me proud to be a person with bipolar disorder.

# About the Author

Brett Stevens is a thirty-one-year-old first-time author who has written this memoir describing his personal experience with Bipolar I disorder. This story started out as a therapeutic exercise to write a narrative of his life, integrating his childhood memories with the visceral accounts of recurrent major psychiatric illness in adulthood. Along the way, he discovered that he has hypermnesia: the incredible ability to remember personal life events with detailed accuracy. As a result, this first-person account details the evolution of psychosis and its impact on his behavior. He is able to recall mental status changes that are textbook definitions of referential thinking, and he describes visual and auditory hallucinations, incapacitating anxiety and paranoia, and grandiose delusions of power, influence, and control.

Brett is the middle of three sons born to an affluent family who lived comfortably in an upper-middle-class neighborhood. He and his brothers attended the neighborhood public school, and all of them played varsity basketball. Their summers were focused on basketball camp, and they all inherited the motivation to achieve in athletics as well as academics. Brett considered himself to be an undersized point guard who had to work harder than his brothers to succeed at basketball. However, he was intensely competitive and found great satisfaction in working toward and achieving his life goals through his mantra borrowed from one of his coaches, "The players who work the hardest will gain the most."

Despite being derailed with three psychotic episodes, he finished college and has found success in three separate careers: professional poker, health club sales administration, and most recently, real estate. He has written a poker blog and developed an online program to teach others how to play. He also competes at amateur chess. He enjoys teaching and training others, and he is deeply committed to helping other people who struggle with Bipolar I disorder.